ARCHITECTURE

THE CRITICS' CHOICE

ARCHITECTURE

THE CRITICS' CHOICE

150 MASTERPIECES OF
WESTERN ARCHITECTURE

EDITED BY DAN CRUICKSHANK

LEFT: Morris Adjmi and Lisa Mahar,
Putnam Lake House, Putnam County,
New York State, 1998–9

AURUM PRESS

First published in Great Britain 2000 by

Aurum Press Ltd

25 Bedford Avenue

London WC1B 3AT

ISBN: 1 85410 720 8

10 9 8 7 6 5 4 3 2 1

2004 2003 2002 2001 2000

This book was conceived, designed and produced by

The Ivy Press Ltd

The Old Candlemakers

West Street

Lewes

East Sussex

BN7 2NZ

Creative Director: Peter Bridgewater

Editorial Director: Sophie Collins

DTP Designer: Angela Neal

Designer: Alan Osbahr

Commissioning Editor: Christine Davis

Copy Editor: Sarah Polden

Senior Project Editor: Rowan Davies

Picture Researcher: Jo Walton

Illustrations in Chapter 1 by Curtis Tappenden

This book is set in 9/14 Franklin Gothic

Printed and bound by Star Standard, Singapore

RIGHT: Severus and Celer, Golden House
of Nero, Rome, AD 64–68

contents

Introduction

We all live in, work in or walk around buildings and experience architecture on a daily basis. The design decisions taken by architects in the near or distant past affect us more directly than any other comparable art or craft. We don't have to listen to opera or look at paintings but we do have to confront architecture. In addition, architecture is unique among the arts for it attempts to combine beauty with utility; it is, as perceived by Roman and Renaissance architects, the attempt to combine 'commodity, firmness and delight' (as suggested by Vitruvius). Architecture shares with sculpture the fact that it is appreciated in three dimensions; it is an art that can be walked up to, around and through, and the materials of construction – be they stone, brick, concrete or steel – can give a powerful tactile pleasure and respond in magical ways to changing conditions of light and weather.

LEFT: Tadao Ando, Naoshima Contemporary Art Museum, Naoshima, 1989–92, 1997.

Yet despite the aesthetic power of architecture and its profound presence in our lives, it remains a subject that is generally little understood or – when it comes to much contemporary architecture – is actually misunderstood. Its stylistic development and aesthetic theories can seem intimidatingly obscure, while talk about different materials and methods of construction appears to make architecture a dauntingly professional and technical subject. This state of affairs is, of course, lamentable. If the art, craft and science of architecture were more generally understood and appreciated, then not only would we all be able to play a more effective role in the debate about the architecture and cities we want in the 21st century, but there would also be an increased understanding and appreciation of the man-made world in which we live.

One way to tell the story of Western architecture is to present outstanding buildings in a manner which is both revealing and inspiring. This is what we set out to do in *Architecture: The Critics' Choice*. The structure of the book is clear and its scope strictly defined. It is organized chronologically, divided into 10 chapters, and deals only with Western architecture or architecture designed by architects based in, originating from or largely inspired by the West. The origins and ethos behind non-Western architecture, be it Asian, African or South American, tell separate stories. The choice of buildings – there is detailed discussion of 150 works from a period covering more than 2,500 years – has been made by 10 authors who are experts in their chosen fields. The authors include architects and academics as well as critics

LEFT: Filippo Brunelleschi, Dome of Florence Cathedral (Santa Maria del Fiore), 1420–36, cupola completed c.1470

ABOVE AND BELOW: Norman Foster, Reichstag, Berlin, 1993–99. View of the dome from the west (above) and sketch of the Plenary Building (below)

from both sides of the Atlantic who, through their informed yet necessarily subjective selection of buildings for this book, give a sense of the immense creative diversity of Western architecture. The perceptive narrative offered by the authors contains not only essential information for newcomers to architecture, but also fresh insights for those more familiar with the subject.

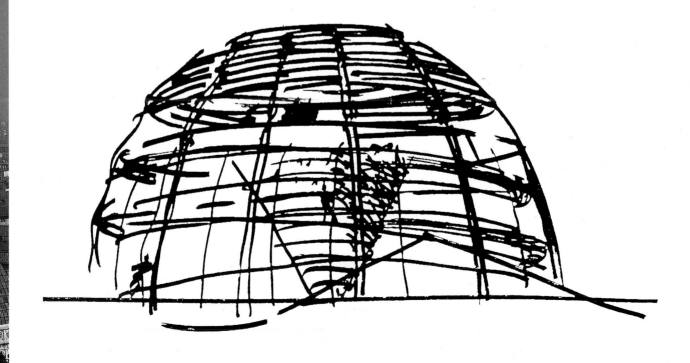

We have selected buildings not only for their intrinsic architectural quality and historic interest but also to ensure that the book covers a wide range of significant and characteristic building types, from cathedrals and palaces to museums, law courts and houses. Excellent but relatively obscure buildings are also included, when possible, alongside more famous examples, in order to add an element of delight and surprise. And so this book works at several levels. It offers an overview of this huge, rich and complex topic, but it also offers very detailed, highly informed personal opinions about individual buildings. It works both as a 'guided tour', led by experts, to some of the outstanding architecture of the world, and as a series of inspirational – and occasionally provocative and opinionated – essays. Needless to say, the choice of buildings has not been easy to make. Discussions have been hard – sometimes heated – but I'm convinced that the choice is a good one, and the text has been strengthened, not weakened, by the pressure put on the authors to distil their knowledge into brief descriptions and explanations. To include informed discussions about so many of the world's best buildings between the covers of a single book is, to my mind, exciting in itself. The fact that this work represents the personal views of 10 architectural experts and is not an objective and comprehensive history of Western architecture means that, inevitably, it has a certain individuality – indeed, an idiosyncrasy. This, in my view, is the

book's greatest strength. There are many would-be objective histories of world architecture but none that manage to tackle this vast subject in such a personal and accessible manner.

This personal approach does, however, mean that geographical coverage can be a little unequal. The authors naturally have their own areas of interest and expertise and these are reflected in their choice of buildings, so that countries peripheral to the main thrust of architectural development – technical and social as well as stylistic and aesthetic – get less attention than those on the cutting edge. Consequently, the regional and vernacular architecture of such locations as the British Isles, Scandinavia and the Iberian peninsula get less attention than, for example, Greece, Italy and France. In addition, there are notable overlaps between chapters, in architects and dates, but these should increase enjoyment and understanding, for they confirm that architecture, like all the arts, does not necessarily develop in a conveniently linear and chronological manner, while the opinions of different authors about the same architect help to present a more rounded and varied picture of the distinct facets and phases of the designer's career.

RIGHT: Walter Gropius, the Bauhaus, Dessau, 1925–26. Balconies on dormitory tower

BELOW: Ada Karmi-Melamede and Rem Karmi, Supreme Court of Israel, Jerusalem, 1986–92

Something should also be said about the issue of architectural style, a subject in which classifications are largely the invention of tidy-minded 19th-century historians imposing a precise development on the unwieldy story of world architecture. The structure of this book is conventional. Chapter one deals with Greek and Roman architecture, and so discusses the origin and development of the classical language of architecture, generally through the construction of monumental buildings. Chapter two is more complex, as the locations, styles and building types dealt with are more varied. It covers Romanesque architecture, the extraordinary and mysterious arrival in early 12th-century France of the Gothic and its later regional developments, and includes entries which range from private houses to churches, cathedrals and entire walled towns. Chapter three is yet more far-reaching in its scope. It starts with the return to classicism in early 15th-century Italy and concludes by discussing classical buildings in 18th-century England and America. Chapter four offers a very personal selection of those classical buildings which are generally termed Baroque. This is perhaps the most enigmatic of art-historical definitions. Conventionally, Baroque begins with the Counter-Reformation classicism of early-17th-century Italy, but classicism with so-called Baroque tendencies – invention, illogicality, theatricality, sinuous sense of movement, richness of decoration – can be found in late-Roman architecture and continues, in various regions, well into the 18th century. Chapter five offers additional insights into late-Baroque architecture while also describing 18th- and early-19th-century Neoclassical architecture in Europe and the United States. Chapter six focuses on those new building technologies which characterize 19th-century architecture and describes the ways in which architects wrestled to combine the potential offered by pioneering materials and methods of construction with a continuing need to make references to past, historic, architectural styles. Chapter seven looks at the decades around the end of the 19th century when historicism – in an extraordinary flourish of belated creativity – started to give way to anti-historical Modernism. Chapters eight and nine deal

with the 20th century, tracing the move from historicist architecture to Modernism – an architectural movement in which ornament was eschewed in preference for an architecture in which function, materials and techniques of construction were honestly expressed – and then onto the eclectic post-war years where Modernism was itself challenged and ultimately rejected. Chapter 10 highlights buildings of the last years of the 20th century which capture the wayward spirit of the time and which suggest directions for the 21st century.

This book is intended to act as a well-informed guide and inspiration to all those interested in architecture. I have been reading and writing about architecture for more than a quarter of a century but have still been delighted and surprised by the fresh ideas and observations herein and the concise way in which the authors have dealt with complex issues. *Architecture: The Critics' Choice* works not only for those familiar with the subject and attracted by a critics' selection of masterworks but also for those who wish to discover more about this remarkable field. All can now enjoy an authoritative book in which learned views are delivered with a clear, personal touch.

LEFT: George Gilbert Scott and W.H. Barlow, Midland Grand Hotel, St Pancras Station, London, 1865–77. Interior view of staircase

ABOVE: Otto Wagner, Karlsplatz Station, Vienna, 1894–1901, detail

The Classical World

Robin Francis Rhodes

The story of classical Greek and Roman architecture begins in prehistory, in the 2nd millennium BC, with the magnificent palaces and tombs of the Mycenaeans on the Greek mainland. And although Mycenaean culture disintegrated around 1100 BC, the instinct for monumental construction and even some of the forms of their architecture survived the subsequent Dark Age and flowered again with the Greeks of historical times.

Monumental architecture was reborn in Greece in the 8th century BC for religious observances, and over the next 250 years distinct regional styles of temple architecture evolved. The coast of Asia Minor, east of the Aegean Sea (now Turkey), was as crucial to the development of Greek culture as the mainland, and as the Doric order evolved as the architectural canon of the latter, so Ionic became the architecture of the former (see glossary for an explanation of the development of ancient Greek architecture and the orders). Similarly, the colonies of western Greece, in Sicily and southern Italy, developed their own distinctive conception of monumental religious architecture. Each of these regional styles evolved not so much as a set of abstract, aesthetic rules – although these were a factor – but as the direct expression of the local religious character and cult practice.

In the mid-5th century BC, Athens attained unprecedented levels of political, cultural and artistic magnificence and became the pivot of the Greek world; in the hands of the brilliant architects of the new Athenian Acropolis, the traditional regional styles were woven into a truly Pan-Hellenic architectural tapestry. Nor were the achievements of the 5th-century Athenians forgotten. Almost immediately, and especially in the Hellenistic kingdoms established by the conquests of Alexander the Great a century later, 5th-century Athenian art and architecture were copied and alluded to as a means of magnifying the grandeur of monumental structures.

With the annexation of Greece by Rome in the 2nd century BC, the foundations of empire were set, and the inspirational power of Greek and Athenian history and art found a new and fertile realm. Traditional forms of temple building handed

LEFT: Unknown architect, Temple of Fortuna Virilis (also known as Temple of Portunus) in the Forum Boarium (cattle market), Rome, c.40 BC

LEFT: Unknown architects, Forum of Augustus, Rome, AD 2

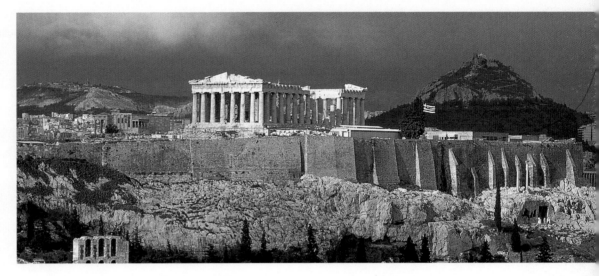

ABOVE: Various architects, the Acropolis (with the Parthenon in the foreground), Athens. Most of the buildings on the Acropolis date from the 5th century BC

down to the Romans by the Etruscans (who inhabited the Italian peninsula from the 8th century BC), and techniques and conceptions of construction dictated by their own invention of a miraculous concrete, were given a monumental facing of Greek decorative forms and materials. From then on, until Rome became a Christian empire in the 4th century AD, the meaning and intention of Roman architectural monuments lay not only in the massing of their elements and in their political, cultural and geographical context within the empire, but also in their particular balance and juxtaposition of Greek and native Roman technique and form.

Because of their great antiquity, most of the buildings of the Greeks and Romans have been destroyed (which is true of many of the works included here). Certainly the original decorative surfaces have very often been badly damaged and their painted colours almost always lost (we would be surprised by the vibrancy of many of the original structures). Similarly, it is only in rare cases that we can associate the name of an architect with a specific building. One problem here is remoteness of time and preservation of written sources, another is the fact that, particularly in Greek times, the architect was often not so much an individual 'genius' responsible for the conception and creation of a building as an organizer of master craftsmen and workmen. Yet in spite of all this, the fragmentary remains of the Greeks and Romans are able to tell remarkable stories of remarkable people who laid the foundations for the history of Western architecture.

Dipylon Vases
ATHENS, GREECE
8th century BC

Architect unknown

The history of Greek architecture as presented here is a history of monumental architecture, and the Greek monumental creation *par excellence* is the temple. Yet the earliest monumental form in Greece was not the temple, it was pottery: the vases that, towards the middle of the 8th century BC, were appearing in the Dipylon Cemetery in Athens (so called after the nearby double city gate).

The shapes of these vases were the same as those used for domestic purposes and their decoration was in the long line of Dark Age development following the collapse of the Mycenaean empire. What was altogether new, however, and what provides invaluable insight into the original nature of the monumental instinct in classical Greek art and architecture, was the scale and function of these vases. No longer were they intended to hold or mix or pour liquids. They marked graves, and in response to their new symbolic, spiritual function their scale ballooned almost insanely: some of these vases (which were fired in pieces) approach 2 m (6 ft) in height! Through their transformation in scale and function, the Dipylon Vases were blown right out of the realm of kitchen crockery and into the sphere of architecture. They became monuments to the dead, the drama of their own physical change reflecting the scale of the spiritual mutation of humankind in the move from life to death. This use of physical transformation as a metaphor for spiritual transformation is at the heart of Greek monumentality and explains why the grandest architecture was originally created in an exclusively religious context.

Greek temples were also emblems of spiritual transition, marking holy places that had been touched by divinity. And like the Dipylon Vases, it was through the metaphor of physical transformation that the temple, as it developed towards the Doric and Ionic orders, became a fitting monument for spiritual mediation between the ephemeral world of humans and the immortal realm of the gods. In its monumental form, the temple represented the metamorphosis of hut-sized, thatched, wood and mud-brick shelters for cult images into buildings larger than any created for practical purposes; the change of common, perishable materials and the undisguised details of their construction into permanent, god-like structures of neatly squared, regularly coursed, carefully joined stone masonry and tiled roofs.

The Dipylon Vases provide insight into the genesis of monumental Greek architecture as an architecture of transition and transformation. They also graphically illustrate the crucial role played by reverence for the heroic past in the development of the monumental arts. The chariot processions and figure-of-eight shields painted on many of the grave pots do not reflect everyday 8th-century Greece. Rather, they recall the heroism of Homer's epic, mythical poems the *Iliad* and the *Odyssey*, and gain monumentality by their association with this semi-divine past. The subsequent incorporation into Doric architecture of rediscovered Mycenaean architectural forms, including details of the columns and entablature, should be seen in the same deferential light.

DIPYLON VASE • NOW IN THE NATIONAL ARCHAEOLOGICAL MUSEUM, ATHENS

Temple of Artemis, Corcyra
CORFU, GREECE
c.580–570 BC

Architect unknown

The island of Corfu, to the northwest of present-day Greece, off the coast of Albania, was an early colony of the city of Corinth and was under Corinthian control when its Temple of Artemis was constructed. A milestone in Greek architecture, this was the first building that was truly Doric. Many if not all of its Doric characteristics had appeared in earlier structures but here they were used for the first time as an ensemble.

The Temple of Artemis was built entirely of stone, covered with a terra-cotta roof, and was conceived on a grand scale at approximately 49 x 23.5 m (160 x 77 ft). The basic structural and decorative elements of standard Doric temples were present: in plan, the temple was a rectangular hall (*cella*), consisting of a front porch (*pronaos*), back porch (*opisthodomos*), and main chamber in which the cult image was housed (*naos*), all surrounded by a continuous colonnade (peristyle) of Doric columns, surmounted by a Doric entablature.

This was not the first monumental temple in Greece but a continuation of the earliest tradition of such architecture. Ancient literary sources and modern archaeology suggest that Corfu's mother city and overlord, Corinth, a city in the heart of Dorian Greece, in the Peloponnese, was the home of Greek monumental structures. In the mid-7th century BC the Corinthians constructed the first truly monumental temples in Greece, a pair of simple, uncolonnaded, rectangular buildings, but complete with grand-scale, neatly cut stone masonry, the earliest datable tiled roofs in the Greek world, and the embryonic form of many aspects of later Doric. It is, therefore, not surprising that the first Doric temple appears in a Corinthian dependency, or that another major element of Greek monumental architecture attributed by the ancients to Corinthian invention

first appears on Corfu: the earliest known pediments (large triangular gables at each end of the building) belong to the architecture of Corfu.

The pediments of the Temple of Artemis carried relief sculpture. In the centre of each, and dominating both it and the viewer's eye, was a pair of carved leopards flanking a huge Gorgon Medusa. Rather than telling a story, these figures were transformed into monstrous emblems, staring out frontally, in direct engagement with anyone who approached the temple. The Gorgon would have been particularly terrifying, for in mythology her horrible gaze always resulted in petrification and death for anyone who met it directly, as her frontal disposition on the pediments demands. Given the dominating nature of the sculpture, both formally and emotionally, it seems clear that there was an intended relationship between this intimidating effect and the concept of divinity as housed in the temple. To judge from the Corfu pediments and the series of similar pediments they introduced into 6th-century Greece, monumental Greek-temple architecture was originally inspired not by the cool rationality of the human intellect, as embodied in human-shaped, Olympian gods, but by a concept of divinity more closely akin to representatives of the older, pre-Olympian, inhuman side of the universe: the awesome irrationality of nature, Mother Earth and the underworld.

ABOVE: The West Pediment of the Temple of Artemis, showing Gorgon and panthers. Now in the Corfu Archaeological Museum.

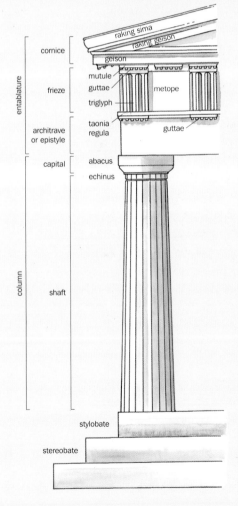

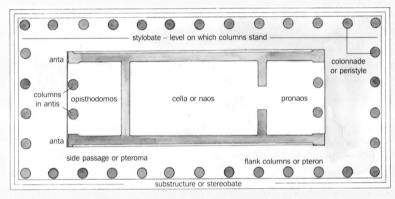

ABOVE AND LEFT: Elevation and plan of a typical Doric temple. The rectangular hall has a central chamber to house the image of the god, which is flanked by two porches. The hall is surrounded by a colonnade topped by an entablature

Temple of Artemis, Ephesus

SELÇUK, TURKEY
c.560–546 BC

Chersiphron
from Knossos

Metagenes
from Knossos,
son of Chersiphron

The Temple of Artemis at Ephesus was one of the Seven Wonders of the Ancient World. In its original incarnation it was also one of the first Ionic temples, made famous by a treatise written by its builders Chersiphron and Metagenes (a work known only from a reference to it by Vitruvius), and by its association with King Croesus (of 'rich as Croesus' fame) of Lydia, who contributed many of the temple's columns.

The Ionic columns were lofty, some with figurative carvings on their shafts, and carried beautifully wrought capitals and elaborately sculpted friezes. But the overwhelming magnificence of the temple was due to a scale completely foreign to Doric architecture. The temple measured some 109 x 55 m (357½ x 180 ft) and was four to five times larger than most contemporary Doric temples on the mainland. Doric temples were monumental but the first Ionic temples in Asia Minor were colossal.

In combination with a low stepped base and its siting in a flat coastal plain, the enormous width and length of the Artemis temple created an overwhelmingly horizontal effect. This and the ambiguous position of the peristyle columns, set well back from the edge of the top step, blurred the boundary between temple and landscape. The resulting sense of continuity between the temple and its surroundings, between constructed and natural, was enhanced by the sheer number of columns (two rows as opposed to a single row in Doric) which evoked the sacred grove in which the temple probably stood. The essentially unbroken procession from landscape to temple was then continued in the spacing of the columns, which widened from the back, along the sides, to the front, with the widest spacing of all on the axis (and so in the centre) of the temple front. And the architectural procession did not end there: echoing the peristyle, pairs of carefully aligned columns extended into the heart of the cella itself, seamlessly integrating exterior and interior.

Unlike the standard Doric temple – which prevents continuity with the landscape and isolates itself from the individual through its higher base, the unambiguous positioning of its peristyle columns at the edge of the top step, its siting on an eminence, and the paralysing effect of its pediment which holds the worshipper at a distance – everything about Ionic consciously blurs the borders between landscape and temple, exterior and interior, even prescribing the paths along which this mingling should occur. And, unlike the Doric temple, whose formal character is consonant with a ritual environment separated from the temple and focused exclusively on the altar in front of the building, the processional qualities of Ionic clearly suggest that rituals also occurred within the boundaries of the temple itself.

Contrasting ideas of humanity's relationship with divinity, as well as different ceremonial and aesthetic requirements, are eloquently expressed in the early temple architecture of ancient Greece. With the Temple of Artemis at Ephesus, the Ionic architecture of Asia Minor is firmly established as an architecture of procession, a form distinct in conception and formal language from the temple architecture of the Doric mainland.

TEMPLE OF ARTEMIS, EPHESUS · SELÇUK *RECONSTRUCTION*

LEFT AND ABOVE: Towering columns with intricately modelled capitals contribute to the impressive stature of this Ionic temple. Standing on a low, stepped base, its scale creates an overall horizontal effect, which allows it to blend into the surrounding Turkish landscape

Temple of Olympian Zeus, Akragas

AGRIGENTO, SICILY, ITALY
late 6th century BC, unfinished

Architect unknown

A third distinctive style of temple architecture evolved in Magna Graecia, which comprised the Greek colonies of Sicily and southern Italy. The peculiarly western Greek conception of monumental religious architecture can be most clearly traced and analysed in the temples of Sicily, and the Temple of Olympian Zeus at Akragas expressed perhaps better than any other the spirit of Sicilian temple cults and the architectural means by which their ritual needs were met.

Its unique form, which included huge man-shaped columnar supports (*telamones*), placed either between the columns of the peristyle or in the interior of the temple, can be partially understood in Doric terms, partially in Ionic; but most useful in analysing its meaning is its position at the end of the extended evolution of Sicilian temples.

In the spirit of competition with the Sicilian city of Selinus, which had recently begun constructing a colossal temple, and perhaps reflecting increasing cultural influences from the rest of Greece in the late 6th century, the Temple of Zeus was constructed on a vast, Ionic scale (more than 100 x 50 m, 328 x 164 ft); its exterior elevation, however, was overwhelmingly Doric, with Doric columns and entablature. Remarkably, the spaces between the columns in the peristyle were filled with stone masonry walls. Looked at in Ionic and Doric terms, this seems strangely eccentric, but placed in the context of the development of Sicilian architecture, it makes perfect sense.

From the beginning, Sicilian cults seem to have been centred on an interior space, a closed back sanctuary in the *cella* of the temple, the *adyton*, a feature clearly borrowed from the architecture of the pre-Greek inhabitants of the island and indicative of the essentially chthonic

nature (that is, focused on the earth, the underworld, and often expressed in mystery cults) of their religion. Over the course of the 6th century, the formal veneer of Doric and Ionic employed by the Sicilians in the construction of their temples was transformed by the peculiar needs of their religion. Most significant was a gradual increase in the depth of the peristyle until it was essentially equal to the width of the *cella*, implying, perhaps, that the ritual significance of the colonnade was becoming equal to that of the *cella*. The result was a temple plan conceived as three parallel halls of equal size: colonnade, *cella*, colonnade. The final step in this equalization came with the addition of screen walls in the peristyle of the Temple of Zeus, which made the colonnades and *cella* equivalent in spatial character as well as in size. This seems to mark the final Sicilianization of western Greek-temple architecture, in which the language of Doric and Ionic have been transformed by the indigenous needs of the Sicilian Greeks into an architecture of the interior, appropriate to the chthonic character of their cults, whose mystery rites seem to have required total privacy. This interior focus suggests that the *telamones* were part of the interior elaboration of the temple rather than exterior supports, as traditionally restored.

Propylaea, Acropolis
ATHENS, GREECE
437–432 BC, unfinished

Mnesikles

The Propylaea was the monumental gateway constructed as the entrance to the Acropolis in Athens. Its form and scale were unprecedented in the Greek world, and even more eloquently than the Parthenon (*see pages 26–27*), its practical, spiritual and political function was expressed in the seamless mesh of the native architecture of the two major regions of the Aegean Sea and of the Athenian Empire: Ionic and Doric.

The Propylaea served as the monumental vehicle of transition between the city of Athens below and the heights of the Acropolis, between the secular world of everyday life and the sacred *temenos* (sanctuary) of the goddess Athena. Through its split-level construction, which stepped up like the rock of the plateau itself, the Propylaea welcomed the final procession of the Grand Panathenaia (*see page 26*) onto the Acropolis.

The transitional nature of the building was expressed most creatively and effectively in its unique western elevation which hailed the procession from afar. Its double pediments, which, like the route of the progress, stepped up from west to east, reflected the changing ground level within the Propylaea, as well as serving as a metaphor for the spiritual alteration that occurred at the border between the profane and the sacred. Indeed, the Propylaea was not simply a *marker* of transition. Instead, through the character of its façade, which projected the spirit of transition and procession far out into the city, and through its outreaching wings, which embraced the advancing Panathenaic procession before it reached the ramp and stairs that led into the building proper, the Propylaea helped prepare those approaching for the transformation that would be required of them when they finally stepped from the outside world into the sanctuary of Athena.

Like the Parthenon, the Propylaea is on the surface a solidly Doric building, resembling a traditional Doric temple with a six-columned façade. But as might be expected in a building whose purpose was essentially processional – and even more so than the Parthenon – the spirit of the Propylaea is distinctly Ionic. As in Ionic temples, the spaces between the columns of its façade are graduated in width, from narrowest at the corners to widest on the axis of the building, where the procession would have passed; and that widest spacing was carried back into the interior of the building by means of successive pairs of columns – Ionic ones. Virtually every detail of the Propylaea, including a contrasting blue limestone course as the top step of the interior staircase, beneath the second pediment and indicating the precise boundary of the Athena sanctuary, was conceived in the service of religious procession.

Finally, the Propylaea, the beginning of the architectural circuit of the Acropolis, also served to foreshadow its end: the cult image of Athena Parthenos in the *cella* of the Parthenon. Just as the statue presented to the Athenians an image of Nike, goddess of victory, on her outstretched hand, so the Propylaea extended on one of its wings a little Ionic Temple of Athena Nike (420s BC), symbol of Athens' success against the Persians, of her advancement as the leader of the Greek world.

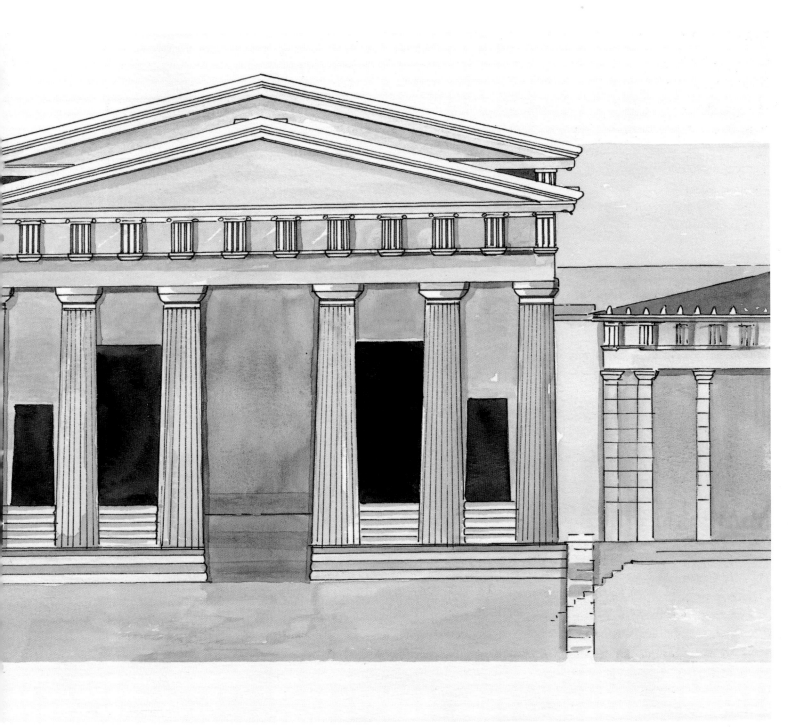

PROPYLAEA, ACROPOLIS • ATHENS *RECONSTRUCTION*

Parthenon, Acropolis
ATHENS, GREECE
447–432 BC

Iktinos
active mid- to late
5th century BC

Kallikrates
active mid- to late
5th century BC

The Parthenon is undoubtedly one of the great achievements of Western architecture, and as a document of history, culture and faith it stands today as the most legible Greek temple ever constructed. It formed the centrepiece of the building programme of the great Athenian general Pericles and the jewel of the 5th-century Acropolis, the citadel on a high plateau containing the main temples of the city.

The Parthenon was inspired by the Greek defeat of the Persians after 40 years of war. It was the most richly sculpted temple of classical Greece, and the themes of its metopes (part of a Doric frieze) and pediments – the victory of the Greeks over the Amazons, the Trojans and the centaurs; of the gods over the giants; of Athena, the goddess of wisdom and civilization, over Poseidon, the god of earthquakes, the sea and the irrational forces of nature; and the birth of Athena, patron deity of Athens and symbol of the city – proclaimed Athens to be the victor over the barbarians of Persia, saviour of Greece, protector of civilization, patron of high culture, and centre of the world.

The Parthenon is often cited as the ultimate achievement of Doric architecture, the pinnacle of the Doric order as it evolved on the mainland. Yet, more profoundly, the new Athenian self-image and world view, as inspired by the miraculous defeat of the Persians and the establishment of an Athenian empire, were here expressed through the traditions of both Doric and Ionic, whose combination in the Parthenon announced the creation of a truly and intentionally international style of architecture.

On the surface, the Parthenon was solidly Doric, with Doric columns and capitals, architrave and frieze, cornice and sculpted pediment. But on a conceptual level the temple resonated with Ionic spirit. First, the eight columns across the façade reflected Ionic tradition (as compared to the typical Doric six). Similarly, the second row of columns within the peristyle at each end gave the impression of an Ionic double colonnade. Also Ionic in spirit, if not in detail, was the gradual widening of the metopes in the Doric frieze on the ends of the temple, from the narrowest at the corners to the widest in the centre, a clear recollection of the graduated spacing of the columns on the front of 6th-century Ionic temples (see pages 20–21). Again, the processional spirit of Ionic was expressed in a continuous Ionic frieze set above the columns of the porches and on the long walls of the cella which carried a carved representation of a procession that moved from the back of the temple, up the sides, culminating in the centre of the front, eastern façade.

The combination of Doric and Ionic in the Parthenon symbolized Athens' new role as mistress of the entire Aegean Sea, eastern Greece and the mainland, as well as her legendary and linguistic connections with the ancient Ionians. But perhaps most important, the incorporation of Ionic procession in the temple was an expression of the native Athenian religion and of the primary religious role of the Acropolis, which it had fulfilled for more than a century: to serve as the climax of the great procession on the city's most significant festival, the Grand Panathenaia, the birthday of Athena.

PARTHENON, ACROPOLIS • ATHENS *DETAIL*

Altar of Zeus, Pergamon

BERGAMA, TURKEY
mid-2nd century BC

Architect unknown

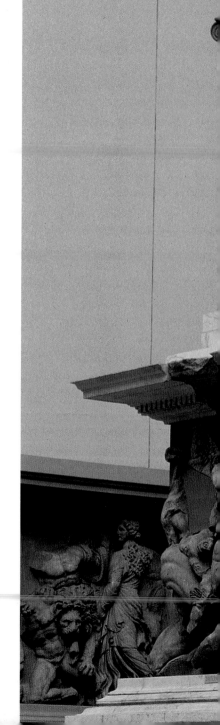

By the middle of the 4th century BC, Periclean Athens had already begun to take on the aura of mythology. Throughout the Greek world people looked back on mid-5th-century Athens, with its magnificent architectural and sculptural creations, its philosophers and playwrights, historians and mathematicians, as a golden age of human achievement. And, as Athens had used myths of Troy, giants, Amazons and centaurs to evoke its own monumental presence, so Greeks of the 4th century and beyond began to elevate themselves and their creations by means of association with Periclean Athens.

The most detailed and comprehensive of these Athenian references were found in the eastern Greek city of Pergamon, the capital of one of the Hellenistic kingdoms of Alexander the Great's successors. Here, the image the city presented to the rest of the world was couched almost entirely in terms of 5th-century Athenian history and art. A series of 3rd-century victories over the barbarian Gauls was likened to the Athenian victories over the Persians and crafted into an image of Pergamon as heir to Athens, protector of Greek culture. When a temple to Athena was constructed on the Pergamene acropolis, it was not in the local Ionic style but in the Doric of the Parthenon (*see pages 26–27*). As in Athens, the Pergamenes dedicated a statue of Athena Promachos (leader in battle) on their acropolis, and one of Athena Parthenos (Athena the maiden), whose sculpted base was nearly identical to that of Athena Parthenos in the Parthenon. And they instituted a religious festival for Athena that was modelled on the Grand Panathenaia of Athens.

At Pergamon, Athenian allusion was applied with academic precision and detail, and nowhere more so than in the great Altar of Zeus, one of the most elaborately sculpted monuments in the Greek world and the centrepiece of the Pergamene acropolis and public image. Like the architecture of the Athenian Acropolis, the Altar of Zeus was a strikingly original creation, consisting on the exterior of an Ionic peristyle supported by a high base that carried dramatic sculpture in high relief. More specifically, it shows the influence of the Parthenon. Both represented the battle of the gods and giants as a symbol of the victory of civilization over barbarism; as on the Ionic frieze of the Parthenon, the proceeding figures moved from the back of the structure to the front, and even up the front steps to the altar; many of the figures on the altar were based on similar ones on the Parthenon; and the carving of the gods was in the idealized style of 5th-century Athens.

All this served to associate Pergamon and her accomplishments directly and literally with Athens. Yet the intellectual rigour with which this association was accomplished was truly original, as was the new life breathed into the traditional mythical conflict by the expressive contrast between the controlled 5th-century style of the gods and the emotion-packed, contorted forms of the giants, who embodied the best qualities of a dynamic Pergamene sculptural tradition.

ALTAR OF ZEUS, PERGAMON • BERGAMA, NOW IN PERGAMON MUSEUM, BERLIN

Portonaccio Temple, Veii

NEAR ISOLA FARNESE, ITALY
c.500 BC

Architect unknown

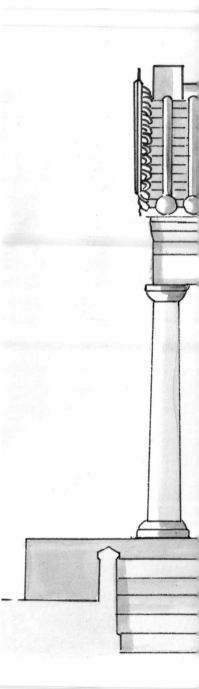

During the 8th century BC, at about the time the great Dipylon Vases were being created in Athens *(see pages 16–17)*, a parallel and closely related culture emerged on the Italian peninsula. The Etruscans were the cultural and political predecessors of the Romans. Like the Greeks, they quickly established a tradition of monumental art and architecture to serve religion, with the temple as a main focus.

The Romans derived their temple architecture from that of the Etruscans, and the Etruscans, in turn, were heavily indebted to the Greeks. Theirs was a columnar architecture, with columns not unlike the Doric, a heavy tiled roof and sculpture. But lacking good local stone, the Etruscans relied almost exclusively on scale and on moulded terra-cotta as the monumentalizing agents in their temple architecture (the main structural materials were wood and mud brick). Corinth, the original home of monumental temple architecture in Greece, seems to have provided the Etruscans with valuable technological know-how in the moulding of terra-cotta. According to Roman tradition, it was brought to Etruria by Demaratos, a Corinthian sent into exile at around the time the Corinthians were constructing their first monumental temples (mid-7th century BC). Demaratos' son was the first Etruscan king of Rome and began the great Temple of Jupiter, Juno and Minerva (the Capitoline Triad) on the Capitoline Hill in Rome. The overseer of that temple as it neared completion at the end of the 6th century BC was Vulca, a famous sculptor from Veii, an Etruscan city near Rome.

The Portonaccio Temple at Veii, just south of the ancient city, was constructed at the time Vulca was active (around 500 BC) and was almost certainly indebted to him and his workshop. It displayed the characteristics that differentiated the

Etruscan (or Tuscan as it is also known) temple from the Greek: heavily proportioned roof, lavish terra-cotta revetment (facing), and, most significantly, a frontal emphasis. The temple stood on a podium approached by steps only at the front, and unlike the framing Greek peristyle, it had columns only on the front porch, set in front of a *cella* that occupied the full width of the podium and half its length.

Yet the Portonaccio Temple was not simply representative of Etruscan temple architecture; it represented it at its finest. Vulca (or another eminent Veiian sculptor) cast some of the finest examples of monumental terra-cotta sculpture in the ancient world to adorn the roof. Unlike Greek pedimental sculpture, which was confined to the gable at each end of the roof, these figures – Apollo, Hercules, Mercury and others – strode back and forth along the ridge of the temple, presenting the narrative of one of Hercules' labours. Vulca's fame for this kind of roof sculpture (*acroteria*) is preserved in ancient accounts of the great four-horse terra-cotta chariot that Jupiter drove on the ridge of the Temple of the Capitoline Triad in Rome.

The Portonaccio Temple can be viewed as a microcosm of Etruscan culture and architecture: inspired by Greek prototypes of architecture, sculpture and myth, it was completely original in its detail, its synthesis, and in its uninhibited spirit.

PORTONACCIO TEMPLE, VEII • *NEAR ISOLA FARNESE RECONSTRUCTION*

Sanctuary of Fortuna, Praeneste

PALESTRINA, ITALY

late 2nd or early 1st century BC

Architect unknown

The Sanctuary of Fortuna at Praeneste near Rome is the most spectacular of the great sanctuaries of the late Roman Republic. Constructed on a series of terraces which rise up a steep slope, it was inspired by similar sanctuaries of Hellenistic Greece. Yet its major significance lies not in the Greek origins of its conception but in its articulation of what became the classic principles of Roman architecture through the remarkable combination of native Italian technology and the classical Greek orders.

Just as important for the evolution of Roman architecture as the adoption of the Etruscan temple form (see pages 30–31) was the invention in the late 3rd or 2nd century BC of a tremendously flexible and durable concrete. It was a synthetic limestone that could be poured and moulded into any form and was much cheaper than the building stones of the Greeks (marbles and limestones), which were hugely expensive to quarry and transport. Concrete allowed the Romans to build extensively and, eventually, in forms completely foreign to the trabeated architecture of the Greeks. The Sanctuary of Fortuna was a landmark in the history of concrete construction: here the seven terraces of the upper sanctuary were united by concrete, producing a monolithic structure which many have been called the first skyscraper.

The Sanctuary of Fortuna was purely Roman in its structure but its appearance was solidly Greek. Its concrete terraces were faced with Doric, Ionic and Corinthian columns and entablatures and stuccoed to resemble Greek cut stone. Just as the Pergamenes ennobled their buildings through reference to 5th-century Athens (see pages 28–29), so the Romans elevated their own structures by cloaking them in the architectural symbols of the cultural glory of classical Greece.

Yet again, Corinth appears as one of the great transmitters of monumental architecture in the Mediterranean. In the 2nd century BC it was the centre of resistance to the Roman annexation of Greece but in 146 BC was sacked by the Roman general Mummius. Every movable piece of art was stripped from the city and brought back to Rome, creating a booming antiquities market and an unquenchable thirst for things Greek. It also caused a profound change in the language of Roman architecture, through the careful combination of traditional forms and construction techniques with a veneer of the Greek orders.

Republican Rome valued moderation, frugality, practicality and local tradition, and the antithetical foreign luxury and decadence that accompanied the influx of wealth from Rome's new conquests was epitomized for many by the deluge of Greek art. The Sanctuary of Fortuna was one of the earliest and most comprehensive combinations of Roman concrete and the Greek orders and can be seen as a kind of architectural metaphor for the subsequent complexity of the Roman character, as Rome was transformed from a local phenomenon to an imperial power: a Republican core given grandeur by a skin of Greek sophistication, with its historical, legendary and mythical associations.

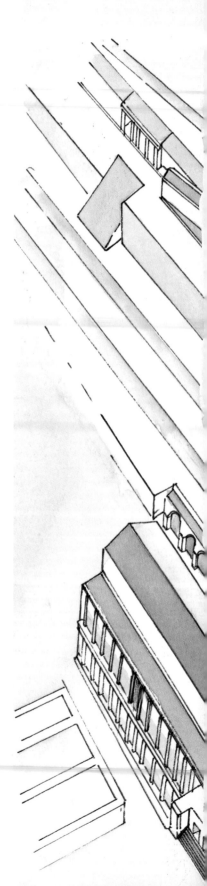

SANCTUARY OF FORTUNA, PRAENESTE • PALESTRINA RECONSTRUCTION

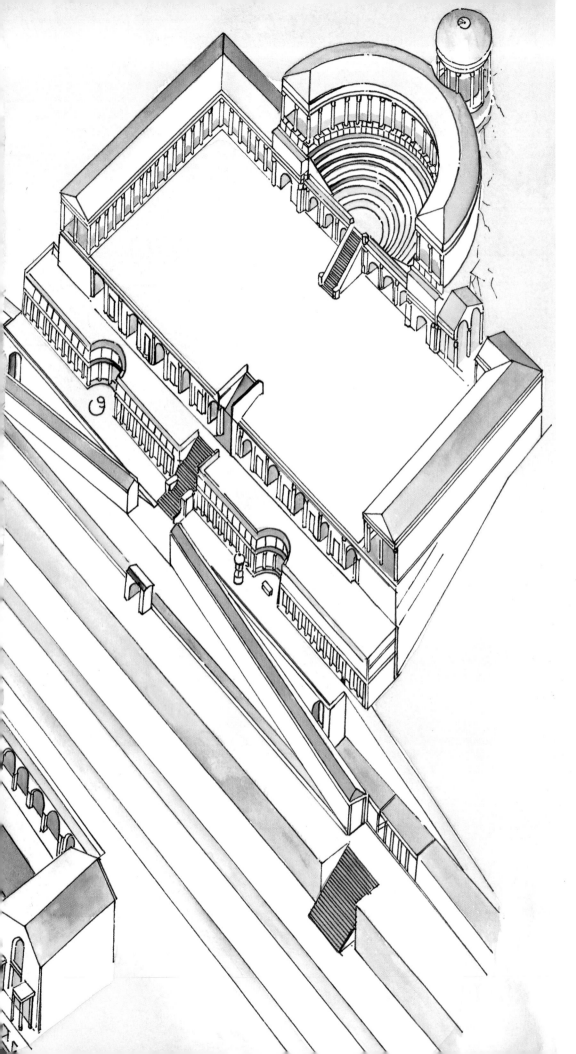

LEFT: The steep terraces of this Roman
temple were inspired by earlier Greek
architecture, which was also the
motivating force behind the appearance
of the columns and entablatures.
However, Greek building materials of
limestone and marble were replaced by a
much cheaper material – concrete

Forum of Augustus | Architect unknown

ROME, ITALY
begun 2 BC

Augustus claimed to have 'found Rome a city of brick and left it a city of marble'. He transformed the Roman everyday into the Grecian monumental. The Roman writer Pliny believed the Forum of Augustus was one of the three most beautiful buildings in the world, mainly because of its lavish use of white and coloured marbles imported from all over the Roman world. It is also the first of the great imperial fora of Rome, and through its skilful manipulation of Greek and Roman materials, forms and history, it stands as the most comprehensive political treatise of Rome's first emperor.

Greek monumentality, particularly in the beginning, was conceived in the service of religion, but in the Forum of Augustus monumental form had a different purpose: the glorification of Augustus and his family. This was achieved through association with classical Greece, the mythologies of the Olympian gods and the Roman people, and the great figures from Roman history. As at Praeneste (see pages 32–33), the most immediately recognizable vehicle of monumentalization in the forum was Greek allusion: the Corinthian columns and entablature of the Temple of Mars Ultor (the avenger), its long, framing stoas (porticoes), and the ubiquitous veneer of marble. But the association with Greece was even more specific, particularly in the copies of the famous caryatids (human-shaped columns) from the Erechtheion (421–406 BC) on the Acropolis in Athens, which appeared in the upper storey of the stoas. Similarly, in the temple itself were placed the Parthian Standards, symbols of the Roman army captured earlier in the century by the Parthians and returned to Rome by Augustus. The Parthians were a barbarian people on the eastern border of the empire, and in his propaganda Augustus equated them with the Persian threat to 5th-

century Greece. As in the famous Prima Porta Augustus (Vatican Museum, the Vatican), a statue of the emperor modelled after the most famous sculpture of 5th-century Greece, Augustus in his forum magnified himself and his accomplishments – and so those of Rome – by association with the monuments and achievements of classical Greece.

The references for the architectural ornament of the Forum of Augustus were classical Greek, but its structural and symbolic heart was Roman. Beneath the marble was Roman concrete, and the plan of its temple was pure Tuscan (Etruscan; see pages 30–31). Behind the columns of the stoas were statues of Romans, on one side famous figures of the Republic, on the other members of the patrician clan of the Julians who traced their origins back to the goddess Venus. Julius Caesar, the political predecessor of Augustus whose image stood in the temple with that of Mars and Venus, had adopted Augustus into the Julian clan. Through this relationship, Augustus was able to claim divine sanction for his rule. And through the Parthian Standards and the depiction of great Republicans he was also able to present himself as re-establishing the Roman peace and returning Rome to the ideals of the Republic.

Golden House of Nero

ROME, ITALY
AD 64–68

Severus and Celer

Augustus presented his divine pedigree in the Forum of Augustus *(see pages 34–35)* and elsewhere, but coupled with that was always a strong expression of the traditional Republican ideals of practicality, economy and pious humility. He could have lived in royal splendour but chose to live in a modest house on the Palatine Hill, next to the simple hut of the legendary founder of Rome, Romulus.

And Augustus could have appropriated the land for his forum, but he negotiated and bought it with his own money. Its irregular border, the result of his inability to strike a deal with certain landowners, forever reminded the Romans of the unwillingness of Augustus to abuse his power by confiscating the land, and stood as a monument to his fairness and respect for the rights of the citizenry.

By contrast, Augustus' successors, the Julio-Claudians (so called after the union of the Julians and another Roman patrician clan), presented themselves as gods and ruled as if all of Rome and her empire were their personal property. The greatest offender, whose behaviour eventually brought down the dynasty, was Nero, and his pleasure-palace stood as the supreme monument to the excess and hubris of the family. The Golden House of Nero (Domus Aurea), designed and constructed by the architect-engineers Severus and Celer, occupied more than 120 hectares (300 acres) of the heart of Rome, land taken by the emperor for his own use after a devastating fire in AD 64. To the disgust of the Roman people, he constructed a huge country estate in the centre of the crowded city, which included an artificial lake, cascading waterfalls, colonnades, a colossal bronze statue of himself, and a sumptuous palace filled with lush wall paintings, moulded plaster, brightly coloured stones and glass, revolving domes and ceilings that sprinkled perfume and flowers on diners below. Nero's reaction to his creation was: 'Now I can finally live like a human.'

Ironically, it was in the most luxurious and self-absorbed building in the history of Rome that cheap, practical, native Roman concrete first began to realize its true potential. Up to this point, concrete had been viewed primarily as a core material or as an aid to construction through its ability to be moulded into arches and vaults. With the Golden House, concrete's efficacy as a shaper of interior space was seriously explored. Unlike the Greeks' post-and-lintel architecture, whose simple structural properties are visible inside and out and are at the heart of its aesthetic, the structural properties of moulded concrete are often hidden, particularly in vaulted interiors where the walls and ceiling present no posts or beams, just a continuous, unbroken surface. Concrete has the power to eliminate the expression of structure from the aesthetic equation. Ironically, in the hands of Nero's architects, who had unlimited funds and creative *carte blanche* to experiment with the novel forms and spatial effects made possible by concrete, this utilitarian invention became a tool of the imagination, and the course of Western architecture was changed. Because of this landmark palace, Roman architecture increasingly became an architecture of complex interior spaces.

GOLDEN HOUSE OF NERO • ROME *INTERIOR DETAIL*

Colosseum
ROME, ITALY
AD 69–96

Architect unknown

Although today the Colosseum (Flavian Amphitheatre) is the most famous ancient monument in Rome, its original political significance is often overlooked. This is ironic because the building was constructed primarily as a statement for the common Roman citizenry. The Colosseum was a house of entertainment, a permanent venue for the gladiatorial combats of which they were so fond. But, more significantly, this celebration of the character and taste of the Roman people was constructed in the heart of Nero's Golden House (see pages 36–37), obliterating the great artificial lake.

By superimposing one of the first monumental constructions of his reign on the hated symbol of the ruthlessly undemocratic Julio-Claudian dynasty, Vespasian, a seasoned general of non-patrician lineage (of the Flavian clan), established himself as an emperor *of the people* and their liberator from tyranny. This message was reinforced by his rejection of the idealized, Hellenized portrait style of the Julio-Claudians – like Augustus (see page 34), they dignified their architecture and sculpture through Greek allusion – with a return in his official portraiture to the unpretentious 'warts-and-all' style of the Late Republic. Vespasian presented himself to Rome as a fellow human being, not as a god. (Work continued on the Colosseum during the reigns of Vespasian's sons, Titus and Domitian.)

Nothing could be more appropriate as a monument to the Roman people than a building constructed using traditional materials and techniques – and so the solution to constructing an amphitheatre in a flat plain (as opposed to digging it out of a hillside) was concrete. Unlike Severus and Celer in the Golden House, the architects and engineers of the Colosseum were not experimenting with the novel spatial effects made possible by concrete; they were concerned with its structural potential. The monolithic qualities of concrete had been known since the time of the Fortuna Sanctuary, Praeneste (see pages 32–33), but in the Colosseum all vestiges of Greek terraced sanctuaries or Greek theatres built into natural hollows in the hillside had completely disappeared. Here, concrete was moulded into an immense, freestanding, multistoreyed structure of vaults, stacked one on top of the other, capable of seating 50,000 spectators. This uniquely Roman building (the Greeks never acquired a taste for gladiatorial combat) was constructed in a uniquely Roman form and technique.

Each storey of the Colosseum is sheathed in the classical orders: Doric on the ground floor, Ionic on the next, Corinthian above, and Corinthian pilasters on the attic. But its monumentality is not drawn exclusively from this reference to classical Greece; the dominating visual features of the building – its massive, elliptical shape and three superimposed tiers of open arches – are purely Roman, the result of its nature as a moulded concrete structure. Rather than hiding behind a Greek veneer, the form of the Colosseum shines through, creating its own aesthetic and delivering its message of traditional culture and values.

Pantheon

ROME, ITALY

AD 118–28

Hadrian (?)

Emperor AD 117–38

The Pantheon is perhaps the most complex and literate architectural synthesis ever created in the Roman world. Following Vespasian's example (*see pages 38–39*), succeeding Roman emperors emphasized their own goals and convictions by associating or disassociating themselves from the works of their predecessors. Thus, Hadrian could associate himself with Rome's Golden Age under Augustus by covering his buildings in the classical Greek orders and by rebuilding monuments of Augustus' reign.

Hadrian also made profound political and religious statements by invoking specific monuments of classical Greece. That he was directly responsible for at least some of the architectural creations of his reign is suggested by the criticism meted out to him by one of his architects, Apollodorus, for the design of the Temple of Venus and Rome (consecrated AD 135) in the Roman Forum. The nature of this criticism also gives an insight into Hadrian's understanding of Greek architecture in its original context and his sometimes literal references to it. Apollodorus was offended by the fact that this colossal building, 136 x 66 m (446 x 217 ft), stood not on a high podium, as Roman temples did, but was barely raised above the plain of the surrounding Forum. This kind of horizontal continuity was unthinkable in Roman temple architecture, but it was perfectly expressive of the nature of the huge 6th-century BC temples of Ionia, after which the temple was clearly modelled.

In choosing to rebuild the Pantheon, Hadrian aligned himself with Augustus and his ideals, for the original temple (dedicated 25 BC; damaged then destroyed by fire, AD 80 and 110) had been a creation of Augustus' right-hand man, Agrippa. Yet in his design Hadrian went far beyond this link. The Pantheon was conceived in two main parts: a triple-colonnaded Corinthian porch that supported a pediment above and whose graduated column spacings spoke of Ionic architectural procession; and a circular *cella* supporting the largest concrete dome ever created in antiquity, a wonderful structure that was originally covered with gilt bronze. Forming the transition between the Greek porch and Roman interior was a Roman arch, whose attic rose above the porch and whose face carried a second pediment. The doubled pediment of the Pantheon façade unambiguously quoted the Propylaea of the Athenian Acropolis (*see pages 24–25*) and, combined with Rome's own powerful architectural symbol of transition, the triumphal arch, formed the most complete expression of architectural and spiritual transition in the classical world. And as the Propylaea led to the sanctuary of Athena on the Acropolis, so the pediments and porch of the Pantheon articulated the transition from the secular world outside to an interior space whose concrete-built dome represented the heavens. In his Pantheon, the Temple of All Gods, Hadrian pursued a universal expression of political, cultural and religious unity through Augustan pedigree and through the sensitive interpretation and combination of some of the most evocative forms in Greek and Roman architecture.

Library of Hadrian

Architect unknown

Hadrian was a philhellene of the first degree who preferred Greece and the east to Rome, and his deep understanding of the forms and spirit of classical Greek architecture profoundly influenced the design of his monuments at home. But as the Pantheon shows *(see pages 40–41)*, he was no slavish imitator of things Greek; nor did he fail to appreciate the unique architectural character and accomplishments of his capital, the indigenous architecture of imperial Rome, which, in turn, he took to Greece.

As might be expected of such a student of Greek art and culture, Athens was a favourite city of Hadrian's. No longer the centre of power it had been in the 5th century BC, its architectural treasures still stood, and it had long been a kind of university town where Roman patricians sent their sons to be educated. Significantly, then, for its place in the living museum of Athens and as an expression of Hadrian's commitment to the intellect and to the study of classical antiquity, one of the enduring monuments of his reign was the great Library he built at the foot of the Acropolis.

Pausanias, a traveller of the 2nd century AD, whose descriptions of the cities and monuments of Greece have been tremendously influential in our understanding of antiquity, called the Library the most magnificent of Hadrian's creations in Athens. The building was lushly appointed with coloured marbles. In form, it was a large rectangular enclosure lined within by porticoes and containing a long pool surrounded by gardens. In one of the short walls was the axial entranceway to the complex; directly opposite, behind the portico, was a series of large rooms. The main, central room was certainly a library, but other activities seem to have been accommodated within the structure, possibly including theatrical performances,

lectures, exhibitions and other cultural pursuits. Whatever the details of its function, human intellect rather than an Olympian or imperial cult seems to have been the focus of Hadrian's Library.

With the Pantheon and the Temple of Venus and Rome, Hadrian manifested his understanding of classical Greek architecture in the city of Rome. Conversely, with his Library he seems to have introduced into the architectural fabric of Athens one of the imperial fora of Rome, the Forum of Vespasian (AD 71–79, the Templum Pacis), which it closely resembled. Yet in its architectural details – the freestanding pedestal bases of the façade columns of the enclosure wall, the two-stepped architrave and the cornice consoles above, the drafted edges of the masonry, the stone of the interior colonnades – the Library of Hadrian was representative of the entire Roman Empire, particularly the Greek east. By combining Roman form with a setting and function so specifically Athenian, Hadrian suggested the integration of the classical Greek and Roman vision; and through the judicious use of architectural details and materials indigenous to other parts of the empire, his Library was an unambiguous statement of both the dissolution of regional differences and the international character of the Roman Empire.

Basilica of Maxentius

ROME, ITALY
AD 307–12

Architect unknown

Beginning with the Emperor Hadrian, the primacy of Rome as the centre of the empire steadily diminished until, finally, the capital was moved from Rome to Constantinople (Istanbul) by the Emperor Constantine in AD 330. The last of the great imperial structures of Rome was commissioned by his immediate predecessor and the last pagan emperor, Maxentius: his colossal Basilica (also known as the Basilica Nova) is one of the masterpieces of Roman architecture.

Maxentius' Basilica was sited on the Sacred Way in the Roman Forum. It stood close to two other famous basilicas in the Forum, the Basilica Aemilia and the Basilica Julia, and was perhaps intended in part as a formal response to another immense vaulted structure directly opposite, Hadrian's temple of Venus and Rome, which was rebuilt by Maxentius after the fire.

The basilica was an ancient Roman building type, dating back into the Republic, which was developed for housing law courts. It was also used to symbolize the emperor and the might of the empire, as in the great imperial forum of the emperor Trajan (dedicated AD 113; architect Apollodorus of Damascus, active late 1st–early 2nd century AD), where the famous Basilica Ulpia stood as its central structure. The Basilica Ulpia, like other traditional Roman basilicas, was a rectangular building with a nave and two side aisles, covered with a pitched wooden roof, and lit by clerestory windows at the top of the nave walls. The Basilica of Maxentius was also lit by a clerestory and consisted of a nave and two side aisles, but here the nave was covered with three massive concrete cross vaults and the side aisles with three corresponding barrel vaults. Clearly, Maxentius' Basilica was looking beyond traditional

Roman basilicas for inspiration and towards another important, indigenous Roman building type, the great imperial bath. More than any other structures, the imperial baths of Rome (*thermae*, which included gardens, gymnasia and libraries as well as pools) had exploited the new understanding of concrete that followed the innovations in Nero's Golden House (*see pages 36–37*). In the Basilica of Maxentius, Roman builders demonstrated complete mastery of concrete construction, in the soaring height of the nave and its vast span, and in the vaulted side aisles which not only moulded large unbroken spaces but also buttressed the massive vaults of the nave.

The Basilica of Maxentius stood as a magnificent, synthetic creation at the end of the line of development of two important and popular types of public building in Rome, the basilica and the imperial bath. It also stood on the cusp of a new era, one that would be crucial to the religious observances and the architecture of the subsequent medieval period. Under the Christian emperor Constantine, Christian architecture found imperial sponsorship, and the Roman building type to which the early Christians turned as the most appropriate architectural expression of the ritual needs of their church was the basilica.

BASILICA OF MAXENTIUS • ROME

Early Christian, Romanesque and Gothic

Robert Harbison

In the period covered by this chapter (c.400–c.1600), Christianity grows from an eccentric sect to a cultural force that replaces Roman Imperial administration as the main binding principle across Europe, including northern and eastern areas that had been immune to Roman influence.

It really comprises three periods: Late Empire, when the centre of gravity moves from Rome to Constantinople, whose influence stretches from Greece to Russia; the so-called Dark Age of the Romanesque, when classical influence fades and pagan energies are incorporated into nominally Christian art; and finally the flowering of Gothic, a genuinely original architectural style, with roots in northern France but spreading throughout the West. After the conversion of the emperor Constantine in 312, Christianity became the state religion, in command of greater resources and able to build. The earliest Christian buildings are adaptations of Roman forms; more adventurous circular and vaulted schemes are reserved for martyriums (marking a site that bears witness to the Christian faith, such as the grave of a martyr), shrines or memorial structures, while churches are simple rectangles, or basilicas. In the East this distinction

BELOW: Cathedral of Notre Dame, Chartres, 1194–c.1220. West front showing (left) a spire added in 1507

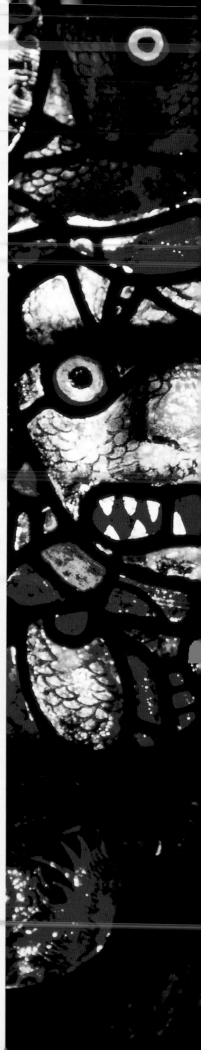

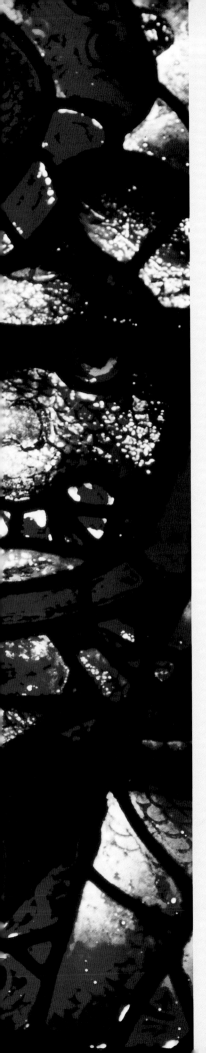

LEFT: Architect unknown, St Mary's Church, Fairford, Gloucestershire, 16th century. Detail of early-16th-century stained glass window by Barnard Flower and others showing the Last Judgement

ABOVE: Architect unknown, Town Hall, Regensburg, Germany, 13th century–18th century

breaks down; ruins of inventive domed churches are known to exist in Syria. This development culminates in the capital of the Eastern Empire, Constantinople, where the greatest Byzantine building, the church of Hagia Sophia, fuses longitudinal and central schemes.

In the West, where the Roman Empire disintegrated earlier, the development was different, with a kind of reversion to tribal preferences. Artefacts survive which combine biblical references, Christian parables and pagan myth (6th–12th century). Even when working on Christian themes, Romanesque artists and craftsmen appear to live in the world of beast-fables, and their solid earthbound buildings are carved with the nightmarish life abhorred by St Bernard of Clairvaux (who founded the strictest form of the Cistercian order in the early 12th century) and banished by the earliest Gothic.

We can point to precise places where Gothic began. There are ribbed vaults at Durham Cathedral (1093–1133) in England and an integrated façade St Etienne at Caen in France (after 1120), but the first time these elements are used wittingly to produce Gothic effects, of structural clarity and relative weightlessness irradiated by light, is at St Denis near Paris (c.1135–44), the project of Abbot Suger, who is the nearest thing to the inventor of Gothic. The challenge was immediately taken up and a quick succession of refinements followed in large churches built in the Ile de France, a compact territory around Paris controlled by the king: Sens, Laon, Paris, Chartres, Reims, Amiens and half a dozen others. Within 70 years, in an amazing explosion of cultural energy, all these cathedrals were under construction and the style had spread to England, Germany, Bohemia and Spain.

Regional variations provide much fascination; late Gothic vaulting in England and Germany, for example, is a wonderful story in itself. The clear structural messages of early Gothic buildings became buried under virtuoso displays of decoration and deceptive pseudo-structures like English fan vaults, which make stone ceilings look like fragile membranes. In England at least, the end of Gothic coincided with the end of the old Catholic religion in the 16th century, but the catalyst to change was different in different places. Having lasted, evolved and transformed itself over 400–500 years, Gothic finally gave way to new impulses and ambitions.

S. Apollinaire Nuovo

RAVENNA, ITALY
late 5th century,
c.550 mosaics revised

Architect unknown

Early in the 5th century, the emperor Honorius moved his residence from Rome to Ravenna on the Adriatic Sea, which from then on played a key role in Early Christian architecture, first under Galla Placida, who governed for her son Valentinian, then under Theodoric, a Gothic king, and finally under Justinian, a Byzantine emperor. Cultural currents meet in the baptisteries, mausolea and churches from these three periods.

Arians, the Greek deniers of the divinity of Christ, were favoured by Theodoric and the church of S. Apollinaire was begun as the king's palace chapel under an Arian bishop. Syrian traces have been detected in the design of the building, but its overall form is recognizably Roman.

S. Apollinaire's basilican layout is typical of the Late Empire, usually seen in law courts or audience halls, and so serving secular functions. By comparison with the domed and vaulted type represented by Hagia Sophia (see pages 50–51), basilicas are straightforward, unmysterious spaces: undivided rectangles, well lit by clerestory windows (in the upper part of the wall), whose flat ceilings make them feel even more like simple boxes. Early Christian basilicas in Rome often add lean-to aisles separated from the main space by arcades. At S. Apollinaire spaces between the columns are larger than usual, making it feel less earthbound.

But the most remarkable feature here is the mosaic which covers the wall surface above the arcades. Glass mosaic may have been invented by Roman craftsmen, but its use in Christian contexts is something entirely new. In spaces like this, walls are dematerialized by the figures which stand out against the shimmer of a gold ground. Here at S. Apollinaire the most archaic portions of mosaic are at the top, complicated scenes from Christ's life contained in box-like frames, interspersed with repeated decorative panels, beneath which come larger frontal figures, punctuated by windows. Then appears the most compelling band, a long hypnotic procession of white robed figures, martyrs on the right and female saints on the left. Here the colours become simpler, reduced to white, green and gold. One set issues from a busy port, the other from a rendering of Theodoric's palace, but they are both leaving the earth behind to arrive in heaven at the other end of this short journey.

Much of this range, though not the architectural starting points, is the work of a later period, around 550, when the Eastern Orthodox Church held sway, but the joins are not easy to identify. Warring sects, Arian and Orthodox, have been harmonized, and the flat basilican setting vibrates with hieratic Eastern ritual. The two processions are heavenly visions but they also reflect the ordinary services that took place in the space beneath them in the 6th century.

Ravenna remains the best place to experience the encounter of two forms of early Christianity, Western and Eastern, where the monuments are not overwhelmed as they are at Rome by the stronger flavours of succeeding centuries. Theodoric executed the philosopher Boethius, and Justinian suppressed competing cultures, but the religious buildings built by both of them exude a powerful spirituality.

Hagia Sophia
ISTANBUL, TURKEY
532–37

Anthemius of Tralles
first half of the 6th century

Isidore of Miletus
first half of the 6th century

The emperor Justinian sponsored one of the architectural wonders of the world in Constantinople: a huge imperial church, replacing an earlier one destroyed during a popular revolt. Hagia Sophia (Holy Wisdom) was designed by two scientist-architects whose backgrounds suggest a synthesis of East and West, Christian and pagan. Anthemius was a natural scientist and mathematician from Asia Minor, and Isidore had taught at the Academy in Athens before it was closed by Justinian.

The heart of the building is a single domed space. From outside it rises in ordered tiers, its magnificent singleness of effect not much spoiled by heavy buttresses added after earthquake damage. Hagia Sophia has lost some outlying parts, like the atrium, or open court, through which it was originally entered, and has picked up others, like the pavilion for Islamic ablutions on the same side. The four minarets (slender towers) at the corners were added at various times in the building's five centuries as a mosque; since 1935 it has been a museum.

Now the interior is reached by a sidelong route, broaching the double narthex, or vestibule, at its narrow end. The narthexes are rich, dim, confined spaces; by contrast, the main space bursts on the viewer with the force of a vision. The space is rectangular but feels round, declining in gentle waves from the high shallow dome which floats overhead, dissolved by light let in by the many windows around its base, which then strikes curved ribs completely clothed in gold mosaic. Spatial and structural novelty, combining central and rectangular plans by means of half domes that leave the main space completely free, are disguised by rich facings and distracting embellishments such as side galleries.

Lower down, the walls are sheathed in coloured marbles that fired a 6th-century courtier, Paul the Silentiary, to extravagant comparisons in his poem about the building. Their purples, greens, greys and pinks reminded him of the sea stirred by oars, of snow flurries, of milk and ice, forests and stars. The panels conceal the structure – square stone piers supporting the dome, and brick walls and vaults – and make the edges of the space seem vague, even insubstantial.

Signs of Hagia Sophia's conversion to a mosque are surprisingly unobtrusive. Huge metal disks with Arabic inscriptions hanging below the pendentives are swallowed up, and the reorientation towards Mecca at the east end, so common in the Byzantine churches of Istanbul, simply adds a geometrically precise layer of cultural interest. Mosque furniture of high artistic quality has rightly been left in place.

This building, although it has no later rivals in size or magnificence, inspired the Ottoman type of mosque with a central dome and the domed churches in Orthodox lands, including Russia. St Mark's Basilica in Venice (1063–94) is another outstanding example of influence from the East and incorporates in its fabric sculptures looted from Constantinople, a brutal kind of flattery.

Stave Church of St Andrew
BORGUND, NORWAY
after 1100

Architect unknown

Norwegian stave churches are a unique survival. Other northern countries must have had numerous wooden churches but they tended to be replaced by stone buildings when increasing sophistication or wealth permitted, or they rotted away because their wooden members were dug into the soil. In England, a single Anglo-Saxon wooden church remains at Greenstead in Essex (some timbers date from c.850), while in Norway a total of 30 survive out of an estimated thousand. The stave church at Borgund, however, is the only one that stands unchanged since medieval times.

Stave churches were built between 1100 and 1300. The origins of the type remain mysterious; is it a survival of an old form of pagan temple, with a chancel added to house the altar? Or a crude provincial adaptation of the Roman basilica? Or a land form inspired by the joinery of Norse sailing vessels? No actual pagan temples survive, even in ground plan, so deriving stave churches from earlier structures remains guesswork. Nonetheless, its main constructional features do not seem related to southern precedents.

The key elements are masts held together by braces one storey up and mortised, or slotted, foundation timbers, which are not buried in the ground but laid on foundation stones. At Borgund, 12 masts form a roughly square central space surrounded by a narrow aisle. Beyond this is the lower chancel with its rounded end, the latter assumed to be a Gothic embellishment of the Romanesque core. Likewise the pentices, or low lean-to porches, around the building and the little chancel tower are considered 'Gothic' additions.

At Borgund the overall effect is remarkably integrated; roofs rise above each other like the bony ridges of a slumbering creature, covered in shingled fur. The walls are well shrouded by low-hanging eaves, their boards laid vertically, adding to the powerful sensation of height. From the gable ends wiry beast-heads strain upwards, like animated attempts to make contact with the elements. Even today, many of the remaining stave churches that have not been moved to museum-villages inhabit wild and lonely valleys.

Of these churches, Borgund is not among the most richly endowed with carving. The interior is dark, lit by small openings high up, so light struggles through the wooden rafters to fall among the masts. Braces between the masts resemble antlers and, as always, what carving there is summons up general animal energy, tangling itself in knots, swirling densely around the entrance. Now, many of the best doorframes from stave churches, tree-trunk-wide fringes bearing lively inscriptions on either side of a narrow opening, are preserved in museums in Oslo or Bergen.

Like many vernacular buildings, including some Anglo-Saxon remains, the stave churches do not really belong to the cycle of styles. As late as the 17th century, at least one master builder was producing credible versions of the stave format. This is not Gothic Revival but fairly unselfconscious survival of Gothic practice into modern times.

STAVE CHURCH OF ST ANDREW • BORGUND

Porch and Cloister of St Pierre
MOISSAC, FRANCE
c.1085–1125

Architect unknown

The Abbey of St Pierre at Moissac in southwestern France had been overrun successively by Arab, Norman and Hungarian invaders before it allied itself with the great Burgundian Abbey of Cluny in 1047. In the 12th century it became the most powerful abbey in its region, a stop on the way to the great pilgrimage centre of Santiago de Compostela in Spain, and the proprietor of valuable dependencies.

Under energetic abbots, a new church was built in the late 11th century and embellished with one of the most elaborate and dramatic cycles of Romanesque sculpture known. Later wars and the French Revolution took their toll, so that now only the porch and cloister of the largely 12th-century church survive. From a distance, the porch looks like a piece of military architecture, heavy and four-square with massive stone battlements. The tower in rosy brick which rises above it is a later addition. Sheltered within the overarching tunnel of the porch is a series of carved narratives without equal. They express a world view by turns savage, morbid and ecstatic to modern eyes. Walls in front and on both sides bristle with writhing and colliding figures on different scales, at different heights, while the central doorpost consists of six threatening beasts standing neatly on each other's heads. Looking past them, the eye is caught by angular old men seemingly about to step out and deliver an admonishment.

This is an art which sets out to rouse, even shock the viewer. At the centre is a vision from the Apocalypse, with a huge staring Christ enthroned, his feet on clouds. Clustering around him are four winged emblems of the Evangelists, two long twisted angels, and the Twenty-four Elders, plainly uncomfortable, who fill the rest of the space. Their

heads and knees turn every which way as they crane to follow the awful events about to unfold. Most of them have forgotten the viols they should be playing and the cups they all carry (Revelation 5:8). Movements pulse through the carved draperies like a turbulent wind or an electric current. On the left wall below this are grisly scenes of torment and wrongdoing, on the right key moments in the life of Christ.

The monks' cloister which lies beyond this porch is another world, with a huge cedar in its central plot of green. Here 76 sculpted capitals at an intimate scale and at eye level tell a confused pandemonium of stories taken from Old and New Testaments and popular legend in no discernible order. Also mixed in are energetic animal and vegetable subjects. In spite of the Christian source of most of them, there is an exuberant licence in the way the incidents are combined. Such schemes represent impressively sustained and co-ordinated labour, but it was not long before churchmen questioned the appropriateness of such violence and negative emotion in a religious context. To us, it is exactly this intrusion from what we call the unconscious that makes the unbridled Romanesque work gripping. In the 1850s the cloister lay in the path of the Bordeaux–Sète railway and narrowly missed being torn down.

Fountains Abbey
NEAR RIPON, GREAT BRITAIN
c.1138–1247, tower c.1500

Architect unknown

Fountains Abbey was founded in a lonely valley in 1132 by 13 monks fleeing from the laxity of St Mary's Abbey, York. They applied to come under the stricter Cistercian rule, and St Bernard of Clairvaux, an important force behind the first stirrings of Gothic in France, sent his deputy Geoffrey d'Ainai to advise on a number of issues, including architecture. Before long, Fountains was the richest Cistercian house in England, possessing large farms with a substantial income deriving in part from 15,000 sheep.

This combination of austerity and prosperity is reflected in the surviving remains of the abbey. The church of grand proportions and beautifully tailored masonry is so plain, it is hard to decide whether it is Romanesque or Gothic. The arches of the nave arcades are pointed – typical of Gothic – but the piers are undivided and un-Gothic in their solid bulk. At the east end the design becomes less monolithic but is still severe, in an unusual eastern transept with slender piers dividing it into two equal bays. Neither the nave nor the transept show any signs of vaulting; aisles had transverse, slightly pointed barrel vaults. So it is conceivable that this mighty space was covered with simple wooden roofs, in the nave at least. Outside, too, plainness rules, in regular square buttresses along the east end, and in the long wall of the dormitory on the west, also punctuated by striking buttresses.

Of all surviving abbeys, Fountains' buildings give the best idea of what a large English monastery was like. The scale is impressive throughout, with noble vaulted spaces for key functions like the refectory, dormitory, infirmary and chapter house. The quarters for lay brothers are much larger than for monks, reflecting the relative numbers in the abbey's heyday. Impressive engineering locates the infirmary over a river which flows through the grounds, here divided into four streams running under barrel-vaulted foundations. At Fountains, the abbot did not enjoy the luxurious accommodation found at Castle Acre Priory, Norfolk (extended c. 1350). Late in the abbey's history, though, the abbot had become such an important personage that granges across the north were adapted as his seats in country-house fashion.

At the Dissolution of the Monasteries in 1539, Fountains and its accumulated wealth passed to the king, Henry VIII, who sold the buildings and grounds within a year to a local magnate. An earlier plan to make the church a cathedral serving Richmondshire had been dropped in favour of another dissolved abbey at Chester. In the 17th century the owner cannibalized the ruin to build a small prodigy house which survives nearby. Late in the 18th century Fountains entered the final stage of its history, being incorporated by a local landowner into a landscape garden. It excited the interest of antiquaries, who cleared debris and excavated buried parts of the structure, while picturesque constructions appeared against its sides. Like Rievaulx (begun c.1140), another large Cistercian abbey nearby, Fountains had become a large found-ornament or folly, stirring up vivid, imprecise dreams of the Gothic past.

Laon Cathedral

LAON, FRANCE
c.1155–1220

Architect unknown

Laon was the capital of France before Hugh Capet moved it to Paris when he became king in 987. So, like most of the early Gothic cathedrals ranged within a 130-km (80-mile) radius of Paris, Laon boasts a connection with the French monarchy. The old town perches on an abrupt rocky outcrop in the middle of a flat plain and thus remains far more intact than most French cathedral towns. So it is partly Laon's setting and partly the unusual consistency of its early Gothic church which explains why it takes the place here of Chartres, Bourges or Amiens (all begun between 1180 and 1220).

Moving from Romanesque to Gothic is moving from darkness to light, from the obscure to the legible, from terror and awe to comfortable acceptance. Or at least one sees open, relaxed forms in the airy towers of this building, which make heavenly ascents look feasible. And instead of monsters there are 16 oxen leaning out halfway up the façade, to commemorate the animals' help during construction. Sculpted scenes now have breathing space and cover the building – including, on the west front, the faces of 19th-century restorers.

Inside, windows too are an occasion for narratives, some of which descend into homely anecdote; the story of a corrupt official is among the most interesting. Stained glass is rightly thought to be one of the trademarks of Gothic. Heavy walls become transmitters of light, not bright but smouldering, even on sunny days, suggesting semi-mystical visions. Later Gothic got carried away by such visions: the great East Window (1405–08) at York Minster is the size of a tennis court and needs a double frame of stone ribs to support it; while Sainte-Chapelle in Paris (c.1239–48) has walls turned entirely into translucent coloured panels – here architecture becomes the medium for non-architectural effects.

On such a huge scale, stories told in the windows become swallowed up, but even at a more accessible size, many of the plentiful stories in large Gothic buildings remain hard if not impossible to read, as if to suggest that human capacities should not limit the reach of human conceptions. Similarly, many of the structural innovations of Gothic – skeletal ribbed vaults, rib-like 'flying' buttresses, heavily perforated walls – are more symbolic than practical in their ultimate aim: they suggest an architecture that is freeing itself from the ground, and create spaces where all is focused on a single goal which remains out of physical reach, in the high curved wall at the crown of the apse for example. Laon is different from the later cathedrals in the flatness of its end wall, and thus represents a more earthly phase than the beatific culminations of the high apses of Chartres, Amiens and Beauvais (1225–72).

But Laon conforms to the model of a strongly longitudinal space which draws the worshipper powerfully towards the east end, a movement broken at the transept, a cross axis which again is more symbolic than functional – the whole structure is an enormous sign of the cross, a sublime translation of suffering into tranquillity.

Ely Cathedral
ELY, GREAT BRITAIN
1082–1353

John Cementarius
mason, probable designer
of octagon
active 1322–26

William Hurley
carpenter, probable designer
of lantern
active 1319–died 1354

E el-eye (eel-isle) refers to a time when the town occupied an island in the flooded Cambridgeshire fens. In the haunting flatness of this landscape, Ely inhabits a ridge, so the cathedral is visible for many miles. It is perhaps the most eccentric of English cathedrals, its outline strangely varied. The tallest accent is a tower at the west end, flanked originally by a pair of turreted transepts (only one survives). The overall effect is clotted, defensive and castellated rather than church-like. Then comes an immensely long nave, crowned at the crossing by Ely's most original feature, the famous octagon.

This was added in 1322–28 after the earlier central tower collapsed. No convincing precedent has been found for this structure. From outside it creates a riot of diverse forms which penetrate deep into lower stages of the building, with large diagonal windows crossed by flying buttresses. There are more diagonals above, as the two upper octagonal stages, one stone and one the wooden lantern, are placed askew on each other. So there is shifting play between the elements. Inside, the octagon causes a surprising burst of light at the end of the heavy Romanesque nave, and the two-tier effect is more enigmatic than on the exterior.

The octagon is followed by the chancel, an outstanding example of early Gothic decoration, richer than this style usually is, with dark Purbeck marble accents and carved leaves springing on capitals and jutting from corbels between the arches. At the east end are two wonderful late Gothic chantry chapels, Bishop Alcock's (begun 1488) and Bishop West's (1525–33). These are like miniature buildings inserted into the fabric, with fan vaults and lacy, perforated walls, crawled over by carved tendrils among which mottoes hide. The best feature at Ely is still to come, an almost detached Lady Chapel (1321–49), thrown out from the main structure to the northeast and entered from the north transept. Ely is a good place to compare early and mature Gothic, or, in the terminology used for English medieval architecture, Early English and Decorated. The choir is early and the Lady Chapel mature.

The lavish space of the Lady Chapel is strangely bland in plan: a loose rectangle, like a barn or a shed. However, the unremarkable space is transfigured by carved decoration and light that floods in from large windows, now clear, but formerly filled with richly coloured glass. Carving in this chapel defeats not only analysis but also the senses trying to apprehend it. The format is simple, a row of niches along the lower wall, deep enough to form seats and thus in some way to be inhabited. Each is roofed with a vaulted canopy covered in stone foliage that sways and bulges as it leaves the wall and rises to a peak. Within the canopies there are divisions and subdivisions like a geometrical riddle, and in the spaces between there are figures and scenes, full of life though defaced. The gnarled effect created by the carving resembles a natural process: the Lady Chapel at Ely epitomizes the Romantic notions of Gothic as a style inspired by vegetable growth.

ELY CATHEDRAL • *ELY LADY CHAPEL*

Aigues-Mortes
FRANCE
1241–1300

Architects unknown

Aigues-Mortes (Dead-waters) is a geometrically regular new town conceived in the 1240s by Louis IX to provide France with a port on the Mediterranean that could compete with the natural harbours of Genoa and Barcelona. In 1248 the king set off on a crusade to the Holy Land from Aigues-Mortes; 20 years later he returned to the town, intending a second crusade, got as far as Tunis, caught typhus and died.

For a time the town prospered in spite of its unfavourable situation in the middle of malarial marshes, battered by winds. In fact, the original argument for building sturdy town walls was defence against the wind rather than human enemies. These walls, the most striking feature of the town today, were begun in the 1270s. Aigues-Mortes was swiftly populated by people from outlying areas, drawn by exemption from taxes and privileges like the salt franchise. Thus, soon after its founding the town had a population several times greater than it has ever had since and functioned as an important link between the East, the Mediterranean coast and the interior of France. However, trade had begun to decline long before the final blow in 1481, when Provence and its port of Marseille were incorporated into France. Now Aigues-Mortes became known mainly for epidemics and ingrained poverty.

Aigues-Mortes is the most complete survivor of the hundreds of new towns built in southwestern France in the 13th and 14th centuries, many of which have disappeared. The absolutely flat terrain made it possible to create a textbook city, whose straight edges are bounded by sheer walls against which almost nothing has been built, inside or out. These walls only engage with the city at the upper left-hand corner where the military presence was lodged. The town is visible at a great distance, surrounded on every side by a low horizon and a virtually featureless landscape. Its buildings do not show above the 10.5-m-high (35-ft) walls, except for the 30-m-high (98-ft) Tour de Constance, the keep, from the top of which a fire could be seen in Nîmes, some 30 km (20 miles) away. These walls continue unbroken for so long before being punctuated by one of the 15 towers that, rather than presenting unbroken strength, they look paper thin. Inside, main streets run unobstructed between the six opposing gates (two north and south, one east and west), and it is possible to walk the unbroken circuit around either the inside or outside of the walls, a kind of completeness and clarity in the plan which is somehow deadening.

If the projectors of the ideal cities of the Renaissance had known Aigues-Mortes they might not have been so keen on regular plans, although admittedly their favourite concentric or star-figures seem at first powerfully different from rectangles, like the difference between basilican and central-plan buildings. Whatever charm Aigues-Mortes has now is due to the abstract beauty of military architecture and, even more, to the surrounding weather, to which it is unusually hostage. Whether rising from the mist or shimmering under a pitiless sun, isolated in its marshy plain, the city appears as a vision, or a perfected geometrical artefact, separated from life.

AIGUES-MORTES • FRANCE *DETAIL OF TOWN WALLS*

Tallinn Old Town

ESTONIA

flourished 14th–
16th centuries

The Old Town of Tallinn is probably the best preserved late-Gothic town in northern Europe. Approached from the sea, it is dominated by the spiked towers of medieval churches clustering around a steep castle hill and still enclosed in old walls. It has had a chequered history: settled by Estonians in the 10th century, conquered by the Danes in the 13th, who lost it to a German military order, won it back, sold it to another German order, who lost it to another, who were defeated by the Swedes in the mid-16th century, who lost it in turn to the Russians in the early 18th century.

After the First World War, a 20-year period of independence was followed by Soviet, then German, then again Soviet occupation from 1944. Estonia gained independence in 1991.

The Gothic town survives from Estonia's heyday in the 14th–16th centuries as a trading centre in a key position between East and West. The flavour of the streets is influenced by the mixture of peoples. Although the distinct districts established for different nationalities and trades only survive in street names, the stamps of different rulers are all around, in Russian churches from three periods, clean Neoclassical villas from the Swedish occupation like a gust of colder air, and in solid German merchants' houses.

This ethnic complexity finds an echo in the virtually unchanged street pattern, which seems a maze at first but has its main arteries, disguised somewhat by deferring to the terrain as no modern street would. Parallel to Lai (Wide) runs Pikk (Long), both lined with the tall, practical dwellings of merchants, with open stone-floored halls at ground level and ample storage for goods under the gables. The plots are long and narrow to allow the owners to keep animals and grow vegetables in space later occupied by workshops. Between the main streets run a confusing variety of smaller lanes, some of which are too narrow for cars. On a map it all looks rather consistent and rational, with a pronounced northeast–southwest orientation, but someone trying to find their way around for the first time could easily end up going in circles.

The main routes and open spaces predate the buildings, which become a kind of infill and often assume arbitrary forms, after which secondary routes had to be forced through the town to cope with the resulting congestion. By such unromantic means Tallinn Old Town arrived at the intimate, dense and confusing structure so prized by modern tourists.

As with Venice, Tallinn's urban form owes a great deal to later stagnation, including its frustrating slumber during Soviet times. Medieval variety was replaced by a uniform torpor, although Toompea, the upper town, has always been quieter still, like the unearthly setting of a Kafka story. Cultural diversity resurfaces today in the embattled Russian community gathering in 18th- and 19th-century churches – the largest, Alexander Nevsky Cathedral (1894–1900, Slavic Gothic Revival), like a nightmare from an Eastern tale – to re-create a world a long way from Protestant Europe.

Ightham Mote
NEAR SEVENOAKS,
GREAT BRITAIN
c.1330–40, 1470s onwards

Architects unknown

Ightham Mote is a small 14th- and 15th-century manor house in a secluded position which looks like a perfect medieval survival. It sits in its ring of water and from almost any vantage point reveals a blend of mellow stone, brick and half-timbering, in seemingly accidental proportions. Although the house has undergone many alterations over the centuries, its scale, layout and materials remain remarkably unchanged. The moat has had a preservative effect; it makes this a difficult building to add to.

The oldest wing lies across a cobbled court from the gatehouse and originally contained the great hall, the solar, or living room, a chapel and a kitchen. More than a century after the first stage of building, the two parts were joined to form a more or less regular quadrangle. This introduced to the building the sense of enclosure which Ightham Mote embodies so strongly, a courtyard surrounded by buildings surrounded by a moat – an empty space, a wall of buildings, a deep border of water. To visitors from later centuries it must have seemed that the Middle Ages themselves lay hidden inside these barriers, out of reach beyond the slender bridges.

In fact, the most important interiors remain substantially intact: the great hall with its high original roof, the 'new chapel' with its painted ceiling from the 1530s, the crypt of the old chapel with an impressive ribbed stone vault. Perhaps the most atmospheric of these is the new chapel, where the wooden barrel vault is covered with early-16th-century heraldry in faded colours. One expert believes this may have been salvaged from one of those impromptu pavilions thrown up for a royal tournament, which would make it a precious relic indeed. However, cleaning has suggested that it was painted in place by no fine artist but a local

sign painter. The secular subject matter and early records show that the room was probably a lavish guest chamber originally. All the panelling and other fittings were brought from elsewhere, to create a chapel which is a historicist dream.

The National Trust, which has owned the house since the mid-1980s, shows various rooms furnished as they would have been at different dates: the housekeeper's room in 1880, the library in 1960. Partly this makes a tendentious point about continuity, but it also echoes a constant feature of this or any other dwelling, large or small, which is that the inhabitants' demands keep changing. Already in the 15th century Richard Haut was adding new wings to escape from the undifferentiated commotion of the great hall, which combined too many functions, hereafter to be distributed among smaller spaces. Even in its earlier phases, Ightham showed evolving notions of what domestic spaces are desirable.

The original inhabitants would not have lived a luxurious life here. This is seen most clearly in how they used the surrounding land (which was only laid out as ornamental grounds in the 19th century) for vegetable and fruit production, with pigeons and fish raised for food in the dovecote, the moat and the large, non-ornamental ponds.

House of Jacques Coeur

BOURGES, FRANCE
1443–50

Colin Le Picart
mason, active during
the 15th century

Jean de Blois
carpenter, active during
the 15th century

Jacques Coeur rose from modest beginnings to become the owner of a fleet of ships trading with the East from Aigues-Mortes *(see pages 62–63)* and financier of the French king. He built a house in his home town of Bourges on the scale of a ducal palace. Coeur himself was probably responsible for many aspects of the design, including the most original features, the intricate plan and the inventive decoration.

Coeur acquired a site which included three round towers of the Gallo-Roman walls of the city. These provided the beginning of solid foundations and gave a military aspect to the rear elevation. On the street side, by contrast, a flamboyant display was mounted, capped by towers partly inspired by chateaux portrayed in the *Très Riches Heures* of Jean, Duc de Berry (Musée Condé, Chantilly, c.1413), a masterpiece of manuscript illumination. In the centre of this front an equestrian statue of the king (removed during the French Revolution) was placed between two false windows in each of which appears a carved figure opening the window and looking out onto the street, thought to be portraits of Coeur and his wife.

An imposing gatehouse, with a large chapel window on the upper floor, leads to an arcaded courtyard diversified with stair-towers. On the left are the public parts of the building while to the right are the kitchens and family quarters, a plan far more clear-headed in distinguishing different functions than others of its time: Coeur applied his genius for rationalizing complex activities to home and business alike. The house also incorporates ingenious technical features, like the reuse of heat from the kitchens to warm the private quarters and good access to the water supply for bathing. Enough of the decorative scheme survives to show that inhabiting this house would have been like living in a medieval manuscript surrounded by emblems and allegories. But as well as heraldic devices and mottoes, chimneypieces, walls and windows displayed references to the owner's business career in the form of ships and exotic shrubs and trees to represent the spice trade. All this remains firmly emblematic, but, indoors and out, portraits also abound. The three-dimensional sculpted figures shown conversing on a carved balcony over one of the main fireplaces have the faces of family and friends.

To build his house, Jacques Coeur used the master mason and the master carpenter of the king, Colin Le Picart (also mason of Bourges cathedral) and Jean de Blois, and many formal ideas are copied from aristocratic residences like the Duc de Berry's at Mehun-sur-Yèvre (begun 1367, now a ruin), but in its ideas of comfort and its idiosyncratic decoration, this building is recognizably a bourgeois production.

In the end, Coeur did not get to enjoy it. By the time the work was finished he had been arrested and the house confiscated by the king. Coeur escaped from prison and was last heard of on the isle of Chios, part of an expedition fighting the Turks. His house later reverted to his grandson before becoming the town hall and then law courts, functions it fulfilled for 250 years before it was turned into a museum in the 1930s.

Siena Cathedral

SIENA, ITALY
second half of the
12th century–1317, 1355–76

Nicolà Pisano
c.1220/25–before 1324
Giovanni Pisano
c.1245/50–before 1320

Giovanni di Cecco
active 1363–97

Almost any major building from the period would serve to demonstrate that Gothic was not truly at home in Italy because of the classical echoes that were never entirely banished, and also because the main structural principles of Gothic had little appeal where desire was lacking to create tall, slender, airy spaces, flooded with light. Siena Cathedral is a prime example of this resistance.

The present building was begun in the 12th century as a Romanesque structure. Sculpture of alluring richness on the lower part of the façade seems to be a mixture of Hellenistic and Romanesque: the wild energy of the one is contained by the conventional banding of the other. At a higher point on the façade another sensibility intervenes, provoked by the example of Orvieto Cathedral (begun 1290) with its colourful two-dimensional front, to turn architectural elements like gables into pictorial surfaces. So the architect at Siena threw up a billboard of peaked forms embellished with marble trimmings, which the 19th-century critic John Ruskin, when he met them in Venice and so nearer the sea, compared to sea-foam. The whole impression is of a luxurious, non-architectural confection, made of something other than building materials.

Completion of the church was delayed while a hugely ambitious plan was pursued (1317–55) which would have made the present nave only one transept of a gigantic building, much of whose form is traced on the ground to the right. Eventually this dream was abandoned and the nave was drastically heightened. In the space between the arcade and the new vault a cornice was run with the busts of 172 popes lurking underneath, an eccentric version of the classical motif of rosettes between consoles (brackets).

Certainly Siena Cathedral uses typically Gothic moulded piers, and if we redefined the style to include illusory colour effects, the building would qualify handsomely, for walls and pillars inside and out are coated in heavy bands of black and white marble, creating horizontal divisions at odds with structure which make a rich blurred shimmer the dominant effect. In the transepts the rhythm of the bands switches from equal stripes to infrequent dark ones on a light ground. The overall mood is relaxed, garish and whimsical.

There are two important Gothic sculptural ensembles in the church, Nicolà Pisano's pulpit and Tino da Camaio's tomb for a cardinal, but works from later periods stand out more strongly, like the famous floor with large pictures made of marble inlay. In this pavement, which involved more than 40 artists, Renaissance and Mannerist designers are following a Gothic scheme, close in concept to the Romanesque designs in Murano (SS. Maria e Donato, 1140) and Otranto (Cathedral, 1160s). The spectator's vantage point on these pictures – cramped, incomplete, steeped in a sensory tangle rather than freed by a rational Renaissance overview – harks back to medieval notions of the place of the individual. Elsewhere in the building, however, signs abound that Italian artists never fell completely under the Gothic spell, and were therefore the first to emerge from it.

Church of St George
VORONET, ROMANIA
1488 church built,
1547 exterior decorated

Architect and artists
unknown

In a small part of a northern province of present-day Romania, 14 painted churches survive that are unique in the world. All but the last date from the first half of the 16th century, long after the Turks had taken Constantinople and spread through Greek, Bulgarian and Serb lands. Northern Moldavia in this period remained independent but isolated, and Byzantine art enjoyed an afterlife there when it had been extinguished in its original heartland, medieval forms surviving into the 17th and even the 18th century.

Most of these little churches still inhabit a sparsely populated, forested landscape, where winters can be extremely harsh. Yet after more than four centuries, paintings continuously exposed to the weather have stood up remarkably well and retained much of their intense colour.

Between the eaves and a stone course along the ground, every inch of the exterior of the church of St George at Voronet is covered with pictures. Only a few small windows are allowed, and the painters seem to begrudge the space, barely interrupting their designs for the openings. The effect has been compared to profuse Romanesque carving in places like Moissac (*see pages 54–55*) or to Eastern carpets, but in fact it is unlike either of these dense, figured effects. The difference at Voronet is that there is no main focus; each side and every level is important. The whole surface is divided into horizontal bands, like a mummy wrapped in its linen shroud, even when, as on the west end, an entire elevation is given over to one scene. This is the famous Last Judgement, enlivened with Eastern iconography and allusions, unfamiliar to Western viewers, such as heaven as a walled garden with crowds anxious for admission, or troops of Turks and Tatars waiting to be judged, or the sky like a scroll being unrolled by angels.

On the south side, the Tree of Jesse escapes from the horizontal divisions, but only by becoming a highly dispersed field where the ancestors of Christ look like scattered constellations spread thinly in the night sky. Here is an intense blue background; elsewhere madder (dark red) or ochre are the dominant colours, chosen from a basic set of vegetable or mineral pigments. Some of the secrets of why the colours have lasted have recently been unravelled. The underlying plaster is mixed with flock, flax and hemp tow (separated fibres), while the pigments are bound with cow bile and thickened with egg yolk, not water, altogether forming a very durable bond.

Aside from the fact that the church was built at the behest of a king, Stephen the Great, and decorated for the most senior churchman in the province, Metropolitan Grigore Rosca, the technical proficiency and the inventive exuberance that takes the entire building surface as its field show that this Moldavian painting is not a form of folk art. Some may feel the result to be anti-architectural, but it was just the latest variation of the Byzantine wish to dematerialize the fabric of buildings. Turned inside out, these churches resemble some ornate Indian temples which the worshipper circles before entering, only to find a dark, cramped interior.

CHURCH OF ST GEORGE • VORONET

Batalha Abbey
BATALHA, PORTUGAL
1388–1530s, abandoned

Afonso Domingues
died 1401

Huguet
died 1438

Mateus Fernandes
active 1490–died 1515

Batalha Abbey in central Portugal was built to commemorate the Battle of Aljubarrota which took place nearby in 1385. João I drove out the invading Spaniards under Juan I of Castile and marked his victory with this grandiose complex which was further enlarged by his successors. The result, the work of at least three main architects, is one of the prime monuments of late Gothic in Portugal.

Afonso Domingues is responsible for the layout and lower stages of the construction (1388–1402). Huguet heightened the nave and added the chapter house and the funerary chapel of João I (the first royal pantheon in Portugal), with a glorious star-vault (1402–38) recalling the lantern at Ely. But the work of Mateus Fernandes the elder is the most remarkable, consisting of another large funerary chapel of octagonal plan and cloister screens (inserted into the arcading around the cloister) of fantastic elaboration (c.1490–1515).

These last were carried out in the years when Manuel I was briefly the richest ruler in Europe, enjoying huge profits from trade with the Indies. The Manueline style he sponsored often incorporates references to maritime adventures, in projects like the monastery at Belém (1502–19), the jumping off place for Eastern voyages. The decorative apogee of Manueline exuberance occurs at Tomar, where Diogo Arruda (active 1508–31) gave a new window to the choir of the Cristo church (1510–14) which seems to be encrusted with objects dredged up from the sea: sponges, ropes, seaweed. Corner turrets are treated like huge sleeves clasped by giant garters, a reference to the award of the Order of the Garter to Manuel by the English king, Henry VII. But the structural peak of the style would have been Mateus Fernandes' chapels at Batalha, now called Capelas

Imperfeitas (unfinished), the most significant centralized structure in all of European Gothic. The great octagon never received its vault, but the vestibules and the large portal on the eighth side are of breathtaking complexity.

The inner face of this portal consists of two arches threaded through each other, a simpler trefoil and a twisting combination of curves with dangling or protruding cusps, emphasizing the points where the curves break. Such a geometric tangle is only the beginning, because the arches turn into multiple series of lacy vegetable columns, like a body that has mostly been consumed by parasites, leaving a fragile skeleton behind.

The cloister screens, later than the cloister itself and variously attributed to Fernandes, Diogo Boytac (active 1498–died ?1528) or Arruda, are further instances of art as essentially an immobilizing puzzle, where forms are trapped within forms, stalks stick to each other like burrs, and even crosses have flanges which catch and impale. The story of Gothic has been told as the development of tracery, by Ruskin among others; in the cloister at Batalha, we trace a regression from elaborated window forms towards the closing up of all the openings again, with the extravagant screens, in a tantalizing impediment to vision. After Manuel's death such fantastic forms were quickly put aside for the clarity of the early Renaissance.

BATALHA ABBEY • BATALHA *VIEW OF CLOISTER*

St Eustache, Paris

PARIS, FRANCE
1532–1640

Architects unknown

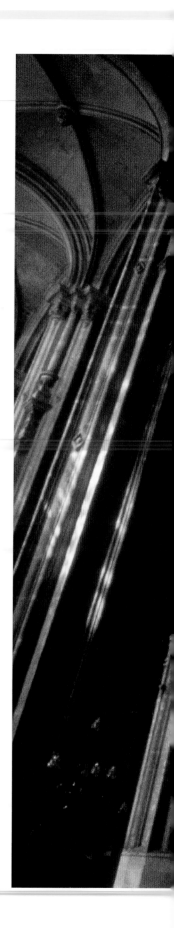

The large church of St Eustache in Paris is remarkable for the way it combines Gothic and Renaissance forms and motifs. Although it was planned in an extremely congested urban site, the patronage of François I, who took a detailed interest in the design, made sure that it rivalled the cathedral of Notre-Dame (begun 1160) in scale and in many details of its plan. Formerly it jostled the great covered market of Les Halles on the south, while butchers' shops lined the rather cramped and lopsided space to the west. Now the market has been levelled to make a concrete garden.

So the exterior of St Eustache is sadly denuded; only at night does it loom impressively as it once did from its urban setting. Inside, the space is fantastically high and the arcades are unlike any others, for within the purely Gothic frame every detail is classical. The cluster-piers consist of numerous little Corinthian columns which seem to leap about at different levels, sometimes stretched to absurd thinness, sometimes squashed to miniature dimensions. No picture can convey the variety and eccentricity of the decorative detail; such unselfconscious exuberance seems thoroughly unclassical. As you walk around the church, you get the distinct feeling that such a combination should be impossible, but at the same time you take pleasure in seeing such daring carried out on this vast scale.

The building of the church continued for more than 100 years, including a long stoppage (1586–1615) during and after the Wars of Religion. Although there must have been many supervisors of the building works, and although some historians claim to see stages of development towards a more austere classicism, the result is remarkably homogeneous within an essentially unhomogeneous hybrid principle.

There are moments which are more Gothic, like the transition as one enters the ambulatory (the curved aisle behind the high altar), where the arcades become narrower and more pointed, and moments which are less, like the western bays of the nave. These are cleaner in appearance because they were rebuilt after a fire in the 19th century by the architect Victor Baltard (1805–74), better known for iron-framed buildings in Paris, including Les Halles (1854–66, demolished) and the church of St Augustine (1862–71). In these more spacious bays, classical details are more like themselves and less obviously pressed into the alien medieval format.

Lovers of Gothic have not always been pleased by the licentious effects of St Eustache; the great French theorist and architect Viollet-le-Duc imagined all its ceilings brightly painted and its windows filled with coloured glass, after which he thought it would resemble a fairies' palace rather than a Christian church. Even a devotee of this building must admit that it does not seem to take its own ideas that seriously, indulging instead in a form of play, on too large a scale to be considered frivolous, but forgetting that Gothic architecture had ever been a transmitter of spiritual truth.

ST EUSTACHE • PARIS *VIEW FROM NAVE*

Renaissance and Palladianism

Steven Parissien

The appearance in 1420 of Filippo Brunelleschi's first Florentine buildings heralded a new era in architectural design. In place of an anonymous, Gothic style which had evolved organically from the cross-fertilization of Christian and Muslim cultures, Brunelleschi and his successors offered a pristine, rational, classical doctrine based on the buildings and teachings of ancient Rome. Many Roman monuments still stood as evidence of the changing aesthetics and construction techniques of that era.

More importantly, Renaissance architects not only had antique philosophical texts to guide their approaches to design but also had a practical manual to the architecture of the early empire in the form of the 10 books of *De architectura* (*On Architecture*) by the Roman architect Vitruvius Pollio (c.90–c.20 BC). The only complete architectural treatise to survive from antiquity, it was rediscovered in 1414. The popularity and success of Renaissance classicism, however, depended less on the innate appeal of

classical proportion and rationality than on the invention of the printing press. Alberti's *De re aedificatoria* (*On the Art of Building*; completed 1452, published 1485) constituted the first theoretical work on Renaissance architecture. Using Vitruvius's text as the basis for his work, Alberti adapted the antique practice to accord with modern humanist scholarship. But its immense influence lies not in the cogency of its arguments but in the fact that in 1485 it became the first work to appear from the new printing presses. Thereafter, the spread of Renaissance classicism depended not so much on individual monuments but on the style's promulgation via the printed word. Books such as Vignola's treatise on the five orders of 1562, Serlio's seven books on architecture (begun in 1540 but not published as a whole until 1584) and Palladio's *Four Books of Architecture* of 1570 represent significant landmarks in Renaissance architecture.

The emphasis laid on printed texts also helped to promote individual designers as celebrities – a process encapsulated in Giorgio Vasari's *Lives of the Artists* of 1550. This helped to foster the stereotype of the agonized creative genius, an unhelpful image which Michelangelo, in particular, did much to promote, and which persists to this day.

LEFT: Filippo Brunelleschi, Dome of Florence Cathedral (Santa Maria del Fiore), 1420–36, cupola completed c.1470

The full force of Renaissance classicism did not reach northern Europe until the 1620s and 1630s – when much of the continent was racked by the Thirty Years War. By the 1560s, classical details, gleaned from imported books and prints, were being applied somewhat indiscriminately to public buildings in the Low Countries and to private houses in England. It was only with the Queen's House in Greenwich (1617–35) by Inigo Jones and the Mauritshaus in The Hague (1633) by Jacob van Campen (1595–1657) that unambiguous Renaissance erudition and classical proportions were properly introduced to northern Europe.

In Britain, Renaissance classicism tended to be viewed through the prism of the architecture of Andrea Palladio. Palladio's publication in 1570 of his *Quattro libri dell'architettura* (*Four Books of Architecture*) was the key to his admittance to the English-speaking pantheon (even though no proper English translation was available until 1716). Inigo Jones, in the Caroline court of the 1620s and 1630s, and Lord Burlington and his Palladian disciples a century later, plundered this work far more comprehensively than any other architectural text of the Italian Renaissance. The direct simplicity of Palladio's plates and prose won the hearts of the Anglo-Saxon world, and his user-friendly volumes were ideally suited to the jobbing architect,

LEFT: Michelangelo Buonarroti et al, Dome of St Peter's, Rome, 1585–1590

ABOVE: Andrea Palladio, Villa Capra ('La Rotonda'), near Vicenza, 1550–1551, detail

who was probably no learned Renaissance Man. Cleverly, Palladio had eschewed many overt references to his Renaissance predecessors; Bramante's Tempietto was one of the very few modern buildings not by Palladio which he illustrated in the *Quattro libri*. To the Anglo-Saxon world and – through the preponderance of publications about the architect – to this day, the history of Renaissance architecture is primarily the tale of Andrea Palladio.

Capella dei Pazzi, Santa Croce

FLORENCE, ITALY
1442–c.1465

Filippo Brunelleschi
born Florence 1377
died Florence 1446

Brunelleschi has long been regarded as the first great architectural figure of the Renaissance. He initially trained as a draughtsman for silk weavers, as a sculptor and as a goldsmith, but by 1415 he had turned his attention to architecture. By 1420, having taught himself the rudiments of design and construction, he was masterminding the hybrid Gothic-classical dome of Florence Cathedral, a project which introduced classical forms and classical construction techniques into 15th-century Italy.

The Capella dei Pazzi was commissioned by Andrea di Pazzi as a chapter house (the site in a religious foundation where clerical business was discussed) for the 13th-century church of S. Croce, where many of the Pazzi family had been buried. Planned after 1429, funds were not made available for the project by Pope Eugenius IV until 1442. The result was one of the first truly classical buildings in medieval Europe, a structure which looked directly to antique sources not just for its plan and form but also for its detailed vocabulary and coloration.

The exterior is unmistakably classical, the principal elevation, with its low dome and slender columns, ignoring centuries of Gothic tradition by espousing the language of republican Rome. The composition is not, however, entirely successful. The porch's graceful, widely spaced Corinthian columns support an overly heavy attic, which provides an uncomfortable contrast with the understated assurance of the dome and cupola behind. In fact, the porch was probably added later and it has been suggested that Brunelleschi's original design did not envisage a porch at all. Whoever its author, care has been taken to integrate the decorative scheme on the porch's barrel vault – glazed ceramic decoration from the celebrated della Robbia factory – with that adopted for the interior.

The interior itself has long been lauded as one of the masterpieces of the Early Renaissance. The plan is tripartite: the porch-vestibule leads to the nave – a simple, tunnel-vaulted rectangle of a square-and-a-half, surmounted by a 12-part dome and cupola – which in turn terminates in a square chancel, provided with a smaller dome. The nave is lit by the central cupola which rises, most impressively, one storey above the entrance porch, and by four tall windows which look out between the porch's six columns. On the nave's walls, the dark grey stone used for the main architectural elements – the Corinthian pilasters, the entablature and the great arches – stands out against the pale grey of the wall spaces in between. This monochrome scheme is enhanced below the painted frieze by della Robbia roundels containing ivory-coloured carvings of the apostles; in the spandrels between the vault's arches, however, it serves to highlight the garish colours of the large maiolica representations of the evangelists, the design for which has, surprisingly, been attributed to the brilliant sculptor Donatello. Perhaps it was these rather overemphasized features that Michelangelo was thinking of when he referred to the capella as being couched in a 'cheerful modern style'.

Palazzo Rucellai
FLORENCE, ITALY
1453–c.1460

Leone Battista Alberti
born Genoa 1404
died Rome 1472

Alberti was the model for the proverbial 'Renaissance Man'. A playwright, musician, painter, archaeologist, mathematician, lawyer and athlete as well as an architect, he excelled in everything. Perhaps understandably, his manner was rather aloof. He preferred, for example, never to visit his building sites, contenting himself with the theory and planning of his buildings rather than their actual construction.

Alberti's contribution to the architecture of the Renaissance lies perhaps more in his published treatises than in his executed structures. His monumentally important book *Della pittura* (1436, dedicated to Brunelleschi) – the first theoretical study of the arts of the Renaissance – served to educate and influence generations of European architects. Nevertheless, a few buildings do survive which enable us to judge the nature of Alberti's genius and vision in three dimensions.

The illegitimate son of a Florentine banker, Alberti worked in Rome from 1432 and was appointed papal inspector of monuments in 1447 by his principal patron Eugenius IV. His Florentine banking connections also brought him into contact with the ambitious banker Giovanni Rucellai (1403–81), who commissioned him to build a grand new town palace.

Rucellai was one of Europe's richest businessmen and a leading patron of 15th-century Florence. He wanted a city-centre residence which not only reflected his wealth but also underlined his innate taste and generous patronage of the avant-garde. Alberti provided just that. The plan of the house was not entirely original – its restrained, eight-bay sandstone façade was grafted onto existing houses, as was the Florentine practice – yet its relatively austere decoration represented something entirely new. For the first time since

antiquity, classical elements were applied to the external wall of a private, secular building. The façade was rigorously organized into classical bays and three superimposed orders were applied in a recognizably antique manner – the first time this concept had been used in the Renaissance world. Above the Doric order of the ground floor is a rich Corinthian order, reflecting the grand nature of the spaces on the *piano nobile* (main floor) behind, while above are simpler Corinthian pilasters, indicative of the more private function of the rooms on this floor. Although the ground floor is higher than those above, the pilasters appear to be of roughly equal height through Alberti's clever use of a high plinth, which also gives the façade an appropriate visual solidity. The square-headed Vitruvian doors – a departure from the customary round-arched openings – add a note of ancient severity. And the façade terminates not in subtle eaves but in a huge, overbearing cornice which provides an optical balance with the pronounced plinth. Deep rustication covers the building; the stones of the top storey are smaller than those of the ground floor, exaggerating both the height of the building and the illusion that the basement extends further forward than the floors above. In all, the Palazzo Rucellai is a solid statement of the aesthetic genius of the greatest theoretician of Renaissance architecture.

PALAZZO RUCELLAI · FLORENCE

Tempietto, San Pietro in Montorio

ROME, ITALY

1502

Donato Bramante (Donato di Pascuccio d'Antonio)

born Monte Asdrualdo 1444
died Rome 1514

onato Bramante has long been revered as the first great architect of what has been perhaps unhelpfully termed the 'High Renaissance'. Certainly he was the first to try and adapt ancient forms and solutions to modern conditions, relying less on Vitruvius than on his own genius and invention. In Book IV of his *Quattro libri dell' architettura*, Palladio declared that Bramante 'was the first to bring to light good and beautiful architecture'; certainly no one exerted a greater influence on the Renaissance architects of the 16th and 17th centuries.

Born near Urbino, the son of a farmer, Bramante showed a gift for painting and perspective at an early age. In 1472 he went to Milan where he worked as both painter and architect, alongside Leonardo da Vinci, for Duke Lodovico Sforza until 1499. Following the French invasion of Lombardy, he fled south to Rome and entered the service of the popes, working first for the unscrupulous Borgia, Alexander VI, and subsequently for the martial Julius II. As moral exemplars, both pontiffs left much to be desired; as patrons of the arts, however, they were outstanding. Encouraged by their generous funding of his architectural schemes, Bramante began constructing a new St Peter's Cathedral and rebuilding the Vatican.

But perhaps Bramante's most successful and influential composition is the small but perfectly formed Tempietto in the cloister of the church of S. Pietro in Montorio, a mile to the west of St Peter's. The site was believed to be that of St Peter's martyrdom, a significance to which Bramante's circular composition (originally intended to be echoed by a new circular cloister) brings emphatic attention. The concept of a circular temple was not new; the 2nd-century BC Temple of Vesta stood nearby. However, Bramante

devised his temple to be considerably more assured and solemn than its ancient model. A Doric order was used, in contrast to the Temple of Vesta's Corinthian, and the columns are placed on a continuous plinth, itself raised on three steps, which give the illusion of height and majesty to the building and ensures that it is not overshadowed by the high cloister walls. Each Doric column of the colonnade is answered by a Doric pilaster on the wall of the temple. The single room, its plain interior dominated by a relief of the crucifixion of St Peter, is raised above the level of the colonnade, and its Roman Doric frieze of triglyphs and metopes, overlaid by Christian imagery, represents the first Renaissance attempt to incorporate this feature in a correctly classical form. However, Bramante departed from antique precedent in extending his central drum skywards and providing it with a tall dome, a stroke of genius which gives this tiny structure greater presence than its dimensions would suggest and, at the same time, indicates the site's direct alignment with heaven. In a cramped site, Bramante had not only revived but had actually improved upon an antique form, creating a gem that has rightly been termed the greatest monument of the Early Renaissance.

Château Chambord
BLOIS, FRANCE
1519–c.1555

Domenico da Cortona
(Domenico Bernabei)
born Cortona c.1470
died Paris c.1549

Some 20 years after Bramante's solemn, austere and antiquely derived Tempietto had been created, Renaissance classicism was being adapted to suit distinctly local temperaments and tastes in France's Loire Valley. Francis I decided to build a grand hunting lodge at Chambord in 1519, four years after beginning a similar project nearby at Blois. Work was soon disrupted by the outbreak of war with Charles V's Holy Roman Empire and by Francis's ignominious capture at the Battle of Pavia in 1525.

Chambord was the French medieval château spectacularly updated to meet at least some of the aesthetic and proportional requirements of the Renaissance. The language used was classical, even if the spirit and execution of the building were far removed from the restrained classicism of Alberti or Bramante. The large round towers that frame the central block and terminate the wings of the 156-metre-long (512-feet) principal front are set with correctly proportioned pedimented dormers; at their summits, however, classical discipline disintegrates in a profusion of quasi-antique chimneystacks, pedimented turrets and soaring, Mannerist cupolas. The detailing may be Italianate, but the bravado and exuberance of the whole composition is decidedly unacademic, only incidentally antique and emphatically French.

The original concept of the château has been attributed to the Italian architect Domenico da Cortona, a pupil of Giuliano da Sangallo (1445–1516) who visited France in 1495 as one of the 22 Neapolitan artists invited by King Charles VIII. Sangallo soon left but Domenico stayed, becoming a French citizen in 1510. A wooden model for Domenico's Chambord project survives, its plan eerily similar to that of Sangallo's Medici palace (1485–97?) at Poggio, near Florence. However,

the château as executed was quite unlike the contemporary buildings of the Italian Renaissance: French architects probably adapted Domenico's masterplan to local customs and practice.

The château's central block or keep is a square divided into four equal parts, the huge central hallway forming a Greek cross, recalling the plan of Bramante's St Peter's in Rome. Each of the quarters has one large room and two smaller closets and a round turret at the outer corner. In the centre of the cross is a freestanding spiral stair, a daring feature, already used at Blois, which replaced Domenico's more conventional suggestion of straight flights in one of the arms of the cross. This splendid invention has two interlocking stairs, one for ascent and one for descent, an ingenious solution to overcrowding traced to the sketches of Leonardo da Vinci, who died in France in 1519. The staircase also acts as a structural support and carries the great lantern which top-lit the hall.

Francis I was so pleased with Chambord that he took his former jailer, Charles V, to visit the château. And in England, Henry VIII mimicked the building's size and vision – particularly the glorious roofline – with a similar fantasy-palace at Nonsuch in Surrey (begun 1538, destroyed). Chambord clearly impressed the whole of Christendom.

Palazzo Canossa
VERONA, ITALY
c.1530–1675

Michele Sanmicheli
born Verona 1487
died Verona 1559

In contrast to the humble origins of many of his contemporaries in Renaissance architecture, Michele Sanmicheli was the son of a successful mason and sculptor based near Lake Como in Lombardy. Propelled into the architectural profession at the age of 16, he subsequently worked not only on the Italian mainland but also on commissions in the islands of Corfu and Crete.

As his career prospered, Sanmicheli developed a keen interest in military architecture which led him to design numerous fortified gateways and, ultimately, to replan the fortifications of the Vatican and of Venice – although not before the Venetians had arrested him as a spy. These commissions had in turn a marked effect on his civil architecture, which as the years progressed became increasingly bold, brutal and three-dimensional.

By 1526, Sanmicheli had settled in Verona and attracted the patronage of the wealthy and highly influential Ludovico Canossa, Bishop of Bayeux, who was a close adviser of Pope Leo X and who soon asked Sanmicheli to build his family a new town palace. The architect's response was to take the innovations of Alberti's Palazzo Rucellai (see pages 82–83) and reinterpret their pioneering classicism in a more robust and grandiloquent manner. The result was one of the most powerful and confident expressions of the Renaissance classical manner ever executed in Europe.

Sanmicheli's Palazzo Canossa borrowed its superimposed orders and regular bay divisions from Alberti. However, the articulation of Sanmicheli's façade was far more emotive than that of the great theoretician. His high, rusticated base and the suggestions of plain, massive 'Venetian windows' or Serliana provided the street front with an aura of grandeur and haughtiness. And the seven-bay façade of stuccoed brickwork was not divided into three, as at the Palazzo Rucellai, but merely into two enormously high principal storeys. The upper storey's round-arched windows were flanked by coupled Corinthian pilasters which served to convey an impression of solidity and strength – indeed, of confidence and success; their effect was enhanced by the novel treatment of the storey's outer corners, where the final pilaster overlaps its partner to create a powerful book-end. At the top, an immense balustrade, crowned by giant statues, helps to cow the passer-by.

Behind the haughty façade lies a ground-floor loggia and vestibule of equal size. Above these, on the piano nobile, is the saloon. Beyond, two wings stretch out to the River Adige; slightly lower in height than the façade, their two principal floors are divided by a low mezzanine, all three floors being provided with far more domestically scaled dimensions than the façade's huge subdivision implies. The Doric-colonnaded wings were most likely intended to form an enclosed courtyard; however, by the time the palace was completed in 1665–75, this concept had been rejected in favour of retaining a view of the river. Even if this aspect of Sanmicheli's vision was countermanded, the palace, and particularly its unforgettable façade, remains one of the most intense and emphatic expressions of Renaissance design.

PALAZZO CANOSSA • VERONA DETAIL

St Mark's Library
VENICE, ITALY
1537–c.1610

Jacopo Sansovino
(Jacopo Tatti)
born Florence 1486
died Venice 1570

Born in Florence, the son of a mattress-maker, Jacopo Tatti trained in Rome as a sculptor under Andrea Sansovino, whose name he adopted. In 1527 he moved to Venice, where he was encouraged to turn his mind to architecture. Having won the support of the Doge, Andrea Gritti, in 1529 Sansovino was made procurator of St Mark's – a post which effectively made him responsible for all public works in Venice.

One of the city's most pressing needs was for a new building to house the libraries of Francesco Petrarch and Cardinal Bessarion, bequeathed to the republic in 1362 and 1468 respectively. The government also wanted to enhance the city's ceremonial centre by opposing the medieval Doge's Palace with a distinctly modern structure, which would publicly associate the republic with patronage of the best contemporary design while creating a more evocative ceremonial space. Sansovino's library achieved both goals. In some senses it even exceeded its brief: although always intended to be lower than the Doge's Palace, its opulent classical virtuosity tends to overshadow the more sedate, Gothic forms of the palace opposite.

St Mark's Library is adjacent to the piazza's existing medieval campanile (the bell tower, at the base of which Sansovino placed the daringly polychrome marble Loggetta of 1542). The ground floor behind the 21-bay Doric arcade housed shops and the floor above the great library and Sansovino's own Procurator's Office. For the main-floor façade, Sansovino allied Vitruvian proportion and strict classical hierarchy to unabashedly lavish ornament. It was a composition of immense power and depth, the Ionic half-columns of the window frames being set behind larger, flanking columns and the window openings themselves being set

deep in the wall. Elaborately carved keystones and reclining sculptural figures in the spandrels fill each bay. The deep frieze above is equally busy, being adorned with obscenely bulky swags and punctuated by eccentric, round-cornered openings, while atop the crowning balustrade are perched heroic statues of Olympian gods and, at the four corners, tapering obelisks. Architectural signage was a familiar concept to Sansovino: in the central bay two enormous caryatids mark the entrance to a pilastered and coffered vestibule, which in turn leads to the long reading room or *salone*. Here, in a space vividly decorated by Salvi, Sciavone, Titian, Veronese and Tintoretto after 1556, round-headed windows alternate with the large, painted panels, while on the ceiling trompe l'oeil beams playfully mimic the genuine structure. The spectacular transition from the powerful façade via the stone-coffered ceiling of the vestibule to the illusory architecture of the building's centrepiece is a stunning visual tour de force.

When part of the reading-room vault collapsed in 1545, Sansovino – who blamed an unusual frost – was thrown into prison, but by the time of his death, the building had restored his reputation. The 19th-century historian Jacob Burckhardt considered the library 'the most splendid work of secular architecture in modern Europe'.

Villa Poiana
POIANA MAGGIORE, ITALY
1540–c.1557

Andrea Palladio
(Andrea dalla Gondola)
born Padua 1508
died Vicenza 1580

Apprenticed to a stonemason at 13, Palladio was to become perhaps the most celebrated architect of the Western world. The architect Gian Giorgio Trissino (1478–1550) gave him his new name (an allusion to the goddess of wisdom, Pallas) and by the mid-1530s Palladio was working with Trissino in Padua and training in Vicenza as a bricklayer and stonemason – hands-on experience which enabled him to switch between the two materials with ease. Having won his first commission in 1536, over the next 40 years Palladio transformed the faces of Venice, Vicenza and the Veneto.

Palladio's first villa commission came partly through luck. Bonifacio Poiana was a leading Vicentine citizen who knew the young architect through his wife, Allegradonna, who worked in the service of Signora Poiana. The wealthy couple had a 15th-century home in the countryside near Montagnana, to the west of Padua, but in 1540 they asked Palladio to design a modern villa across the road. Originally surrounded by a garden, an orchard and a pond, today Palladio's masterwork stands forlornly beside characterless fields.

The plan Palladio devised for the villa's *piano nobile* was deceptively simple: four rectangular spaces, all roughly forming double cubes, arranged around two staircases. The cross-vaulted hall was placed across the front entrance; the barrel-vaulted saloon, of equal size, stretched lengthways towards the rear; two equally shaped rectangles formed the two public rooms reached at either end of the hall – the one to the right given the grand name of *Sala degli imperatori* (Emperors' Room); and the central block was completed by two smaller, square rooms at the rear. Some elements on the original plan were not executed: only one of two wings was built, and a colonnade and small wing pavilions were omitted.

The two main elevations are remarkably plain, relying on their restrained geometry and the effect of their uninterrupted wall space, whose render was originally delicately incised to suggest ashlar blocks (hewn stone with straight edges). The entrance is in effect one large Venetian window, the arch above the central opening being decorated with five large circular indentations. The central three bays project slightly, dignified with a small flight of steps and surmounted by an audaciously broken pediment, pierced by a high window originally intended to ventilate the attic granary. (Today, both attic windows at the front and back are crudely blocked up.)

Inside, the principal interiors were luxuriously frescoed. It is probable that Palladio designed the scheme in the Emperors' Room, as the trompe l'oeil niches with depictions of Roman emperors appear in the illustration of the Corinthian Hall in Book II of his *Quattro libri*.

The overall result is engagingly simple and assured; honest, unglamorized features borne out of an honest philosophy of design. The Villa Poiana established the pattern of Palladio's mature style and provided the benchmark by which subsequent villa designs would be judged.

VILLA POIANA • POIANA MAGGIORE

Piazza del Campidoglio
ROME, ITALY
1544–1660

Michelangelo
(Michelangelo
Buonarroti Simone)
born Caprese 1475
died Rome 1564

Like Alberti, Michelangelo was astonishingly gifted in a bewildering variety of fields. An accomplished poet, sculptor and painter, he had already created a stunning portfolio of works – among them the sculpted *Pietà* (1497–1500) and *David* (1501–4), and the Sistine Chapel ceiling (1508–12) – when given his first architectural commission in 1514 (the chapel at Rome's Castel Sant'Angelo). His manner, however, made Alberti look approachable. Vain and antisocial, he alienated even the grandest of his patrons. Yet Michelangelo remains a touchstone for artistic integrity and architectural vision.

In 1544, shortly before his appointment as chief architect to St Peter's in Rome, Michelangelo was commissioned to redesign one of the centres of imperial and papal Rome, and his Piazza del Campidoglio remains one of the most inspired and original examples of Renaissance planning. At its centre lay the antique statue of the legendary emperor Marcus Aurelius, moved by Pope Paul III from the Lateran Hill to this Capitoline site in 1548. Michelangelo provided the statue with an unusual oval frame, which helped to dilute the trapezoidal form of the piazza and lend an overall impression of symmetry to the space while also accentuating the height of this relatively small statue. Michelangelo had already provided the 15th-century Palazzo Senatorio behind the statue, which housed the city's administrative offices, with a remodelled façade and, most significantly, an imposing double staircase. The latter was a masterstroke which provided the piazza with a dramatic visual termination, diverted attention away from the palazzo's oversized basement storey, and underlined the theme of ascension.

In 1561 work began on remodelling the Palazzo dei Conservatori, the piazza's western boundary and the home of the city's guilds. It was given a giant order of Corinthian pilasters on high pedestals that terminated in sculptures lining a bold balustrade. On the principal floor, each of the unusually wide bays contains a window framed by aedicules with daringly broken segmental pediments – except for the central bay, which is filled with one vast window framed by an even more audaciously broken triangular pediment. On the ground floor, smaller Ionic columns support the flat beams – not customary round arches – which frame the entrances to a deep arcade. The whole composition is one of great intensity, the dramatic contrasts of light and shade being heightened by the colours of the masonry: the pale grey travertine of the pilasters, columns and pediments contrasting with the rust-red brickwork.

The Palazzo dei Conservatori was completed by Giacomo della Porta (c.1537–1602). In 1603 work began on the new Palazzo Nuovo to the east, the façade mirroring that of the Conservatori; it was not finished until 1660. By then the hilltop site was famous as the archetype of grandiose town planning, and the evocative celebration of Roman virtues which Michelangelo had devised had become a model for the glorification of Louis XIV and his absolutist contemporaries.

PIAZZA DEL CAMPIDOGLIO • ROME *VIEW SHOWING THE PALAZZO SENATORIO, CENTRE*

Basilica
VICENZA, ITALY
1549–1614

Andrea Palladio
(Andrea dalla Gondola)
born Padua 1508
died Vicenza 1580

Vicenza had a collection of medieval buildings in its centre which functioned as the base for civic government (*palatium civitatis*). In 1546, Palladio was put forward by his mentor and patron Gian Giorgio Trissino – who aimed to make his protégé Vicenza's city architect – as the ideal candidate to rebuild the site as one, harmonious whole. Having defeated the other schemes for the new basilica, Palladio's solution was to unify the oddly shaped site – a long, irregular rectangle – in an engagingly simple way.

He decided to clothe the *palatium* in two tiers of Venetian windows, the bottom loggia of which would be phrased in the Tuscan order and the top in Ionic. Jacopo Sansovino had adopted a similar solution for St Mark's Library in nearby Venice (*see pages 90–91*). However, Palladio's walls were not actually connected to the building behind but formed separate, transparent entities – arcades only infrequently and almost incidentally associated with the walls and windows beyond. Their Venetian windows could also be widened or contracted as space permitted; thus, what appears to be a series of similarly sized bays is actually a collection of openings of varying widths, whose simple elements and unusually large voids – even the spandrels tend to be pierced with a circular hole, or 'ouzel' – prevent casual observers from detecting any dimensional differences and give the site as a whole the illusion of classical uniformity. In a similar vein, the buttressed piers at each corner (excepting that which abuts the existing campanile) only possessed the illusion of regularity. The site's complex, irregular corners were made to appear right-angled by Palladio's employment of three closely packed columns at these crucial junctures. Above the entablature, the balustrade was lined with statues emphasizing the regular divisions

between each of the basilica's bays. The architect thus conjured the image of classical correctness out of an asymmetrical plan.

Work began on the project in May 1549. Each bay, executed in local limestone, was subcontracted to two masons. Work continued slowly but steadily on the lower storey until 1561, when an economic crisis precipitated by failed harvests prompted the city council to suspend the work for two months; thereafter work progressed more slowly and Palladio's wages were cut. The project was stopped again in 1570, when all available funds were used to help finance Don John of Austria's naval expedition against the Turks, in defence of Western Europe – a campaign which culminated in unexpected victory against the Ottoman fleet at Lepanto – and Palladio left Vicenza for the richer pastures of Venice. The final arches were completed in 1614.

Palladio had no doubt that the finished article would wear well, suggesting that it stood comparison with 'the greatest and most beautiful [buildings] that have been created since classical times, both for scale and decoration as well as for material'. As a gifted compromise it was a stunning achievement; as a composition of simplicity and assurance it remains, in civic terms, unparalleled.

ABOVE: Original floor plan for the Basilica by Andrea Palladio.

San Giorgio Maggiore

VENICE, ITALY
1566–1611

Andrea Palladio
(Andrea dalla Gondola)
born Padua 1508
died Vicenza 1580

The tiny island of San Giorgio, lying at the end of the Giudecca Canal and opposite the civic centre of Venice, had been provided with a church from AD790. By the 16th century the site had acquired a group of monastic buildings to which was added a cloister and a plain refectory. In 1560 Palladio was employed to improve the refectory, which he did by adding cross-vaulting, lunette windows and an internal cornice. Six years later work began on a new church to Palladio's design, intended to replace the now undersized and dilapidated medieval basilica on the site.

Palladio's plan reflected the tripartite nature of the Trinity: a spacious, rectangular basilica, behind which lay a small, square presbytery and, screened by heavy Corinthian columns, a horseshoe-shaped retrochoir. Although the plan of the basilica-nave was based on that of the ancient Basilica of Maxentius in Rome (*see pages 44–45*), even to the extent of placing the domed crossing one bay to the west of the presbytery, it was also strictly functional. Palladio had been asked to allow as much of the congregation as possible to witness communion; thus, the basilica's unusually wide, cross-vaulted aisles, apsidal transepts and slender crossing piers, together with the placing of the choir behind the altar, all served to allow uninterrupted sight lines into the presbytery and its altar. Nor was the humanistic element forgotten in Palladio's vast nave. The majestic giant order of Corinthian columns and pilasters which supports the dome and vault is brought down to earth by the more appreciable scale of the half-sized order which supports the niches and nave arches. Yet Palladio's interior is deliberately austere and understated, the monochromatic whites and greys of the nave being relieved only by the terracotta-coloured squares of local marble in the floor.

Outside, the plain brick wall of the body of the church terminates in a west front of white marble, originally a freestanding portico. This façade represents a vast stage-set and, along with S. Maria della Salute (1630–87; Baldassare Longhena, 1597–1682), is the most impressive piece of civic sculpture in Venice. Designed to be seen across the water from the Doge's Palace and the Zattere, its superimposed temple fronts (a concept Palladio borrowed from Giovanni Maria Falconetto, 1468–1535), featuring the same interplay of giant orders and half-columns as the nave, give the composition a multilayered, strongly three-dimensional aspect. The façade is not especially ecclesiastical in its imagery. Its outer temple front, for example, is based closely on the triumphal arch form – a swaggering symbol whose demonstrative ostentation presents a shocking contrast with the undemonstrative brickwork behind. At the same time, however, its dimensions clearly and honestly reveal the building's plan – the widths of the nave and aisles being reflected in the façade's bays. Moreover, it serves as a fabulous advertisement for the vigour of the Venetian Republic and for the enlightened Renaissance patronage of its leading citizens.

Place des Vosges | Architect unknown

PARIS, FRANCE

1605–c.1638

What is now known as Paris's Place des Vosges but was originally called the Place Royale originated in Catherine de'Medici's scheme of 1563 to build a grand new square of fashionable terraced houses on the site of the old royal palace of the Tournelles. (The palace had morbid associations for Catherine, who abandoned it after the death of her husband, Henry II, from injuries sustained in a tournament held there in 1559.) The outbreak of the French Wars of Religion in the 1560s, which Catherine did much to help precipitate, forced the project to be shelved.

However, in 1603, the victor of the conflict, Henry IV, revived the scheme in order to provide the medieval heart of Paris, the Marais, with a central parade ground and place to promenade. A plan was drawn up by an unknown architect to the king's specification and individual plots of four bays in width were then sold to well-to-do buyers – with the proviso that the elevation of each new house should correspond to the overall design. The scheme attracted many of the lesser aristocracy and wealthy bourgeoisie who could not afford their own Parisian hôtel but who wanted a town house in what swiftly became the most fashionable quarter of the capital.

Each house is marked by a separately defined and steep mansard roof, punctuated by two large, square-headed dormer windows and two small oeils-de-boeuf (projecting oval or round windows) – which today have mostly been enlarged far beyond their originally modest dimensions. Below are two storeys of equal height, faced in brick with stucco dressings and provided with 'French' windows – effectively, glazed doors – extending right down to the floor (a novel practice which did not reach Britain and North America until the end of the 18th century), and at ground level

is a continuous stone arcade. To the north and south the central houses, built at the instigation of Henry IV himself, are a storey higher, giving the development a central emphasis and rescuing each range from the boredom of repetition – an effect which Sir John Summerson was later to term 'one damn Georgian house after another'.

The square was completed around 1638, and a statue of Louis XIII – who had succeeded his assassinated father Henry IV in 1610 – was placed in the centre. This statue, along with most existing public sculpture, was destroyed during the French Revolution, after which the square was renamed; its uninspired replacement dates from 1825. Nevertheless, the form and detailing of the Place Royale had exercised an enormous influence on 17th- and 18th-century urban architecture. As its finishing touches were being made, Inigo Jones was adapting the design and materials of its four ranges for his new 'piazza' in London's Covent Garden (1630–31), which also included an arcade. This, the first true London square, became in turn the ancestor of the much imitated Georgian terrace and square. Henry IV's imaginative project was to spawn children of which even its ambitious progenitor could not have dreamed.

Banqueting House, Whitehall

LONDON, GREAT BRITAIN
1619–22

Inigo Jones
born London 1573
died London 1652

Inigo Jones introduced Renaissance architecture into Britain – nearly two centuries after its glories had been revealed in the works of Brunelleschi and Alberti. Abandoning the healthy, eclectic English tradition of mixing Gothic and classical forms, Jones turned to the inspiration of Italian order and proportion. He chose as his model Andrea Palladio – an architect who had been dead for 40 years and whose buildings were already considered rather austerely old-fashioned in his native country.

Jones was the right man in the right place at the right time. The son of a Smithfield clothworker, he was apprenticed to a joiner and subsequently became a picture framer and costume designer. His costume designs brought him to the notice of James I's court, which had recently taken up masques with great enthusiasm. Jones quickly attached himself to the heir to the throne, Prince Henry, and then, after Henry's untimely death in 1612, to the greatest English connoisseur of the day, the 2nd Earl of Arundel. In 1615 Jones became Surveyor-General of the King's Works, a tailor-made post which he held until 1642.

After the second Banqueting House at the rambling Tudor Palace of Whitehall had burnt down in 1619, Jones was swiftly appointed to replace it (Arundel was one of the commissioners). For the building's principal façade, Jones, in imitation of Michelangelo's Palazzo Senatorio (see *pages 94–95*), emphasized the three-dimensionality of the composition by using three differently coloured limestones: golden Oxfordshire for the basement, brown oolite for the bays above, and pale grey Portland for the columns and pilasters. (This pleasing effect was eradicated by Sir John Soane when he refaced the whole building with Portland stone two centuries later.) The middle three bays

were intended to be topped by a pediment but a subtler effect was achieved with a slight projection and the use of engaged columns rather than pilasters. The bays were wider than had been the practice of Palladio and other Italian cinquecento architects, but Jones displayed his Renaissance orthodoxy in using superimposed orders in the correct hierarchical manner, with the plainer (Ionic) supporting the more elaborate (Corinthian).

The interior is a simple Vitruvian double cube, with a slender gallery marking the division between storeys. This form had no precedent in Renaissance design, although Jones had used the same idea at the Queen's House in Greenwich, begun two years earlier. In 1638, Rubens' painted ceiling panels celebrating the wise government of James I, commissioned 18 years earlier, were installed, putting an end to the staging of masques in the hall as the torches used for lighting would have left soot on the precious canvases.

Following the English Civil War (1642–48), Charles I was executed at the Banqueting House in 1649: for many, the building epitomized the venal influence of Catholic, Italian taste on a Protestant king and court. Yet the physical and stylistic impact of the Banqueting House was huge: Canaletto's views show its dominant presence in the 1740s.

BANQUETING HOUSE · LONDON

Peckwater Quadrangle, Christ Church
OXFORD, GREAT BRITAIN
1706–14

Henry Aldrich
born London 1648
died Oxford 1710

While the Place des Vosges remains the ancestor of most of the classical urban developments of the 17th, 18th and 19th centuries, the terraces and squares of Georgian Britain and Colonial America owe their Renaissance grammar and vocabulary to a more immediate inspiration. No grand city square or terrace, one of the most influential buildings of the English Renaissance is an Oxford University quadrangle.

At Peckwater Quadrangle in Christ Church college, the grandeur and coherence of a Renaissance palace front was thoughtfully and deliberately applied to the humble dwellings of undergraduates and dons. And its author – the designer who perhaps more than any other brought the precepts and forms of Renaissance Italy and Jonesian London to 18th-century Britain – was not a professional architect or mason but a don.

Henry Aldrich was in many ways an Oxonian reincarnation of Alberti. An Oxford theologian who became Dean of Christ Church and vice-chancellor of the university, he wrote learned texts on fields as diverse as Greek, logic, heraldry, mathematics, music and architecture. He is known to have visited Italy and at the time of his death was preparing a major work on Vitruvius and Palladio, *Elementa architecturae civilis*, which was published in 1789. Peckwater Quad was not Aldrich's first architectural essay; he had already devised the church of All Saints for Oxford High Street, a competent exercise in sedate Wrennian classicism which was begun in 1701. The erection of both buildings was sensibly left to an expert, the local mason William Townesend, whose distinguished family were to oversee the construction of countless Oxford monuments, often designed by inexperienced amateurs, for decades to come.

But nothing in Aldrich's past prepared his contemporaries for Peckwater Quad. Each range of 15 bays was devised according to the hierarchical precepts of Renaissance Italy. Thus a rusticated basement is surmounted by two ashlar floors, each bound by a giant order of pilasters or (for the pedimented, five-bay centrepiece) engaged columns. The larger, upper-floor windows are dignified by alternate segmental and triangular pediments, suggestive of a grand Renaissance *piano nobile* but in fact screening student rooms. For the windows, however, Aldrich did not use traditional cross-framed openings but double-hung sashes, invented in the mid-17th century and first widely used by Sir Christopher Wren in the 1690s. Thus technological innovation and domestic convenience were successfully harnessed to Renaissance proportional theory. On the south side, the courtyard was left open to accommodate a new college library, designed in a more ebullient, Michelangelesque manner by Aldrich's fellow don George Clarke (1661–1736) and built after 1717.

Not everything about Peckwater Quad is exemplary; the corners where the ranges join are cramped, yet its importance to Anglo-Saxon classicism is enormous: at the time, most new additions to Oxford colleges adopted a Gothic style, more redolent of the 15th than the 18th century.

PECKWATER QUADRANGLE, CHRIST CHURCH COLLEGE • OXFORD *DETAIL*

Marble Hill House
**TWICKENHAM,
GREAT BRITAIN
1724–29**

Roger Morris
born London 1695
died London 1749

Marble Hill is perhaps the prototypical Palladian villa. Designed with Italian antecedents in mind and adhering closely to Renaissance proportions, its taste, simplicity and comparative economy provided a template for generations of architects and builders. Devised as a pleasant Thames-side retreat 10 miles from central London, it was built for Henrietta Howard, Countess of Suffolk, a former mistress of the Prince of Wales. Here, Henrietta gathered a court of local literati, including the poet Alexander Pope, the satirist Jonathan Swift and the playwright John Gay.

An early scheme for the house by Colen Campbell (1676–1729) survives, its 1-3-1 rhythm echoing not only Palladian villas (*see pages 92–93*) but also Campbell's recent Whitehall town house for Lord Herbert. Campbell was Lord Burlington's first architectural advisor but by 1724 he had been dropped and the Marble Hill commission, which Burlington effectively disposed of on behalf of the Prince of Wales (later George II), was directed instead at the architectural double-act of Lord Herbert (Campbell's former patron and later 9th Earl of Pembroke) and Roger Morris. For all their projects, Herbert, the confident, well-connected aristocrat, acted as the link between client and executing architect, Morris, who had trained as a bricklayer and carpenter and was ill-at-ease in grand company. Campbell's resentment at his usurpation is evident in the plates of Marble Hill which appeared in 1725 in volume III of *Vitruvius Britannicus* (not actually a commentary on Vitruvius but a gazetteer of the nation's recently built country houses), where Morris's name is conspicuously missing.

Morris appears to have done little to alter Campbell's planned elevations, aside from introducing a pilaster portico on the principal (north) side. Inside, Morris's plan reflects the simplest of Palladio's villas, the ground and the main floor being centred respectively on a square hall and cubic saloon which echo the regular, neo-Palladian proportions of the principal façade. The hall features ostentatious plaster beams linking the four Doric supports, in the manner of a rustic Veneto home. The staircase, constructed from Honduran mahogany recently liberated from the former Spanish colony, is couched very much in Inigo Jones's Renaissance manner of a century before. And sited at the top of the staircase, the Saloon or 'Great Room' is festooned with sumptuous gilded plaster decoration, executed by the gifted James Richards, which makes the room seem larger and grander than its modest dimensions would suggest. The Saloon's overdoors and overmantel contain capricci of the sites of Ancient Rome which Henrietta, as a woman, was prevented from seeing at first hand.

In 1727, Jonathan Swift used Marble Hill and another of Morris's simple, cubic villa designs as prototypes for the ideal Arcadian retreat in his *Pastoral Dialogue*. And today, after careful renovation work, Marble Hill remains perhaps the purest expression of Palladian form in Britain.

MARBLE HILL HOUSE • TWICKENHAM *SOUTH FRONT*

Redwood Library
NEWPORT, RHODE ISLAND,
UNITED STATES
1749–58

Peter Harrison
born York 1716
died New Haven, Connecticut 1775

One of the last countries to attempt to emulate the architectural achievements of Ancient Rome and Renaissance Italy was Colonial America. Here, however, the pleasant, rural nature of much of the settled countryside and the occupations and economic status of many of the colony's richer citizens created conditions for classical architecture remarkably analogous to that of 16th-century Italy. Accordingly, the coastal colonies became particularly fertile ground for the transplantation of the Palladian villa, examples of which had by the 1750s appeared from Connecticut to the Carolinas.

In order to properly recapture the theory and practice of the Renaissance, wealthy villa owners and their less affluent neighbours sought advice from the architectural pattern-books which had become so numerous in recent decades. And occasionally they were able to profit from the ingenuity and imagination of émigré architects. Peter Harrison was one of these, an Englishman who, finding work scarce, emigrated in 1740 to Newport, Rhode Island. Here he not only traded wine, rum, molasses and mahogany, brought from the West Indies and largely bound for Britain, but also taught himself architecture using pattern-books by authors such as William Salmon, Batty Langley and the Halfpenny brothers. Fortified by their example, he embarked on a career which was to make him North America's first significant architect. Harrison chose as his template not the fashionable complexities of contemporary European Rococo, nor even the sophisticated Palladianism of his native England, but the unambiguous order and proportion of the Italian Renaissance.

The remarkably assured Redwood Library was, astonishingly, Harrison's first work. The library was named in honour of Abraham Redwood, a Quaker who had donated the sizable sum of £500

to buy books for the town. The library is determinedly neo-Palladian in its orientation, preferring to cite Palladio's Veneto villas rather than the bland commercial temples of Palladian London. Harrison's design celebrates the very details of Palladio's projects: the timber walls, for example, are grooved and painted to imitate rusticated stone. The Doric portico recalls the rustic west portico of Inigo Jones's St Paul's Church, Covent Garden of 1630; like Jones's work, it was, for the time, remarkably Italianate in its inspiration – few architects in America had assayed such uncompromising neoclassicism in the 1740s. The short, low wings suggest those of many of Palladio's rural villas. And while the three Venetian windows at the rear of the library recall the north elevation of Chiswick House, London (1725–28; Richard Boyle, Lord Burlington, c.1694–1753), they also allude to similar features at far older sites such as the Villa Poiana (see pages 92–93).

Altogether, the restrained purity of Harrison's design shows remarkable talent and conviction. And 30 years later, the country's first major native-born architect, Thomas Jefferson, was to use Harrison's pioneering designs as the basis for his visionary architectural philosophy.

The Baroque

Christian Norberg-Schulz

'Baroque' was for a long time a derogatory term. It was used to denote something strange, exaggerated and unnatural, a stylistic tendency that was seen as a degeneration of the orderly style of the Renaissance. This attitude, however, helps us to understand why and where the Baroque came about.

Baroque was the artistic expression of the Counter-Reformation and so was originally a Catholic phenomenon. In 1540 Ignatius Loyola founded the Jesuit order (the Society of Jesus) and in his Spiritual Exercises (1548) formulated a method of arriving at religious participation by using all the senses. The Council of Trent (1545–63) established the means to oppose the Protestant movements and the idea of a new participatory art was laid down by the bishop of Milan, Carlo (Charles) Borromeo. He maintained

that the centralized 'ideal' plan of Renaissance churches was pagan and opted for the Latin cross, with a wide nave that becomes a 'hall of prayer'. This aim was realized in the first Jesuit church, Il Gesù in Rome, 1568–76, begun by Giacomo Barozzi da Vignola (1507–73) and completed by Giacomo della Porta (c.1533–1602). The façade by the latter emphasizes the central entrance,

BELOW: Engraving of St Peter's Square in Rome during the sixteenth century; artist unknown

LEFT: Giacomo Barozzi da Vignola and Giacomo della Porta, Il Gesù, Rome, 1568–76

inviting people in, and inside the visitor experiences a 'total work of art', where dynamic architecture becomes a frame for vivid paintings; the ceiling truly appears to be a vision of heaven. On a larger scale, Pope Sixtus V carried out a grandiose plan in 1585–90 to present Rome as a living *città santa* (holy city), linking the various holy sites by a system of straight roads.

Gian Lorenzo Bernini played an essential role in the development of the Baroque, both his sculpture and architecture expressing the grandeur and emotional power of the movement. Bernini developed the concept of the *theatrum sacrum* (sacred theatre), already seen in Il Gesù, evoking a tangible holy presence.

The Baroque idea of arriving at public participation through persuasion, however, was not restricted to Rome and Italy. As a general movement it spread to other Catholic countries, first to the main powers France and Austria, and after the Thirty Years War (1618–48) to southern Germany. Surprisingly, it was also echoed in Nordic countries. Lutheranism, after all, was not as austere as Calvinism, and a certain openness to art as a means of participation also distinguished the Anglican Church in England. Finally, the Baroque blossomed in Russia in the reign of Peter the Great.

And so the Baroque became a universal expression of those 'systems' which, during the 17th and 18th centuries, competed to offer man a spiritual path. In its most intellectual form, often expressed through the reversal of established rules and motifs, Baroque became Mannerism; in its final form, before the advent of Neo-Classicism,

ABOVE: Engraving depicting Pope Sixtus V's proposal for converting Rome to a *città santa* (holy city), c. 1585

it evolved into the decorative and ornate Rococo. Beyond the spiritual, the magnificence of the Baroque made it an ideal language for grand secular buildings.

Leading architectural historians have offered valid interpretations of the Baroque 'style', starting with the influential Heinrich Wölfflin in the late 19th century. Paul Frankl systematically explained the Baroque treatment of space and built form, while another student of Wölfflin's, Sigfried Giedion – who was to become my teacher in Zurich after the war – related Baroque dynamism and spatial openness to Modern architecture.

S. Andrea al Quirinale

ROME, ITALY
1658–70

Gian Lorenzo Bernini

born Naples 1598
died Rome 1680

S. Andrea was built by Gian Lorenzo Bernini as the church of a Jesuit college, where ardent monks and missionaries were trained, and so its architecture and pictorial decoration are highly persuasive. Outside we are invited in by concave lateral walls, while a convex flight of stairs surmounted by a semicircular portico makes interior space pour out. A large rectangular aedicule replaces the traditional church façade.

This aedicular portal, with its framing pilasters, unifies interior and exterior space. Although the solution seems dynamic, all the elements are relatively simple and Bernini never made use of distorted forms or metamorphoses favoured by other Baroque architects. In this sense he is still a 'classical' architect. His two smaller churches, both outside Rome in Castelgandolfo (1658–61) and Ariccia (1662–64), represent the same simple and great manner of his mature work.

The plan of S. Andrea, a transverse oval, is original. Oval plans had been used since the second half of the 16th century, but always with the main axis pointing towards the altar. The oval unites longitudinality and centralization, that is, the two original principles of ecclesiastical architecture, and so encompasses the concepts of the path and the goal. This suggests that the altar should be placed at the centre rather than at the end of the main axis, but, in fact, it was rarely sited there in centralized Renaissance churches, and when it was the clergy protested. The centre was symbolic rather than functional, representing the union of heaven and earth.

Does Bernini's transverse oval contradict these precepts? Its use has been explained by the shallowness of the site, but Bernini could have employed a circle surrounded by chapels as he did in Ariccia. Instead, he created a subtle interplay of directions. The transverse axis is blocked at either end; it does not run into chapels but is stopped by tall, structural pilasters. The shorter 'main' axis is emphasized by an arch over the entrance that rises into the dome, and by a richly ornate presbytery which is centred on the painting of St Andrew's crucifixion by Pietro da Cortona (1596–1669). This is surrounded by a host of gilt angels, and the light pouring in from an invisible source above makes it seem like a vision. The horizontal axis offers a dynamic interpretation of the earthly domain, in accordance with the Baroque spirit.

Bernini was a pivotal figure in the evolution of the Baroque. Originally a brilliant sculptor, he succeeded Carlo Maderno (c.1556–1629) as the chief architect of St Peter's in Rome in 1624, and in 1657 designed the piazza in front of the church, one of the greatest achievements of European architecture. At S. Andrea, St Andrew's ascension to heaven is represented by a highly expressive sculpture by Bernini's pupil and assistant Antonio Raggi. The saint is received by angels that fly into space across the cornice of the lantern. Thus the whole *theatrum sacrum* tells a coherent, vivid story. And the dome, with its uniform geometric pattern and its gilding, contrasts with the earthly domain. It seems to rest on garlands held by other angels and so looks like a gift from heaven, making the sacrifice of the saint meaningful.

S. ANDREA AL QUIRINALE • *ROME INTERIOR*

S. Ivo della Sapienza
ROME, ITALY
1642–50

Francesco Borromini
born Bissone 1599
died Rome 1667

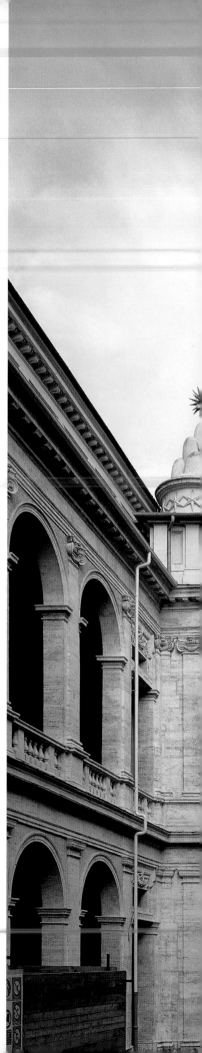

The most original yet troubled genius of Roman High Baroque, Borromini first worked as a stone carver before becoming a committed architect and, like his great rival Bernini, dedicated his energies to Rome. In his first work, the tiny, oval church of S. Carlo alle Quattro Fontane (1637–41), with its rhythms and undulations, he expressed his wish to reinterpret the elements of architecture, formal and spatial.

In 1642 Borromini began the church of Rome's Old University, S. Ivo alla Sapienza. The *theatrum sacrum* is absent; no saint ascends to heaven and no angel flies into space, but it still has an affinity with Bernini's S. Andrea al Quirinale (*see pages 112–13*). The down-up theme is present, as is the concave-convex relationship in the treatment of the exterior. Here, however, they form a vertical development, making the volume expand, contract and almost breathe as the eye rises up.

S. Ivo completed the two-storey university courtyard, which was articulated by pilasters and archivolts (mouldings along the arched contours). Borromini continued this articulation across the concave end wall which formed the church façade. Above this wall the convex drum rises up, not as a static cylinder but as an expansive volume pressed in by bundles of pilasters at six points. The bundles carry concave 'buttresses' resting on the convex surface of the minuscule cupola, and at the top they carry a large lantern bearing a helix. An original invention indeed! But is this a dome or a tower? The answer is both, which touches upon Borromini's unique ability to create new syntheses of the traditional elements of architecture.

The greatest metamorphosis in Borromini's opus happens inside S. Ivo. The plan is developed around a hexagon with alternating apses and convex recesses. The six corners of the hexagon

have double pilasters while the apses and recesses have single ones. The pilasters form a continuous wall articulation under an engirdling entablature, but only the double pilasters continue as structural ribs inside the cupola to carry the lantern. Above the single pilasters are windows. The movement of the entablature is thus carried into the dome by means of the primary ribs, but as the vertical development approaches the lantern, the rhythm calms, to become the perfect circle of the lantern ring. So the basic theme is the transformation of one shape into another and the passage from restless complexity to peaceful simplicity.

The detailing and decoration support this general theme. The alternation of forms around a hexagon means that opposite sides do not correspond and hence the lower part of the interior never comes to rest. But painted stars tumble down from around the lantern opening and ornamental angels appear between the tops of the primary ribs. The rising movement of the complex lower part of the interior is received by heavenly light, symbolized by the stars. The message is therefore essentially the same as in Bernini's church, but S. Ivo gives it an architectural interpretation. Borromini continued to explore such dynamic design ideas, devising an inspired system of interdependent spatial 'cells' at S. Maria dei Sette Dolori (1642–48, unfinished).

SS. Sindone
TURIN, ITALY
1666–90

Guarino Guarini
born Modena 1624
died Turin 1683

T urin Cathedral houses a most unusual chapel, the SS. Sindone or 'Holy Shroud' by Guarino Guarini. Being a Theatine priest, Guarini was sent across Europe to build churches for his order and worked in, among other places, Messina, Paris, Turin, Nice, Vicenza, Prague and Lisbon. In Rome (1639–47) he admired Borromini's work and systematically developed his ideas. Unfortunately most of Guarini's churches have been destroyed, but his treatise *Architettura civile* (*Civil Architecture*, 1737) and philosophical writings help us understand the profound symbolism of his designs.

In SS. Sindone we encounter the Baroque *theatrum* in a new way. Here it is neither illusionary nor architectural but 'surrealistic'. That is, the space seems to belong to another world, a world of mourning where, nevertheless, light filters in from above. Being entirely black, the interior wraps around its hidden gem: the Holy Shroud. This most sacred relic is only shown once a year, but it is always present in Guarini's interior. Rarely has a space been created that so effectively makes a deep unfathomable content manifest.

As a centralized space, the SS. Sindone adheres to the Early Christian conception of the mausoleum. Having to incorporate three entrances, two from the cathedral and one from the Royal Palace, Guarini divided the circle into nine sections, spanning six of the bays with large arches (on which the dome rests) and using the remaining three for the entrances. Guarini introduced small circular transitional spaces where the ramps leading from the cathedral meet the chapel. These penetrate the main area, a device that is commonly found in late Baroque architecture, where such elements of a spatial composition often become interdependent and a 'pulsating' body results. (Guarini's project for

S. Filippo in Casale, 1671, is an infinitely extended grid of cells, circular and square, with internal convex sides.) But SS. Sindone does not pulsate. As a mausoleum it shuns the impression of organic movement to become a manifestation of eternity.

The space rises up to receive light from above. Defined by light, architectural space here returns to light. And so the upper part of the dome consists of a seemingly infinite number of superimposed, staggered segmental ribs, each spanning from the centre of a rib below. Light filters through small windows between them. In most of his projects, Guarini transformed the cupola into a system of interlacing ribs, a theme he probably took from Moorish buildings he saw in Spain on his way to Lisbon; in Turin, the solution can also be seen in his S. Lorenzo (1668–87). The light which enters through the remarkable dome of SS. Sindone transforms the surfaces below into vibrating patterns, where six-point stars dominate; even the floor is set with stars. Thus, the lower 'earthly' area is integrated with the 'heavenly' dome – and so this is another interpretation of the basic relationship encountered in SS. Andrea and Ivo (*see pages 112–15*). The chapel was damaged by fire in 1998 but is undergoing restoration.

SS. SINDONE • TURIN *INTERIOR VIEW OF DOME*

St Margaret

BREVNOV, CZECH REPUBLIC
1709–15

Christoph Dientzenhofer

born Rosenheim 1655
died Prague 1722

A few miles west of the Castle Town in Prague there is a great Benedictine monastery church by Christoph Dientzenhofer dedicated to St Margaret. Here the spatial system of interdependent cells, suggested by Borromini and developed by Guarini *(see pages 114–17)*, is fully accomplished. Dientzenhofer probably knew the work of Guarini, as in around 1690 he went to Marseilles to build a chapel and would have passed through Turin. Moreover, Guarini's treatise on architecture was circulated in 1686.

In 1684 Christoph's brother Georg (1642–89) began the Kappel shrine near Waldsassen, on the road from Franconia to Bohemia, with Christoph as an assistant. After Georg's premature death, his younger brother settled in Prague where he became the leading architect for the first two decades of the 18th century. His first major work, the monastic church of Oboriste (1699–1713), is derived from Guarini's Immacolata Concezione in Turin (1673–97), but in the chapel of the castle in Smirice (1700–13), Christoph introduced more original ideas. Here, space has become an open system of mutually dependent cells, contained within an undulating outer wall. The openness of the system is shown by the lack of a continuous interior entablature; rather, the vault appears as a *baldacchino* (canopy) on stilts, with secondary in-filling wall sections between the vertical members (a solution derived from the late-Gothic *Wand-pfeiler*, wall-pier, as seen, for example, in the Vladislav Hall in Prague's Castle). The system was developed on a grand scale in St Nicolas in the Lesser Town (Malá Strana, Kleinseite) in Prague (1703–11). Here, Christoph introduced a truly original idea: where the spatial cells expand on the floor, the corresponding vaults above contract, creating a displaced, syncopated rhythm.

Christoph's development of the series of cells culminated in St Margaret in Brevnov. The main disposition of this church is biaxial, consisting of symmetrical spaces around the transverse axis. With the addition of a presbytery, however, the general longitudinality is assured. The outer wall is articulated by large Ionic pilasters, broken only at either side by deep recesses flanked by columns, making a strong relation between inside and out.

The interior appears as a succession of tall wall pillars filled by secondary, neutral surfaces, which are curved to indicate the oval cells of the spatial composition. Being syncopated, the structural parts of the vault are not simple, transverse arches but a composite form derived from two double-curved arches. The vault itself splits open and heavenly, painted scenes appear. Thus we return to Bernini's *theatrum sacrum*, and Brevnov indeed represents a great synthesis of the essential conceptions of the Baroque.

Christoph's younger brother Johann (1663–1726) designed the splendid Benedictine abbey church in Banz (1710–19), across the border in Franconia, which has a similar syncopated system and heavenly images in the vault. The brothers' work was continued in Franconia by Neumann and in Bohemia by Christoph's son, Kilian Ignaz.

ST MARGARET · BREVNOV

St John on the Rock

PRAGUE, CZECH REPUBLIC
1729–39

Kilian Ignaz Dientzenhofer
born Prague 1689
died Prague 1751

Prague is one of Europe's great Baroque cities. It does not, however, possess a comprehensive plan like Turin, but rather comprises a large number of Baroque 'episodes': palaces, churches and gardens. After the Catholic victory over the Calvinists at the White Mountain (Bila Hora) west of Prague in 1621, Bohemia remained outside the ravages of the Thirty Years War and building activity went on.

The Catholic general Count Waldstein (Wallenstein) erected an immense residence in the Lesser Town and other aristocratic families followed, using mostly Italian architects and craftsmen. New churches appeared and old ones received new interior decoration. Counter-Reformatory zeal was the common denominator, and in Prague it met a highly expressive local tradition. The result was a dynamic architecture which reached its zenith in the work of Kilian Ignaz Dientzenhofer.

Dientzenhofer's father, Christoph (*see page 118*), sent him to Vienna to study with Hildebrandt (*see pages 132–33*). When he returned to Prague in 1717 he completed his ailing father's work and began a splendid independent career. Kilian did not continue the pursuit of syncopated spatial organization but took another Guarinian method as his point of departure: the principle of pulsating juxtapositions (*see page 116*). This means that the cells which make up a spatial whole alternately expand (for example, to form an oval) and contract (to form a rectangle with convex sides). The idea first appears in the church at Pocaply, north of Prague (1724), and culminates with St John on the Rock, whose dramatic location is enhanced by the double-flight staircase leading to the entrance.

Dynamism is expressed by the concave-convex-concave movement of the façade, where the concave sections are due to the diagonally placed towers. These have a 'wild' termination typical of local Baroque. The plan is developed around a central octagon (slightly elongated) with internally convex sides. Secondary ovals could have been added on the transverse axis but these are actually only present on the longitudinal axis. The transverse limits are closed off by neutral walls between piers, marking a new interpretation of the *baldacchino* motif of Christoph. Now the central cell has become the hub of an open multilateral system, where secondary spaces may be added or taken away in all directions. The system may also form a simple, longitudinal succession of cells, as in the Jesuit church of Oparany (1732–35).

In Kilian's major buildings, the wall piers on the diagonals are united by wide arches that form one composite pier containing a window, suggesting the building stands within a luminous space. The secondary walls on the transverse axis are pierced by large chasuble-shaped openings, a theme already used at Pocaply. The *baldacchini* of St John on the Rock are decorated with heavenly scenes. Thus the *theatrum sacrum* is present as a heavenly domain which comes down to rest on earth. And, in fact, Kilian's dynamic interiors are surprisingly focused on the floor plan, his later works tending towards the dominant rotunda form, which became the main thrust of Baroque development during the 18th century.

Vierzehnheiligen
BANZ, GERMANY
1743–72

Johann Balthasar Neumann
born Eger 1687
died Würzburg 1753

The great pilgrimage church of Vierzehnheiligen is beautifully located above the river Main, opposite the monastery of Banz. It is generally considered the culmination of Baroque ecclesiastical architecture and completes the mode of spatial composition suggested by Borromini and developed by Guarini and the Dientzenhofers *(see pages 114–21)*. Its architect, Johann Balthasar Neumann, belonged directly to this tradition.

Born in Bohemia, just across the border from Franconia, Neumann grew up as Christoph Dientzenhofer's St Clare was being built in his home town. Banz was close by and its master, Johann Dientzenhofer, later became Neumann's mentor. In 1717 Neumann visited Vienna and northern Italy and he also went to Paris and met leading French architects such as Gabriel Germain Boffrand (1667–1754) and Robert de Cotte (1656/7–1735), both of whom contributed to the development of the Rococo decorative style.

And so Neumann had the ideal professional background to add to his great talent, and in 1719 he was appointed court architect to Prince Schönborn, for whom he began to plan the great Residenz in Würzburg (1719–44). During the early years in his post, Neumann worked closely with Johann Dientzenhofer, but he soon had his own design office with several assistants, designing buildings for a large part of southern Germany.

A few of his works stand out as particularly important, bearing the mark of Neumann's own attention to their design. Vierzehnheiligen (Fourteen Saints) is his masterpiece. Taking the form of a Latin-cross basilica, its relatively restrained exterior has a tower façade. Between the towers a convex *ressaut* (projection) suggests a more animated interior, and on entering the building, a seemingly infinite, radiant space is revealed, consisting of a series of oval *baldacchini*. These are defined by huge columns and pilasters, some freestanding within the perforated outer wall. A strong effect of *Zweischaligkeit* is created: a double spatial system where the inner, structural area is immersed in a continuous, luminous surround.

But the plan is most unusual. The dominant centre is not at the crossing of the longitudinal and transverse axes but further back. At the crossing, the vault is cut away by four convex lateral spaces, allowing the oval in front to expand. Such expressive syncopated interconnection would have been impossible without the Dientzenhoferian method. And this was not the planned effect. The supervisor of the project (and Neumann's rival), Gottfried Heinrich Krohne, had made the foundations of the presbytery too far to the east, and so the location of the altar no longer coincided with the crossing. In 1744 Neumann solved the problem, transforming the nave into a dominant, oval rotunda, and so uniting all the basic concepts of the Baroque church into a singular synthesis.

Vierzehnheiligen is the only major church of the period with Rococo decoration throughout. The elaborate altar is placed freely within the rotunda. The whole is a unique scheme in which the space becomes a frame for a mysterious inner world.

VIERZEHNHEILIGEN • *BANZ INTERIOR DETAIL*

In der Wies
STEINGADEN, GERMANY
1744–54

Dominikus Zimmermann
born Gaispoint 1685
died Wies 1766

Among the numerous sanctuaries and pilgrimage churches of southern Germany, those by Dominikus Zimmermann are supreme examples of *Gesamtkunstwerke* (fully synthesized works of art). Where Bernini achieved remarkable illusions in his interiors, Zimmermann suggests immediate reality. He showed that he was not only an architect but, in a literal sense, a builder, a creator, and also a masterly stucco-worker.

Zimmermann's first masterpiece, the church of Steinhausen (1727–31), rises above a village near Biberach. Its white and colourful interior, calm and yet saturated with life, is unforgettable. What Steinhausen promised was realized in an even more enchanting way by the pilgrimage church In der Wies (In the Field), located at the foot of the Bavarian Alps, not in a village but forming the 'head' of a small monastery. In front of the main entrance to the church, Zimmermann built a house for himself which today is an inn. Steinhausen and Wies are closely related but also quite different. Both were planned as longitudinal ovals with freestanding piers inside. These piers rise right up to the vault, and the space thus appears as a centralized *Hallenkirche*. The Central European 'hall-churches' from the late Middle Ages did not have the traditional basilican section but were built as unified spaces with piers standing like trees in a forest (Schinkel made this comparison at the beginning of the 19th century). As in the works of the Dientzenhofers (*see pages 118–21*), a Gothic note is therefore present, although all the parts stem from the classical tradition.

In both churches, the oval vault carried on piers is like a vast *baldacchino*, surrounded by a radiant ambulatory. An ambulatory was necessary in pilgrimage churches but it was often attached to the outside of the building or erected as an independent structure. In Steinhausen the outside wall still has a tectonic character, being subdivided by tall pilasters. In the Wies church, however, it has become a thin membrane-like 'envelope', pierced by numerous freely shaped windows which emphasize its non-structural character (reminiscent of Kilian Ignaz Dientzenhofer's chasuble-shaped openings). Only on the convex façade do applied columns signal the entrance.

The interior is an unsurpassed essay on essential architecture. The piers of Steinhausen have become pairs of slender columns, whose roundness is contradicted by 'shadow-edges' at the corners, another Gothic feature. As the church of a monastery, a deep presbytery has been added, where the late Baroque *Zweischaligkeit* (*see page 122*) reaches a climax; the splendid goal of the worshipper where everything dissolves into a celestial vision of light. The presbytery is one of the few fully three-dimensional pieces of Rococo architecture in existence, the exuberant decoration enhancing the sense of rejoicing. Baroque rhetoric is here substituted for a 'presence', which was ultimately the ambition of the whole epoch. In the Wies church, one really enters heaven, as believers once did in medieval cathedrals, but now the celestial quality also saturates everything earthly.

St John Nepomuk
Z'DAR, CZECH REPUBLIC
1719–22

Giovanni Santini
born Prague 1667
died Prague 1723

The development of the late Baroque style in Central Europe included some unexpected phenomena. In some ways, the aim of the Counter-Reformation implied a return to the Middle Ages. Then, Catholic architecture defined the 'international' style, and so Gothic features reappeared in the works of the Dientzenhofers and other architects, but acting as principles rather than clear forms. Giovanni Santini, however, used Gothic motifs in combination with classical elements, creating a surrealistic effect.

Santini (or Johann Santin-Aichel) was of Italian extraction and trained in Italy. He worked in Prague at the same time as Christoph Dientzenhofer (*see pages 118–19*). In 1702–1706 he rebuilt the Cistercian Abbey in Sedlec near Kutna Hora (Kuttenberg), which had been destroyed during the Hussite Wars (1419–36), and in 1712–26 reconstructed the Benedictine Abbey in Kladruby. For both he was asked to use a *more gotico*, a Gothic style, to recall the monastic tradition of the Middle Ages, and achieved a highly personal effect by applying Gothic ribs to the vaults of the churches. These have no structural function but are simply 'drawn' on the surfaces. Other Gothic motifs were also used and an intriguing mixture of styles was the result. Santini's purely Baroque works are based on similar non-structural principles; the large pilgrimage church at Krtiny in Moravia (1713) and his last work, the monastic church in Rajhrad near Brno (1722), show no interdependence between the spatial elements, and the applied classical members are cut off as they rise up. Baroque forms are indeed present, but not as 'pulsating' *baldacchino*-like bodies.

Among Santini's works his St John Nepomuk shrine on the Green Mountain at Z'dar in Moravia is particularly fascinating. The centralized building is derived from the five-pointed star, which according to legend appeared around the head of the saint when he was found floating in the Vltava (Moldau) River under the Charles Bridge in Prague. (John, the confessor of the queen, refused to divulge her secrets to the king and so was thrown into the river from the bridge. He became the patron saint of bridges, and many in southern and Central Europe carry a Nepomuk statue. He even stands on Ponte Milvio in Rome.)

The exterior has a very particular composition of concave and convex forms, but it lacks Baroque plasticity. In fact, the most surprising property of the building is the absence of the dynamism that is suggested by its star-like plan. The structure appears static, but at the same time strangely surrealistic. The interior has a similar quality, being enclosed by a neutral surface broken by Gothic openings and applied, non-structural ribs.

The works of Santini are full of striking contradictions. Within a church, heaven remains inaccessible and the architecture presents a tragic air. Santini must have foreseen the disintegration of the European anthropomorphic tradition, where human emotions were evoked in architecture, and his works became a combination of memories rather than an expression of belief.

St Stephen, Walbrook

LONDON, GREAT BRITAIN
1672–79

Christopher Wren
born East Knoyle 1632
died London 1723

Few can match the output of Christopher Wren as an architect, yet he had no formal training in the field. He had, however, a good classical education, including a thorough knowledge of Latin, but mathematics and astronomy were his main interests. He also had a fine inspiration in Inigo Jones, whose classical works, such as the Banqueting House in Whitehall *(see pages 102–103)*, he greatly admired.

In the 1660s, Wren turned from his first passion, science, to architecture. In 1665 he visited Paris where he saw Bernini's designs for the Louvre (1665–66, unexecuted) and visited Guarini's St Anne-la-Royale (1662 onwards, destroyed) and the suburban palaces of Vaux-le-Vicomte *(see pages 130–31)* and Maisons (1642–51; François Mansart, 1598–1666). He witnessed the Great Fire of London (1666) which destroyed thousands of houses and more than 80 churches, among them St Paul's Cathedral, and within days had produced a typically Baroque, geometrical plan for the rebuilt city. The Stock Exchange was the main focus, St Paul's played a secondary role, and no large palace was included. But old property boundaries had to be respected and Wren's plan was not realized. In 1670, however, he was commissioned to rebuild the City churches. He built 51, all dating from the 1670s and 1680s. Several were damaged or destroyed during the Second World War, but those that remain offer a vivid impression of Wren's inventive genius.

Since most of the churches do not have much of a façade, the steeples and interiors are of primary interest. Being Protestant churches, the Catholic basilica form is generally abandoned, although an echo is still present in St Bride, Fleet Street. There are no presbyteries; the altar is placed directly in front of the end wall. Yet there is a tendency towards centralization – sometimes focused on a square space – a fundamental conception of the Reformed Church, for which belief in the word of God was central. The interiors are characterized by an elegant lightness which is enriched by the use of slender Corinthian columns.

The dome is a superb centralized form, and in his most accomplished church, St Stephen, Walbrook, Wren placed a classical dome within a grid of repeated bays. To achieve a uniform dome he had to widen the longitudinal and transverse bays in the middle, a device he repeated on a monumental scale in St Paul's (1675–1709). Thus, St Stephen's unifies several of the traditional elements of ecclesiastical space: the nave, the transept, the cross and the circle, and, because of its 'rich simplicity', may be considered Wren's most convincing ecclesiastical achievement.

Wren's churches present an array of steeples in the cityscape. These show a wealth of solutions, some with Gothic elements. St Vedast in Foster Lane uses concave and convex profiles which recall Borromini. But most of the steeples are based on superimposition and not 'organic' growth as seen at S. Ivo's *(see pages 114–15)*. The development of a distinct English exterior architecture was taken up by Hawksmoor *(see pages 146–47)*, whose churches unite classical and Gothic features in masterpieces of surface articulation.

ST STEPHEN, WALBROOK • LONDON *INTERIOR*

Vaux-le-Vicomte
NEAR MELUN, FRANCE
1657–60

Louis Le Vau
born 1612, place unknown
died Paris 1670

Where the Italian Baroque gave pride of place to ecclesiastical buildings, the French Baroque celebrated the château; a natural consequence of the power of the aristocracy and greater religious confidence in the face of the Reformation. The characteristic Baroque U-shaped plan is rooted in the French tradition of distributing the buildings of a castle around a spacious courtyard (by contrast, the compact Italian palazzo derives from the Roman multistorey apartment house, the *insula)*.

During the Renaissance, French planning was systematized with a *corps de logis* (main building) and wings on either side. The Château d'Anet (1547–52) by Philibert de l'Orme (1500/15–70) is a characteristic example. The U-shaped plan also applied to urban dwellings. These 16th-century buildings were composed on the addition principle, with a repetition of elements horizontally and a vertical superimposition of classical orders. A more expressive note was introduced by François Mansart, who still used superimposition in his Château de Maisons Lafitte, but with a new plastic richness in the juxtaposition of volumes and their detailing. Typically French is the use of steep 'Gothic' roofs, even echoed at Versailles.

The first truly Baroque château is Vaux-le-Vicomte by Louis Le Vau. The castle was built for Nicolas Fouquet, the French finance minister. The opening celebrations were attended by the king, who wondered how Fouquet could have afforded such a splendid palace. As a result, the host was arrested, but Louis XIV brought his architect Le Vau, his landscape architect Le Nôtre and his decorator, the painter Lebrun, to Versailles.

Vaux-le-Vicomte is surrounded by a moat, like a medieval castle. On one side the island comprises a *cour d'honneur*, where the visitor is received, and on the opposite, garden side, the landscape is organized around a longitudinal axis which starts in the main salon of the château and extends ad infinitum. Thus the basic disposition of the Baroque residence was defined through the collaboration between Le Vau and Le Nôtre. The château receives the visitor in the 'urban' *cour d'honneur*, leads him through the dominant centre, the salon, and releases him into 'civilized' nature.

Vaux-le-Vicomte also revolutionized the practical disposition of the plan. Traditionally, the rooms of a palace formed *appartement simple* or *en enfilade*: one room had to be passed through to reach the next, which could be intrusive. At Vaux, the *corps de logis* is doubled. This *appartement double* was of great importance, allowing privacy, which particularly benefited women.

Finally, the façade of Vaux carries a giant order, which had been introduced by Michelangelo and Palladio and given a Baroque interpretation by Bernini. Bernini visited Paris when Le Vau was designing Versailles, but the character of Le Vau's work is not Italian; it still recalls the medieval origin of the French château. It was only with Jules Hardouin-Mansart (1646–1708) that a repetitive structural system replaced the Baroque volumes (for example, the Grand Trianon, Versailles, 1687).

VAUX-LE-VICOMTE • *NEAR MELUN*

Belvedere
VIENNA, AUSTRIA
1713–16, 1721–23

Johann Lukas
von Hildebrandt
born Genoa 1668
died Vienna 1745

Among the Baroque residences of Europe, the Belvedere palace in Vienna is particularly important, both as a total scheme of architecture and gardens and as a highly articulate set of buildings. It is on a sloping site in the green belt surrounding medieval Vienna. The Lower Belvedere (1713–16) looks towards the city while the slope is crowned by the Upper Belvedere (1721–23). Between the two is a 'French' garden, whose first parterre is an earthly piece of tamed nature, while the second brings us closer to the sky. The two levels are connected by flights of stairs, ramps and a waterfall.

The owner, Prince Eugene of Savoy, must take much of the credit for the splendid result, but the plan was executed by the talented Johann Lukas von Hildebrandt, who was appointed first court architect in 1723. Prince Eugene was a military genius. He offered his services to the French King Louis XIV, but being small and not very handsome, he was rejected. Turning to the Austrian Emperor Leopold I, who had a similar appearance, he was accepted, and went on to win great victories against the Turks, and the French. Thanks to his military successes and the feeble character of Leopold's successors, Prince Eugene became the real ruler of Austria and needed a grand residence.

The Lower Belvedere to some extent fulfilled this need. It is centred on a double-height marble hall for receptions, where a large ceiling fresco by Martino Altomonte glorifies Prince Eugene as hero, personality and victor. The rest of the single-storey building comprises rooms for his collections of exotic plants and animals, as well as services for both palaces (including a stable for 60 horses!). The exterior is subdivided by double pilasters in the middle and simple vertical bands on either side. The general light character is appropriate to the function of a garden palace.

The Upper Belvedere develops this character in a splendid way. Not only is the composition of volumes richer but the wall articulation is more sophisticated, being carried all around the building with significant variations. The Upper Belvedere is a masterpiece in diversified unity. The forecourt is not an enclosed *cour d'honneur* but an open space with an ornamental lake in the centre. To reach the entrance, the visitor has to go around the lake and so experience the building obliquely, and thereby its composition of volumes. The portico has a composite, Borrominesque gable while behind, the volume of the main hall rises up between double-height pavilions. Shorter, single-storey wings link this central part to four corner pavilions, which stand out like towers, reminiscent of a medieval castle. The garden façade repeats the general composition but here the main hall is linked directly to the garden. Double pilasters rise over a continuous rusticated base which is echoed inside in the staircase and grotto-like *sala terrena* (a ground-floor garden room). By contrast, the great octagonal marble hall upstairs has splendid coupled pilasters under an illusionary painted vault. The hall has become Vienna's forum for important receptions and conferences.

Amalienborg
COPENHAGEN, DENMARK
1750–54

Nicolai (Niels) Eigtved
born Haraldsted 1701
died Copenhagen 1754

To the northeast of the old, crooked streets of central Copenhagen there is a Baroque city-extension, the Fredriksstaden (begun 1740). Its grid-like system of streets lined with houses from the period is well preserved, and the attractive Amalienborg square acts as an urban focus. The area is named after King Frederik III, whose equestrian statue stands at the centre of the square. The French *place royale*, developed in Paris during the early 17th century *(see pages 100–101)*, was the model.

Fredriksstaden was planned and the main buildings designed by the Rococo court architect Nicolai (Niels) Eigtved, who had worked with Matthaeus Daniel Pöppelmann (1662–1736) in Dresden. Eigtved died before everything was complete; most notably absent is the domed Frederik's Church, which should have terminated the axis from the harbour and so marked Denmark's important role as a seafaring nation (it was built on a reduced scale during the second half of the 19th century).

Eigtved's plan is a milestone in the evolution of the Baroque city. It all started with Pope Sixtus V's plan of 1585–90 for Rome, which aimed to link the holy places with straight streets, both to make it easier for pilgrims to find their way about and to express the role of Rome as a unified *città santa*. Sixtus' urban conception was developed in Turin and Paris, although in Paris the churches no longer served as the primary focus, a role taken over by urban spaces where series of buildings surround statues of the king – and hence the term *place royale*. The wish for geometric integration was carried on in the town of Versailles and led to centralized systems of infinitely extended streets, such as Karlsruhe in Germany (1715). As a rule, the French prototypes have a continuous boundary (at Place Vendôme in Paris, begun 1699, the façades were put up first to ensure continuity, and then the building sites behind were sold). By contrast, the octagonal space of Amalienborg is defined by four similar palaces on the diagonals, designed for aristocratic families. In 1795, however, the castle, Christiansborg, was destroyed by fire and the royal family bought the palaces, where they still reside. A Neoclassical corridor on columns was erected to unite two of the palaces, those of the king and the crown prince. It does not, however, disturb Eigtved's refined architecture.

The palaces are simple volumes emphasized by hipped roofs and have continuous flat façades. Only the three central bays of each building step forward as a *ressaut*, with full columns and tall windows that indicate the importance of the main rooms behind. These windows are arched and have finely modelled surrounds. The columns rise above a delicately rusticated ground floor. A lightness and lack of plasticity endow the whole with a Danish character. Amalienborg square is in fact one of my choices because of the humbleness of the whole. The position of the palaces on the diagonals negates the usual monumentality of the *place royale*, and Eigtved's delicate articulation of the buildings strikes a democratic note which gives them a timeless appeal.

AMALIENBORG · COPENHAGEN

Tessin Palace
STOCKHOLM, SWEDEN
1692–1700

Nicodemus Tessin
the younger
born Nyköping 1654
died Stockholm 1728

Visiting Stockholm after Copenhagen is like encountering a different world. Where the Danish Baroque is distinguished by lightness and elegance, the Swedish is typified by monumental grandeur. This is particularly evident in the Royal Palace, designed by Nicodemus Tessin the younger. Tessin was educated in Rome (1673–78 and 1687–88), where he met Bernini and Carlo Fontana (1638–1714), and around 1680 visited France, which enabled him to study the garden layouts of Le Nôtre.

After his return to Sweden in 1688, Tessin was commissioned to reconstruct and later completely rebuild the Royal Palace (begun 1697). The result was a large Roman palazzo with a *cour d'honneur* towards the old city and a garden terrace over a heavily rusticated wall on the side of Lake Mälaren. A strong solution, if rather foreign in character.

In front of the main entrance to the palace, Tessin built a house for himself. The exterior is simple but well proportioned, with three storeys, an elegant *piano nobile* and rusticated ground floor. Thus far, all is traditional. On entering the internal garden, however, the spaces gain an unexpected complexity and richness. Two trapezoid structures are separated and linked by freestanding, curved walls, where the Doric order of the ground floor is repeated. The sides of the second trapezoid act as corridors leading from the end of the larger, first trapezoid to the *corps de logis*. The corridor wings are lower than the buildings they connect, emphasizing the openness of the garden, which contains a symmetrical labyrinthine parterre that ends in a round fountain, continuing the curved theme. The second trapezoid, defined by three-storey façades, forms a counterpart to the *corps de logis* and contains services, stables and cover for carriages. Its central part, however, looks like a

palace in its own right, with double Ionic columns over a rusticated base. The composition ends with a false perspective. The top storey is shallow, but the decreasing height of the columns gives the impression of imposing, receding height in the building (the same device was used by Palladio in his Teatro Olimpico in Vicenza, 1580–85, and by Borromini in Palazzo Spada in Rome, c.1650).

The garden is a unique example of Baroque spatial planning. The trapezoid side walls diverge, making the space appear wider than it is, and the composition is both unified and diversified, a longitudinal axis and a subtle interplay of spatial tensions running through the layout. Linear rustication surrounds the gardens, essentially Doric on the ground floor and Ionic above. The whole becomes a kind of *theatrum*, not a sacred one, but a 'stage' for the owner, his family and guests to perform on. It is a fundamental Baroque idea to understand the world as a *theatrum*, but Tessin's spectacular achievement is unequalled. (He was in fact a theatrical designer for Charles XII, for which he was made a baronet in 1696.) The composition of this house is still part of the Vitruvian tradition and demonstrates its inexhaustible potential, but it is a surprise to find such an inventive interpretation in the rather austere city of Stockholm.

Karlskirche
VIENNA, AUSTRIA
1716–37

Johann Bernard Fischer von Erlach
born Graz 1656
died Vienna 1723

Vienna has been compared to Saturn: a compact core surrounded by a lighter ring. This pattern was developed after the victory over the Turks at the siege of Vienna in 1683. A green belt was laid out around the medieval city where the well-to-do built 'garden palaces'. Hildebrandt's Belvedere is the most important of these *(see pages 132–33)*, but within the belt a large church was also erected, the extraordinary Karlskirche. Today it is part of the city, but originally it stood in greenery.

In 1713 Austria was laid low by the plague and the emperor promised to build a church if the outbreak would end. Prayers to the Counter-Reformatory St Charles Borromeo were believed to have helped, and so the new church was dedicated to him. In 1715 a competition was held and the court architect, Johann Bernard Fischer von Erlach, won.

The Karlskirche can seem bewildering. The dominant dome undoubtedly makes it Baroque, but what about the Roman triumphal columns? And the classical portico, which can hardly be called Baroque, although its entablature grows out of the volumes behind? The building is a mixture of styles, with numerous references to the past. And indeed, Fischer's conception of architecture was largely historical. Several Baroque architects turned to history, both for inspiration and for creating a synthesis of past and present. Borromini sent an assistant to Ravenna to survey the Byzantine-Roman San Vitale (AD 526–47); Guarini's use of Moorish forms is another example, and in Bohemia and Moravia Giovanni Santini created a 'Gothic' Baroque. (The use of 'Gothick' in England should also be remembered.) But Fischer went further. In 1705 he started to collect information on the buildings of all countries and epochs, and in 1721 published *Entwurff einer historischen Architektur*

(*A Plan of Civil and Historical Architecture*), which contains 74 etchings of buildings from throughout the world, beginning with Stonehenge, moving through Egyptian, Chinese and Islamic works (the first architectural treatise to include these), and ending with his own projects. The illustrations are sometimes quite fantastic, but the idea is clear: his own works represent the culmination of architectural history!

The Karlskirche is a realization of historical synthesis. The Baroque dome, the triumphal columns and the classical portico are brought together as a *theatrum architecturae mundi*. The Baroque towers at either end of the façade recall St Peter's in Rome, as does the narthex (vestibule) which forms a transition to the impressive oval interior. The whole *theatrum* is not just a formal exercise, however, but has symbolic meanings. The portico flanked by the giant columns refers to Solomon's Temple in Jerusalem, while the ensemble brings imperial Rome back to life. The Karlskirche, thus, is a case of *Staatskunst*, imperial art, demonstrating the role of Austria as a primary European power. But it also represents the end of the great 'systems' of the Baroque. Enlightenment is on the way, and Fischer's *Entwurff* can be seen as an early contribution to enlightened knowledge.

KARLSKIRCHE · VIENNA

Sacristy of the Certosa
GRANADA, SPAIN
1732–45

Francisco Hurtado de Izquierdo
born Lucena 1669
died Priego 1725

Spanish Baroque architecture is relatively unknown, in spite of its many monuments and formal extravagance. The very exuberance of the style, where structure is hidden under massed ornamentation, has hampered our knowledge. The traditional elements of bay, apse and dome are there, but are part of an immaterial whole. The dematerialization of Moorish architecture, swathed in decoration, comes to mind, but whereas the Moorish character is still comprehensible, Spanish Baroque is the result of a dramatic, complicated process, originating in the Christian body–soul dichotomy.

To compound the difficulty in grasping the nature of Spanish Baroque, it does not form part of a natural development from early Roman Baroque principles but rather springs from Mannerism. Baroque synthesis, in the sense of Bernini and Borromini (see pages 112–15), is lacking and is substituted by a multitude of dominant effects. In the Spanish Baroque, the theatrum sacrum is fully realized, leaving no distance between the worshipper and the illusion. Here you do not 'sense' or 'imagine', but have to enter the 'stage', giving back your body to light. (Bernini understood this attitude when he made the Cornaro Chapel in S. Maria della Vittoria, Rome, 1645–52, dedicated to the Spanish mystic, St Teresa of Avila.) This art of the interior was echoed outside by ornate portals and embellished window surrounds, which are particularly effective in the white towns of southern Spain, such as Carmona and Ecija.

These highly worked interiors are most typical of the deep south of the country, with its characteristic inward-looking living spaces. Here the centre of the dwelling is the court or patio which, to express the difference between outside and inside, is usually dressed with glazed tiles. Between the street and the court is a small ante-camera, which is left open during the day and which forms the intermediary in the sensitive relationship between public and private domains.

The Andalusian Baroque reached its high point with Francisco Hurtado de Izquierdo, who created interiors of an incredible richness. The sacristy of the Certosa was probably all designed by Hurtado apart from the retable (altar screen), which lacks the vibrating energy of the rest. Pilasters, entablatures and capitals are there, but even the shafts are covered by an ornamentation which jerks and jumps as it moves over the surfaces. Yet the interior has a strong sense of unity. A mellow shade of white throughout (except in the dome), it feels like a miraculous camarín (a small chapel behind and above the high altar in Spanish churches) which swallows you as you enter. Hurtado was already dead when the sacristy was built, but his style is unmistakable: the meeting of structure and light creates 'a world within a world', expressed in both a classical and local idiom. Regional qualities had a profound effect on the emotionally charged Spanish Baroque: further north the structural language is the same, but what was white has become black, reflecting the different tones of the landscape.

Neoclassicism

Gillian Darley

The increasing complexity of the political, commercial, industrial and cultural institutions of mid- and late-18th-century Europe and North America required clients and patrons to commission new and sophisticated buildings reflecting local, regional and national aspirations. The almost unanimous choice of the Neoclassical style, the rational architectural language of the Enlightenment, was, as is so often the case, made in reaction to what had preceded it.

The bombastic excesses of the Baroque, and the whimsy of Rococo, had been seen as synonymous with Roman Catholicism. In reaction, the English Palladians – a distinctively puritan group – followed the eponymous Italian architect, absolutist in their approach to classical antiquity. French architects, too, approached classicism with a strong underpinning of theory reinforced with an academic programme; their Mecca was Rome. But from mid-century and particularly following the end of the Seven Years War in 1763, architects swarmed south to

experience the reality of the great sites of Roman antiquity. For the first time, too, Greek classical architecture began to exert an influence, its admirers taking a fundamentalist approach to the use of the orders. There were models and inspiration for engineers as well as for architects, and a choice between the symbolism of imperial Rome or democratic Athens. There is very little polite Neoclassicism in my selection of 15

BELOW: Thomas Jefferson, Monticello, Charlottesville, 1769–1808

LEFT: John Soane, house at Lincoln's Inn Fields, London, 1792; breakfast room

buildings. In several cases they reflect the taste of John Soane, whose breadth of knowledge of antique precedent and later literature gave him the confidence to deviate from the strict letter of Neoclassical law. He lived in Lincoln's Inn Fields, London, surrounded by mementos of his Grand Tour of 1778–80. These included G.B. Piranesi's views of the Grecian ruins at Paestum in southern Italy, coloured engravings of Pompeiian decorative schemes (first excavated in 1755) and cork models, casts and stone fragments of temples and ancient structures. The exquisite interiors of his house as finally completed in the 1820s and 1830s offer a synthesis of his architectural thinking and his sources of inspiration. The house is also a reminder of the eclecticism which was reflected in many contemporary pattern books, the lingua franca of the building world, especially that of North America where architects were more scarce than texts.

Thomas Jefferson's self-designed house Monticello (1769–1808) was Palladian with a dash of Pliny's Roman villa. Almost as personal as Soane's Lincoln's Inn Fields, Monticello was remodelled after 1796, but this time in the French style. Elsewhere, especially on Capitol Hill, the architect-president put his tastes to the service of an ambitious young country. Equally, under the Prussian monarchy, Schinkel's reinvention of the urban landscape of Berlin was the most whole-hearted of contemporary European classical ventures at this time. Paris, deluded by Napoleonic promises, was less able to deliver the architecture of a great modern city despite a rich seam of

ABOVE: John Vanbrugh, Castle Howard, Yorkshire, 1699–1712; gatehouse

ideas, from the designs offered by Etienne-Louis Boullée (1728–99) to the struggles of architects to convey imperial ambitions in stone. London, invigorated for a period by the civic energies and vision of John Nash (1752–1835), soon relapsed into an institutional phase of late Neoclassicism. Despite a brief Italianate revival, the time had come for the resurgence of the Gothic, a medieval moral revival heralded by A.W.N. Pugin's pleas for old values and 'true' religion.

Seaton Delaval
**SEATON DELAVAL,
GREAT BRITAIN**
1718–28

John Vanbrugh
born London 1664
died London 1726

Few houses are as impressively strange, as wayward and unsettling in their mixture of forms and motifs as Seaton Delaval, looming over the Northumberland coast. Mannerist rustication, Palladian windows, an Ionic portico, laid upon the rudiments of Tudor-castle planning, with rooftop traces of the curiosities of 17th-century Anglo-Indian funerary monuments all appear in this idiosyncratic work by Sir John Vanbrugh.

Among the many duties of the architect, Vanbrugh considered it of paramount importance that 'the Appearance of every thing may exceed the Cost'. He had been a soldier, playwright and an East India merchant, trading in textiles from Surat in the 1680s, so he brought an enormous range of visual references to his architecture, his final, triumphant, choice of profession. The exact nature of his professional relationship with Nicholas Hawksmoor, with whom he entered on an informal partnership around 1700, sharing ideas and collaborating on the great North Yorkshire estate Castle Howard (1700–26), remains imprecise. However, Vanbrugh was heavily dependent on Hawksmoor's expertise to supply the skills which he, a brilliant designer but a novice architectural draughtsman, wanted.

One of Vanbrugh's last works, Seaton Delaval marks the apogee of his distinctive style. It broke with his early penchant for spreading mansions and for details culled from the Baroque. This tall house, with its rusticated temple front and corner towers, its Italian Renaissance features and its odd silhouette, punctuated by massive chimney stacks, balustrades and finials, had no clearly recognizable sources of inspiration, such as an English Palladian house would show. Vanbrugh, in John Soane's opinion 'the Shakespeare of architects', avoided 'the simple elegance of the antique', preferring a

vertiginous 'fire and boldness'. The exposed site, just outside Newcastle looking out to the North Sea, must have enhanced the sense of rawness, and the confrontational architectural language ensures that Seaton Delaval, even hemmed in by development as it is now, is almost shocking.

Vanbrugh was fortunate in his client: 'the Admiral is very Gallant in his operations, not being dispos'd to starve the Design at all'. Although Admiral George Delaval, whose family had owned the estate since the 12th century, died in a riding accident in 1723, his nephew, who succeeded him, continued the commission. Reduced to a shell by fire in 1822, the tight, high form of the central block remains intact. The stern north front is grandiloquent, with its arcaded courtyard, and offers a marked contrast to the gentler south, garden front, softened by an entrance portico. So that the relatively small house was not burdened by stairwells, Vanbrugh placed a pair of oval staircases in the octagonal rusticated towers to the east and west; light poured down from Venetian windows – a touch of elegance amid the heavy masonry. Still more castle than villa, Vanbrugh maximized the dramatic effect of a north-lit, double-height hall leading to a single-storey south-facing saloon – dark giving way to light. Once seen, Seaton Delaval stays in the memory for a lifetime.

SEATON DELAVAL • SEATON DELAVAL *NORTH FRONT*

Christchurch, Spitalfields
LONDON, GREAT BRITAIN
1714–29

Nicholas Hawksmoor
born Tuxford 1661
died London 1736

Christchurch, Spitalfields towers protectively over a dense network of Georgian streets, preserved from redevelopment by the passage of immigrants into and then out of the area – successively Huguenots, Jews and Bangladeshi. In his youth, its architect, Nicholas Hawksmoor, had worked closely with Sir Christopher Wren and then enjoyed a highly productive, mutually inspirational association with Sir John Vanbrugh.

Hawksmoor's appointment as one of the surveyors to the Commissioners for Churches under the 1711 Act for Building Fifty New Churches in the City of London, Westminster and their 'suburbs', the cost to be met by a tax on coal, gave him a perfect opportunity to imprint his strong, distinctive architecture upon London. The churches were to be prominent and preferably on island sites (in contrast to the awkward slots and corners with which Wren had to struggle).

Only 12 churches were built; Hawksmoor designed six and they made his reputation. He was revealed as a master of Baroque spatial ingenuity, steadied by an admiration of Roman antiquity and the sober motifs of its mausolea and public baths – hemispherical windows and blank niches – which created a dramatic play of dark and light. He was intrigued by engravings of classical antiquity and the written accounts of lost monuments such as Pliny's description of the Mausoleum of Halicarnassus (355–50 BC), inspiration for his spire at St George's, Bloomsbury (1716–31). Since many of Hawksmoor's later designs were thwarted or compromised to accord with the Palladian style which swept all before it, his London churches – despite their differing fates and states of preservation – are highly revealing of Hawksmoor's extraordinary architectural personality.

I have chosen Christchurch for its familiarity: a building that tends to be taken for granted, visible from thousands of City office windows. The foundations were laid in 1714, together with those of St Anne, Limehouse (1714–30) and St George-in-the-East, Stepney (1714–29). Its portico, the white Portland stone thrown into high contrast against the darkened recess of the entrance, is mirrored above in a flattened, smaller form on the tower and again, above that, by a lone arch. The spire has been altered but the impression remains; the whole is a monumental presence above Spitalfields market.

The church is majestic, its powerful lines exemplified by the huge dropped keystones of the north and south doorways and a series of stark porthole windows which beat an insistent rhythm around the exterior, despite its relatively modest size. Inside, it is a basilica with a nave and side aisles (with galleries, removed in alterations in 1866), the raised chancel marked by a columnated screen. Hawksmoor was intrigued by the form a church might have taken in the 4th century, 'in the purest times of Christianity', and, despite the solid ornament of the ceiling, the coving of the aisle vaults and the enrichment of capitals and entablatures, Christchurch is a heroically simple solution to the design of a place of worship.

CHRISTCHURCH, SPITALFIELDS • LONDON

The Pagoda, Kew Gardens
LONDON, GREAT BRITAIN
1761–62

William Chambers
born Gothenburg 1723
died London 1796

William Chambers, the son of a Scottish merchant, was born in Sweden and studied architecture in Paris and Rome. He was appointed architectural tutor to George, Prince of Wales (the future George III) in 1757 and in the same year published *Designs of Chinese Buildings*, drawing on his memories of China, which he had visited as a merchant seaman with the Swedish East India Company.

Chinoiserie ornamental buildings were appearing in grand parks and gardens all over Europe, part of the fashion for *jardins anglo-chinois*, and in 1761 Chambers added a Pagoda to the gardens at Kew. The 49-metre-high (160 ft) tower allowed the recently redesigned and replanted royal botanic garden, formed 30 years earlier by Frederick, Prince of Wales, to be viewed in all its splendour.

The core of the building was a tapering, plain stock brick octagon, with a verandah at its foot, broken up by a succession of blank and glazed windows on each storey. It was ornamented by 10 projecting roofs, covered with banded green and white glazed tiles. Scarlet balconies in Chinese fret pattern wound round each storey, while coloured glass dragons with bells in their jaws peered over from the corners of the eaves at every level. A wooden spiral staircase wound to the top and the colourful interiors were decorated with papier-mâché palm trees and a trompe l'oeil sky.

The Pagoda, perhaps based on an engraving of the ancient Porcelain Tower of Nanking, the most impressive in China, was a joyful combination of the Rococo at its most exotic and the current picturesque fashion for wildly eclectic garden buildings: its neighbours were an Alhambra and a Mosque, both lost in the early 19th century. Little now remains, except the red fretwork balconies, to remind us of the impact the spectacular Pagoda

would once have made. The Chinese Teahouse at Sans Souci, Potsdam (1754–57) and the Chinese Pavilion at Drottningholm near Stockholm (1763–69) give a taste of the exoticism of Chambers' Pagoda in its original state. Yet, even relatively plain, it injects a dash of the Orient to the western fringes of London as it towers above the mature cedars and rare arboricultural specimens.

William Chambers' career was assisted by his royal patrons and the publication of his *Treatise on Civil Architecture* (1759, revised 1768, 1791), which became the standard text on the correct use and application of the classical orders. He was an obvious choice to become the first Treasurer of the Royal Academy in 1768, but from 1775 he became engrossed in designing and building the most impressive architectural complex in the capital, Somerset House (completed 1796). Despite a long absence from Paris, Chambers maintained close friendships with leading French architects such as Marie-Joseph Peyre (1730–85) and Charles de Wailly (1730–98), and in so doing provided a living and crucial link between French Neoclassicism and English Palladianism. Pure Roman classicism and an absolute respect for the hierarchy and proper use of the orders lay behind his architectural decisions, and Chambers the purist never again reverted to the light-hearted picturesque eclecticism of the Pagoda at Kew.

THE PAGODA, KEW GARDENS · LONDON

Acquedotto Carolino
CASERTA, ITALY
1753–64

Luigi Vanvitelli
born Naples 1700
died Caserta 1773

The summer palace at Caserta, near Naples, was built for effect, the seat of an absolute monarch, designed on a scale to rival Versailles or the Escorial. But the glory of the complex lies in its immense linear park and water gardens, carved through (and over) the town. The architect was Luigi Vanvitelli and his patron the Bourbon king, Charles VII of Naples. Vanvitelli trained in Rome and came to work on the palace in 1750 – and was still doing so at his death (it was completed by his son Carlo, 1739–1821, in 1774). However, Vanvitelli's true masterpiece was his aqueduct.

Charles VII was an idealistic monarch in his early years, setting up industrial enterprises to provide employment, including the porcelain factory at Capodimonte and a silk works and model industrial town at San Leucio. In 1753 he conceived a highly ambitious engineering project, a 40-km-long (25-mile) aqueduct which could both supply water to the park and provide much needed irrigation to the countryside between Caserta and Naples, an area of remarkable fertility (the *campania felix* of antiquity) but low rainfall and great heat. The royal water gardens, 3 km (almost 2 miles) in length and built on a gradual slope, had a series of sculptured fountains symbolizing the elements and hunting pursuits (in spite of its size, the palace was built as a hunting lodge). These cascades led to a waterfall – and the whole was fed by mountain waters collected by the aqueduct. Much of this huge and technically advanced endeavour was hidden in tunnels or carved through mountains, but the most visible section was the three-tiered brick Archi della Valle, 528 m (1,732 ft) long and 60 m (197 ft) high. Roman aqueducts had survived throughout Italy, but the Pont du Gard (1st century BC) near Avignon in France is the clearest inspiration behind this astonishing structure.

Vanvitelli, the son of a Dutch painter, had gained valuable engineering experience working in the Camera Apostolica (the Papal Office of Works) before his return south. The continuous rhythmic arcading of the aqueduct is only broken by two triumphal arches which allowed the 18th-century highway and now its modern replacements, road and rail, to pass beneath. On the walls of the arches, stone tablets bear Latin inscriptions commemorating the enterprise. Lacing together the two sides of a steep valley like a rigid corset, the aqueduct, though now dry, remains hugely impressive. It is a largely forgotten monument to the vision of a king and the skills of his personal architect, as well as being a heroic recreation of a great Roman structure – a classic Neoclassical gesture and a tribute to the functional brilliance of Roman structural engineering.

The aqueduct was admired by contemporary engineers and architects. John Soane saw it in 1779, and, as the son of a bricklayer who would later become the master of deceptively simple brick architecture, the structure lodged in his memory, resurfacing in designs decades later, such as his first, unexecuted plans for the riverside infirmary at the Royal Hospital, Chelsea (1809).

ACQUEDOTTO CAROLINO • CASERTA *DETAIL OF ARCHI DELLA VALLE*

All Hallows, London Wall

LONDON, GREAT BRITAIN
1765–67

George Dance the younger
born London 1741
died London 1825

All Hallows, London Wall was a medieval City church which survived the Great Fire of London in 1666, only to decay to such a point that it needed urgent rebuilding a century later. Trapped between a bastion on the Roman Wall and a warren of small alleys and lanes, the new church had to be shoehorned into a constrained and asymmetrical site. The architect to whom the task fell was George Dance the younger.

Dance had just returned from six years in Italy and his solution was fresh and lively – the work of an architect fired up by years of study and eager to put his ideas into practice. All Hallows looks back to the structure of the Roman baths and basilicas which Dance knew so well, but translated into a graceful, almost domestic, form.

The church consists of a simple ground plan, a rectangle with an apsidal chapel at the east end and a tower above the entrance at the west. Dance's flair emerges in the balanced, airy interior, the symmetry of which betrays nothing of the difficulties of the site. A young man of independent architectural inclinations, he did not consider himself bound by the strict letter of the classical vocabulary. By simply omitting the cornice, he allowed the decorated vaulting to spring directly and, to his contemporaries, disconcertingly, from a frieze and from the capitals of the columns below. The result is an unimpeded hall with fluted Ionic columns demarcating the perimeter walls, belted by a honeysuckle-strewn frieze. Light pours in from clerestory windows to north and south, punched into the shallow barrel-vaulted ceiling. The apse is unlit and ornamented with lozenge-shaped plasterwork. In pride of place stands an altarpiece by Nathaniel Dance, the architect's brother – the family included noted actors and musicians as well as architects and painters.

George Dance senior (1695–1768) was Clerk of the City Works (in effect architect to the City of London) and designer of the Mansion House (1739–42) as well as several City churches. His son obtained the commission to rebuild All Hallows over the heads of a number of older and more experienced candidates and in 1768 inherited his father's post as well as becoming an architect-member of the new Royal Academy.

Dance's inventiveness within the classical vocabulary and his clear understanding of structure combined to make him a startlingly original and effective architect who designed, at one extreme, the great rusticated fortress of Newgate Gaol (1770–84, demolished), and at the other, the offices at the Guildhall (1788–89), where he devised a stone filigree façade of Indian-style exoticism which was much criticized for its wilfulness. Dance was also a clear-headed urban planner who envisaged routes linking the City to areas both north and south of the Thames, and in the late 1790s designed a number of major works, including docks and warehouses, around the Port of London. His most imaginative but unexecuted scheme was for twin bridges, raised alternately, to replace London Bridge and assist the passage of river traffic. Dance's ingenuity and independence had been clearly signalled in the little church which announced his architectural arrival in London.

ALL HALLOWS, LONDON WALL • *LONDON CEILING DETAIL*

Home House
LONDON, GREAT BRITAIN
1772–77

Robert Adam
born Kirkcaldy 1728
died London 1792

The Neoclassicists Robert Adam and James Wyatt (1746–1813) were professional rivals and the scene of one of their bitterest battles has recently been revealed. Home House in Portman Square was thought to be the work of Adam alone, but it was actually begun by Wyatt. He was awarded the commission by the famously louche and fabulously rich Dowager Countess of Home in 1772 and continued it in a typically lackadaisical fashion for some years before the Countess, by then over 70, settled his bill and turned to Robert and James Adam (1732–94), who finished the job in 1776–77.

No doubt spurred by the satisfaction of ousting his younger rival, whom he had previously accused of filching his designs, Robert Adam rose with aplomb to the challenge of remodelling the house, in spite of the fact that Wyatt's structure was virtually complete and at least partially decorated. Most spectacularly, Adam decided to demolish and rebuild the principal staircase, brilliantly reinventing it within the limits imposed by Wyatt's existing small, almost square, top-lit stairwell.

Adam's stair is set at right angles to the entrance hall, on the so-called Imperial plan, a single flight breaking into two curving arms to meet on the next floor. The stairwell culminates in a leaded oculus set upon alternating Ionic pilasters and columns that formed a piece with the (lost) Doric screen below. From the landing, visitors turned left and began their progress via an anteroom through the principal reception rooms, above all Adam's fabulously glittering Music Room fronting Portman Square which, in turn, led to the Great Drawing Room with its view of the garden.

As a student in the late 1960s at the Courtauld Institute of Art – before it moved to William Chambers' Somerset House – I remember the constant pleasure of rounding the corner from the entrance hall and coming upon Adam's stair as it soared upwards, injecting the whole house with life, a stream of light and a sense of muted, exquisite elegance – so at odds with student life.

The stair retains the main features of Adam's sober-toned decorative scheme, stucco trophies and medallions and painted panels purporting to be bas-reliefs (shallow carvings), carried out by the plasterer Joseph Rose and the painter Antonio Zucchi. Combining his liking for filigree ornament, which appears in the glazing of the dome and the surrounding plasterwork, but adding the sobriety of a classical ornamental repertoire, which extends to the ironwork of the balusters, Adam combines his architectural and decorative mastery to fine effect. For Adam, perhaps the most influential British architect of the late 18th century, was also a great decorator and furniture designer, using classical motifs, gilding and colour with skill and taste.

The staircase at Home House, stately and yet light-hearted, epitomizes the Neoclassical interior at its most urbane and elegant. Robert Adam's stair, so adeptly inserted within the house, is a *tour de force* – the brusque Scot's tart and wordless repartee to the professional shortcomings of the socially adept and charming James Wyatt.

Custom House
DUBLIN, IRELAND
1781–91

James Gandon
born London 1743
died Lucan 1823

The increasing sophistication of commercial and political life during the late 18th century required new kinds of buildings in which the complexity and symbolism of the planning and architecture reflected their function. The remarkable Custom House in Dublin was one such structure, designed by James Gandon who had been apprenticed to William Chambers in London in 1758.

Chambers' Somerset House was already under construction as Gandon began to plan the Custom House. Both buildings had fine riverside sites and were answering a brief to provide large numbers of offices as well as ceremonial rooms. In detail, however, the solutions were markedly different. Chambers looked back to stately French classical precedent while Gandon preferred a more subtle, interpretative classicism, in which proportion and repetition, variation and alternation of motifs rang the changes and allowed the massive building to become a surprisingly discrete whole.

While in London, Gandon, whose family was Huguenot, had caught the attention of a number of Irish peers and well-placed figures who were in a position to dispense patronage. Through them he secured the commission for the Custom House and moved to Dublin in 1781 to embark upon his great project on the banks of the Liffey. It took the determination of the architect and the tenacity of his client, the Hon. John Beresford, to deal with the difficulties that came with the scheme. These ranged from a boggy site to Byzantine political machinations (similar to those suffered by architects working for the federal government in the United States in the early 19th century).

The Custom House complex consisted of administrative offices and grand rooms set around two great internal courtyards. To east and west, the courts were screened by open arcades and the eastern end opened onto the dock, which together with the stores were part of Gandon's brief.

Each of the four façades was ornamented with allegorical and symbolic sculpture, the most elaborate upon the south-facing river elevation, where the arms of the kings of Ireland, keystones representing the rivers of Ireland and the pediment decorated by the union of Britain and Hibernia proclaimed the political reality in elegant but immutable masonry. Above the quadrangle was an elongated dome, surmounted by the figure of Commerce. The principal sculptor was Edward Smyth, and Gandon's workforce was made up of local tradesmen including the Darley family of stonemasons – my own relatives.

Gandon became the architect of choice to the Dublin administration, designing the Parliament House (1785–89) – later the Bank of Ireland – and the Four Courts (1786–1802). His Huguenot background may have led to his work on a model settlement, New Geneva, near Waterford (1783, not executed) for émigré Swiss watchmakers.

Fire destroyed the Custom House in 1921 and much was lost in the rebuilding: the arcades were infilled, the blank niches, which had alternated with windows, were forgotten, and the dome was reinstated incorrectly, so the building is only a shadow of Gandon's powerful original.

Chester Castle

CHESTER, GREAT BRITAIN
1786–1822

Thomas Harrison

born Richmond, Yorkshire 1744
died Chester 1829

Thomas Harrison spent half his life working on Chester Castle. The site had earlier been a Saxon castle and before that a Roman fortress. Upon these ghostly imprints and within the ruined medieval walls, Harrison constructed a civic complex that was the grandest and most impressive Greek Revival citadel in England, visited and admired by architects from the length and breadth of the British Isles.

Although attention tended to focus on the buildings of the capital, London was by no means the only location for significant architecture during the Georgian period. In major cities throughout Britain there was an explosion in public and institutional building and the preferred style was Neoclassical. The new developments were often the work of a single architect or family, for example, in Liverpool that of the Fosters, father and son (John senior, c.1759–1827, and John junior, c.1787–1846), in Edinburgh William Playfair (1790–1857) and in Newcastle John Dobson (1787–1865). Modern versions of Athens rose across Britain.

Thomas Harrison trained in Italy (1769–76). On his return he worked in northwest England, his commissions including churches and civic buildings in Manchester and Liverpool. Chester, an ancient regional centre, capital of Cheshire and a county palatine (possessing royal prerogatives), wanted its own Acropolis, and Harrison, a somewhat maverick architect, was to be their man.

Harrison won the competition for the castle site in 1785 and began to plan the courts and gaol the following year. His brief expanded over the years to include the Shire Hall (1792–1801), barracks and armouries. In 1807 he demolished the outer gateway and drawbridge of the old castle to make way for the Propylaeum (1810–13), the imposing Greek Revival entrance gate and lodges.

The buildings – with their interrelated functions of keeping the peace and the administration of justice – form an enclosure ranged around three sides of a generous courtyard which largely follows the outline of the outer bailey (court) of the old castle. But for the prison and the Exchequer Court, the complex remains intact and in use.

As the years passed, Harrison's approach to the Greek Revival became purer. While the portico to the County Court (1797) was in Greek Doric, the semicircular interior is Roman, with 12 gigantic freestanding Ionic columns surmounted by a heavily coffered, top-lit half-dome, as rehearsed in Paris at the Ecole de Chirurgie (1769–75, now Ecole de Médecine) by Jacques Gondoin (1737–1818). But by the time Harrison was building the Propylaeum, he had settled fully into the Greek Revival. He marked the attic of his Greek Doric gateway with massive masonry blocks, a final flourish to complete the grand composition which had absorbed him for almost 40 years.

The architect Charles Robert Cockerell (1788–1863) described Harrison in the 1820s as 'undoubtedly the noblest genius in architecture we have had – in external architecture chiefly'. Now his remarkable Propylaeum presides over a vast car park, but at least it survives, unlike that at Euston Station (1835–39) by Philip Hardwick (1792–1870), infamously destroyed in 1962.

CHESTER CASTLE • CHESTER

Barrière de la Villette

PARIS, FRANCE
1784–89

Claude-Nicolas Ledoux

born Dormans 1736
died Paris 1806

The girdle of customs houses and warehouses designed to encircle Paris from 1784 onwards was a clear demonstration of political intent: the French authorities wanted to ensure that the collection of taxes was properly policed. The scheme also constituted an extraordinary architectural exercise, carried out by a single architect-visionary, Claude-Nicolas Ledoux.

Ledoux worked in the Département des Ponts et Chaussées (bridges and roadways), the body responsible for the national infrastructure. In that capacity he began a remarkable ideal city to be built at Arc-et-Senans, near Besançon. Although the radial town never went beyond the Saline de Chaux (1775–79), the saltworks which would have provided the economic *raison d'être* for the project, a good sense of what it might have been is conveyed in the handful of existing buildings and the architect's engravings. Ledoux reduced the classical elements to powerful geometrical forms, a virtually Mannerist language which recalled the many unbuilt (and sometimes unbuildable) designs of his compatriot and elder, Etienne-Louis Boullée. Both men took an almost abstract approach to form and volume that was at variance with established French Neoclassicism, although Ledoux did design a number of private houses that were admired at the time (their planning, again, often breaking with convention).

But it was the muscular, radical architecture of the saltworks which informed Ledoux's designs for the 40 barrières (1784–89), the customs houses, the building of which continued after the French Revolution. The Bureau de Pantin, more familiarly known as the Rotonde de la Villette, stood at the intersection of two major routes into Paris. Reflected in the waters of the Bassin de la

Villette, the rotunda had a splendid setting, unlike many of the barrières, which were often located at awkward road junctions or in outlying districts.

As impressive today as it can ever have been, the gigantic butter-toned stone drum is surrounded by a belt of arcading and rises from a heavy rusticated base. The barrières were symbolic architecture, intended by their presence and scale to denote state control. Beyond that, they housed small offices for the bureaucrats of the customs service. The Rotonde de la Villette, like a huge cored apple, contains small utilitarian offices around a central, circular courtyard, dramatically open to the elements.

The visitors who hurried to Paris from Britain after the Napoleonic Wars (1800–15) found many of the barrières still standing. John Soane was impressed above all by the Rotonde de la Villette and in 1819 set his pupil and assistant Henry Parke to sketch it. It became one of his finest illustrations for the Royal Academy lectures.

The boulevards and railway lines which slashed through Paris in the mid-19th century saw the rapid loss of Ledoux's redundant barrières; only four survive, of which the Rotonde de la Villette is by far the most impressive. In an area reclaimed from industry by a host of new cultural institutions, the rotunda provides both a vivid historical memorial and a dash of architectural bravado.

Bank of England
LONDON, GREAT BRITAIN
1788–1826

John Soane
born Goring-on-Thames 1753
died London 1837

John Soane became architect to the Bank of England on the death of Sir Robert Taylor (1714–88). Thus the building programme passed from an elderly sculptor-turned-architect working in the urbane Neoclassical tradition, as typified by Sir William Chambers, to an ambitious young man with only a few country houses to his credit, but who enjoyed the patronage of the Prime Minister, William Pitt the younger.

Shortly after Soane's appointment as architect, Britain went to war with France. The prelude to and duration of the Napoleonic Wars required the Bank, financing the conflict for almost 20 years, to rapidly and dramatically transform itself. Soane seized the opportunity and, from 1792 into the early 1800s, virtually reconstructed and extended what was becoming a 'city within the City'.

Soane was faced with an extremely difficult site. High perimeter walls (which he was to rebuild and further reinforce) meant that the only available daylight fell into the building from above or entered from windows around the many courtyards which punctured the wedge-shaped area. Gradually he replaced almost all of his predecessor's work, including Taylor's great, but leaking, Rotunda, used as the Stock Exchange. Soane retained the circular form – an evocation of the Pantheon (see pages 40–41) – but reworked the structure and detailing, simplifying classical forms and motifs in his own fashion, a novel departure for which he was widely criticized. He also built a series of elegant banking halls – variations upon a theme – in which lightweight domes were cut, extended and sliced to provide illumination for the clerks working below.

Above all, it was Soane's mastery in combining (and separating) the Bank's increasing functions and activities – the printing of bank-notes, storage and transfer of gold bullion, provision of both public access and security – that made the Bank of England his masterpiece. He threaded the site with beautifully detailed, meticulously considered passages, loggias, lobbies and vestibules, while taking its awkward shape, its changes of level and bad drainage in his stride. He also gave the Bank an appropriately proud, imperial, image with the Lothbury Court, where he reverted to the full-blown language of classical Rome and inserted a grand triumphal arch.

Since the Bank was only partially open to the public, Soane commissioned a stream of images of his work from his assistant Joseph Gandy (1771–1843), ranging from perspectives, sections and elevations to romantic fantasies in which the Rotunda lay in ruins. They were displayed at the Royal Academy summer exhibitions and used in lectures Soane gave as Professor of Architecture. At 13 Lincoln's Inn Fields (begun 1812), his house (now museum), they hung from floor to ceiling.

While the Bank of England launched Soane upon a remarkable career, many promised public commissions failed to materialize or disappointed him, and so the Bank remained the vindication of his architectural vision. In 1833, recently knighted but with failing eyesight, he retired. A century later his Bank had been demolished: a shocking act.

Baltimore Roman Catholic Cathedral

BALTIMORE, MARYLAND, UNITED STATES
1805 onwards

Benjamin Henry Latrobe
born Fulneck 1764
died New Orleans, Louisiana
1820

Benjamin Henry Latrobe, born near Leeds, was the son of Moravians, a religious sect founded in Herrnhut, Germany, which set up a network of self-sufficient communities in Europe and America. His mother was from Pennsylvania and his father, an elder of the community, was English. From the age of 12, Latrobe was educated abroad, first in Saxony and then in Silesia.

In 1795, following the blows of his wife's death and acute financial troubles, Latrobe left England for his mother's homeland. Having trained and practised as an engineer and architect in the European tradition, Latrobe had much to offer the United States. The small group of American gentlemen-amateur architects were not able to build the infrastructure for an emergent country, and those professionals who had come from Britain or France were both invaluable and scarce.

Once in the United States, Latrobe's fortunes greatly improved. He worked in Norfolk and Richmond, Virginia before moving to Philadelphia, and from 1800 worked extensively for the federal government on Capitol Hill. In 1805 he won the commission for the new Roman Catholic Cathedral in Baltimore, the basilica of the Assumption of the Blessed Virgin Mary. He designed both Gothic and classical versions ('my habits rather inclining me to the latter, while my reasonings prefer the first') and John Carroll, the English bishop who had been consecrated at St Mary's Roman Catholic chapel at East Lulworth in Dorset (1786–87; John Tasker, c.1738–1816), a pocket Neoclassical church in domestic dress, strongly preferred the latter. The cathedral was finally dedicated in 1821, still incomplete, after a long hiatus before and after the Anglo-American War of 1812, but Latrobe's portico was not added for another 40 years.

The interior is dominated by a double-shell dome which allowed light to filter in through unseen windows as *lumière mystérieuse*. Today, despite the blocking of this secondary lighting – in many ways the dominant factor in Latrobe's design – the interior remains impressive. The plan is a Latin cross, straddled by the dome which soars over almost the full breadth of the building and rests directly on segmental vaults, with lower saucer domes to east and west, although that over the choir was not added until long after Latrobe's death. There are obvious links to the form of John Soane's Stock Office at the Bank of England *(see pages 162–63)*, under construction while Latrobe was in London. In 1815, Latrobe and Maximilien Godefroy (1765–1848), the French civil engineer who became the first professor of architecture in the United States, collaborated on the Baltimore Exchange, a lost gem with a Pantheonesque drum, echoing Soane's Rotunda at the Bank. Godefroy's Unitarian Church (1817–18), across the street from the cathedral, followed the same model.

The structural and spatial sophistication of Latrobe's cathedral is unprecedented in North America for this date, viewed against the typically polite, slightly archaic late-18th-century civic and ecclesiastical architecture. The cathedral, even without its theatrical lighting and with accretions and alterations, is a building of immense grandeur.

University of Virginia

CHARLOTTESVILLE,
VIRGINIA, UNITED STATES
1817–25

Thomas Jefferson

born Shadwell, Virginia 1743
died Monticello, Virginia
1826

The 'Academical Village', the University of Virginia built by Thomas Jefferson, is the epitome of a classical enclave. In his youth, Jefferson had helped design an extension to his alma mater, William and Mary College at Williamsburg, Virginia (1771–76). Soon after his return from Europe, where he familiarized himself with Roman antiquity and the French classicism of the late 1780s, he pursued his dream of building a national university. He consulted the President, George Washington, and other architects such as Latrobe and Robert Mills (1781–1855).

Jefferson, as Vice President of the United States and then as President, 1801–1809, immersed himself in the idea of planning and designing a college, convinced that a number of separate, linked lodges or houses was the ideal structure, rather than a barrack-like building 'equally unfriendly to health, to study, to manners, morals and order'. To that end, he organized his new university in two long, low wings to either side of a grassy, sloping mall. The difficulties of the site meant he had to make a number of changes to his original plans, but the main architectural elements were a series of pavilions or lodges for the professors, in which the classrooms would also be housed, alternating with student dormitories, linked by covered colonnaded walkways. Extra dormitories and six dining halls lay to the rear, behind the vegetable gardens. The two arms faced each other across a terraced grass expanse, meeting at the focal point, the domed library or Rotunda. Jefferson varied the orders on the individual pavilions – a departure from the classical rule which did nothing to interrupt the striking harmony of the whole campus – and the library, a Roman Pantheon looking entirely comfortable in this rural American setting, completed the whole.

The scale of the university was intimate, reflecting the remote location and Jefferson's idealistic emphasis on setting up a familial relationship between the teachers and their handful of students. The materials, warm red brick and white paintwork for the columns, colonnades and Chinese fretwork balconies, and the gently modulated proportions of the low ranges of buildings, give the university a vernacular air, with the crisp delineation of classical features laid upon it. This almost domestic treatment survives alongside the modern campus, which scarcely impinges upon Jefferson's academic mall.

The University of Virginia was Jefferson's brainchild, 'the hobby of my old age', and epitomized his architectural and educational ideas, tested out against his professional peers. The miniature campus, set in the generous rolling countryside of Virginia and still functioning within the university (the Professor of Architecture, enviably, lives in one of the pavilions), remains a memorial both to Jefferson's high aspirations and to his ideal of intellectual intimacy and fellowship. The University of Virginia is a vivid reminder of the foresight and vision of its founder and architect, who died a year after the college opened.

Altes Museum
BERLIN, GERMANY
1823–30

Karl Friedrich
Schinkel
born Brandenburg 1781
died Berlin 1841

From his youth, Karl Friedrich Schinkel had been toying with the idea of a great museum to house the Prussian royal art collection. In 1815 he was appointed surveyor at the Office of Works in Berlin and the prospect of carrying out such a plan became a possibility, Schinkel actively promoting the idea. As the official architect of the post-Napoleonic Prussian capital, he embarked on a number of key public works which helped to emphasize the civic and social virtues of the regime.

Schinkel began by drawing up a comprehensive city plan for Berlin and followed this with a building programme. First came the stern Greek Revival Neue Wache (the New Guardhouse) of 1816–18 and then an impressive theatre and concert hall, the Schauspielhaus, of 1818–21. The last of the city monuments was the Altes (old) Museum. Friedrich Wilhelm III's royal collection – now reunited after its dispersal under Napoleon and expanded by new acquisitions – would be housed in a purpose-built museum and art gallery at a focal point in the city, the Lustgarten (now the Museum Island). Schinkel's new building neatly closed and defined a square, its remaining sides marked by the royal castle, the cathedral and a canal. The Altes Museum was an important piece in Schinkel's urban design and he gave almost as much attention to its siting and presentation in the city as to the detail of its displays and the circulation of visitors.

The front elevation of the Altes Museum, seen as a wall behind the dense trees in the landscaped square (recently reinstated) and designed to be a very public entrance, was marked by 18 Ionic columns and approached by a broad flight of steps. Inside, the stairs continued and were still visible from the square through the open portico. At the centre lay Schinkel's architectural flourish, an enormous galleried rotunda, modelled on the Pantheon in Rome (see pages 40–41), its dimensions reduced by half. More practically, a pair of courtyards to either side allowed light into the galleries at the core of the building. The galleries on the floor above the entrance level were devoted to sculpture, those above again to painting. The public was encouraged to go up onto the roof terrace and view the city from an excellent vantage point. Schinkel and the museum director, Gustav Waagen, agreed that they should approach their task, as they told the king, with the notion to 'first delight, then instruct'.

Schinkel controlled every detail. He was determined that the materials should be the very best, and organized an ambitious programme of symbolic sculptural ornament for the exterior, not installed until many years later. He even specified the styles of the picture frames. Happily, despite the vicissitudes of Prussia and its capital, the Altes Museum has survived and is a remarkable witness to the early-19th-century impetus to introduce the wider public to great art collections, ideally in buildings designed specifically for the purpose. But Schinkel's absorption in the scheme, from the place of the building within his urban plan to his close consideration of the collection, its content and presentation, sets the Altes Museum apart.

ALTES MUSEUM • BERLIN *DETAIL OF PORTICO*

Merchant Exchange
PHILADELPHIA, PENNSYLVANIA, UNITED STATES
1832–34

William Strickland
born Philadelphia, Pennsylvania
1788
died Nashville, Tennessee 1854

The sight of a pale stone Greek Revival building on a quiet corner in Chestnut Hill, Philadelphia, set amid the polite brick domesticity of William Penn's 17th- and 18th-century town, still has the power to surprise. The great Grecian models of civic and democratic classical architecture more frequently reappear in splendid locations, such as Edinburgh's early 19th-century hilltop Acropolis that is Calton Hill or the heroic Philadelphia Museum of Art (1916–28), set on the dramatic outcrop of Faire Mount.

William Strickland, the son of a carpenter, began his architectural career as an apprentice to Benjamin Henry Latrobe but, unlike his able contemporary Robert Mills, did not persevere and left the office after two years. Strickland's first building was the Gothic Masonic Hall in Philadelphia (1808–11), flagged up against the city skyline by a lofty wooden spire. The Hall soon burned down. After this his career foundered until in 1818 he entered and – beating Latrobe – won a competition to design a banking house in 'a chaste imitation of Grecian Architecture, in its simplest and least expensive form'. To the former end Strickland used the Greek Doric style for the Second Bank of America in Philadelphia (1819–24) and to the latter gave the building a marble skin over an entirely brick construction. It was the first Greek Revival building in North America. With its political resonances, in addition to its archaeological appeal, the style became a popular choice for commercial, financial and federal premises, denoting probity and dependability.

Strickland's later Merchant Exchange was an honest stone building of clever and practical geometries. A rectangular block followed the line of the street corner but was given a dash of verve by the curved form of the imposing Exchange Room,

approached by a sweep of steps to either side of the colonnade. For this, the first stock exchange in the country, Strickland ventured away from the temple-fronted norm into a far more inventive version of the Greek, reflecting both the imagery and practical needs of the new building type.

Strickland, who had not travelled to Europe, ensured his accuracy in reproducing details and applying the orders by scrupulously following the archaeological evidence in *The Antiquities of Athens* (vol. I, 1762; vol. II, 1789) by the British architects James 'Athenian' Stuart (1713–88) and Nicholas Revett (1720–1804). Externally, the eaves are marked by a decorative band of Greek naturalistic ornament and above is the crowning feature of the building, a lantern modelled on the Choragic Monument of Lysicrates in Athens (334 BC). The elegance and great strength of Strickland's design, continued in the use of the Corinthian order in the colonnade which wraps the building, is true to the classical sources while also being imaginative and contemporary.

Internally, the semicircular 'apse' of the Exchange Room was elaborately decorated with frescoes and a mosaic floor, now lost. Today, the Merchant Exchange seems sadly run-down, despite its key role in the history of American architecture.

MERCHANT EXCHANGE · PHILADELPHIA

Reform Club
LONDON, GREAT BRITAIN
1838–41

Charles Barry
born London 1795
died London 1860

Following the euphoria induced by the passing of the Reform Bill in Britain in 1832, a group of Whigs and Radicals decided to found the Reform Club in 1836. The next year a site became available on Pall Mall beside the Travellers' Club (1830–32) and Charles Barry, its architect, was the obvious candidate for the new building. As a young man, Barry had taken a three-year tour of Italy and the eastern Mediterranean and his preference for the style of the Italian palazzo was clearly seen in the Travellers' Club.

Barry's palazzo was in complete contrast to its neighbour to the east, the pioneer among the new generation of gentlemen's clubs on Pall Mall, the Grecian Athenaeum Club (1827–30) by Decimus Burton (1800–81). After more than a century of an increasingly archaeologically led revival of classical antiquity, architects were seeking a new approach and the return to the High Renaissance suggested by Barry was a way out of the impasse.

The Reform Club was a late-Renaissance palace, specifically the Palazzo Farnese in Rome (c.1515–after 1546; Antonio da Sangallo the younger, 1483–1546, and Michelangelo). Barry wrapped his building around a generous internal cloister, the courtyard of which he intended to remain open. The Building Committee decided it would be more comfortable and more useful if glazed, and the court became an ornamental atrium, floored in mosaic in the antique style.

The Reform Club remains unaltered – apart from the admission of women members. A flight of steps leads directly off the street and it stands high and grand, its two-and-a-half storeys looming well above the Travellers' Club. With a *piano nobile* nine bays wide and marked by a row of crisply pedimented windows, the smooth grey Portland-stone palace offers a very cool, English variant of its warm-toned, heavily rusticated model in Rome.

The members of the club enjoyed, in addition to the usual amenities – a library and reading room, dining room, billiard and card rooms – a novel introduction of bedrooms on the upper floor, which allowed members from abroad or out of London to stay on the premises.

Ascending the stairs from the Saloon (as the atrium is known), the dominant room on the upper floor is the Library, its windows overlooking gardens to the rear. The glory of the club, it is handsomely furnished in antique fashion and screened by columns, providing a majestic but congenial setting. The Morning Room was dominated by a cast of the Parthenon frieze, familiar and fittingly symbolic of democracy to the classically educated members – who also had the benefit of the most modern facilities, such as central heating.

Barry began the club when he was already working on the Palace of Westminster (*see pages 178–79*), where his predetermined Gothic scheme was, while essentially symmetrical, quite different to his Renaissance Revival palace. Despite his absorption at Westminster, the major public commission of the Victorian era, Barry lavished every care upon the Reform Club, a building which straddles the divide between the old and the new forms of classicism – just as it points, rather more profoundly, to the dawning of universal suffrage.

The Machine Age

Gavin Stamp

Between the French Revolution at the end of the eighteenth century and the advent of Art Nouveau in the 1890s, the 19th century had no distinctive architectural style of its own – and that worried thoughtful architects. But, far from being a period of mere historical revivalism, uninterested in the possibilities of new technology and new materials, it was a time when architects rose to the challenge of planning and gave characteristic expression to a range of complex and unprecedented building types such as the museum and art gallery, parliament house, railway station, town hall and industrial mill.

Style was certainly an obsession. Many architects were content to use different styles for different purposes: classicism for banks, Gothic for churches. But some maintained that progress was possible only when one style was made universal, ubiquitous. In England, Pugin argued that Gothic alone was rational, national, adaptable for all purposes – and Christian. Morality was introduced into architectural choice, reinforced by the influential writer John Ruskin, who also maintained that true architecture needed the vitality of ornamentation that was based on the study of nature. He also encouraged honesty in the expressive use of different building materials, reflecting the contemporary interest in geology and the natural sciences.

BELOW: W.H. Barlow and R.M. Ordish, St Pancras Station train shed, London, 1866–68

LEFT: Eugène-Emmanuel Viollet-le-Duc, Palais de Justice, Paris, 1857–68

Mid-century, a 'Battle of the Styles' raged internationally between classical and Gothic, and the Gothic Revival became a creative, invigorating, progressive force in Britain that eventually influenced Continental Europe and America (hence the preponderance of British buildings in this selection). But even the Gothicists worried that, in a century that had seen such progress in science and engineering, in transport and public health, architects still had to rely on historical styles. Gilbert Scott realized that the problem of his time was knowing too much, 'that we are acquainted with the history of art, a hindrance rather than a help to us as artists'. His stylistic opponent, Alexander Thomson, could also complain that 'with us architecture has all but ceased to be a living art, and the present age, so rich in achievement in other departments, is seen making the most ridiculous efforts to insinuate its overgrown person backwards into the empty shells of dead ages'. Many of the buildings of the period were products of a climate of doubt and uncertainty – about religion and science as well as architecture.

One answer to the dilemma was to elaborate and distort in the name of originality. Another was to be eclectic, combining elements from different traditions, or to gather hints from local, vernacular ways of building. Then there was the challenge set by the works of the engineers, emphasizing the possibilities offered by the products of the

ABOVE: Charles Barry, New Palace of Westminster (Houses of Parliament), London, 1840–1870

Industrial Revolution: cast and wrought iron, together with plate glass. Ruskin may have believed that iron structures could never be true architecture, but enlightened architects knew, as the architect and theorist Eugène-Emmanuel Viollet-le-Duc (1814–79) argued, that iron beams and large windows had to be embraced within their chosen style, and the best of them created innovative buildings in which old and new technologies were happily combined and honestly expressed within their structures.

The Victorian Age produced a wide variety of resourceful and experimental buildings that were resonant of the past while being proudly of their own time: a wonderfully rich and rewarding architecture, full of meanings both literal and symbolic, and decorative but functional.

175

St George's Church, Everton

LIVERPOOL, GREAT BRITAIN
1812–14

Thomas Rickman
born Maidenhead 1776
died Birmingham 1841

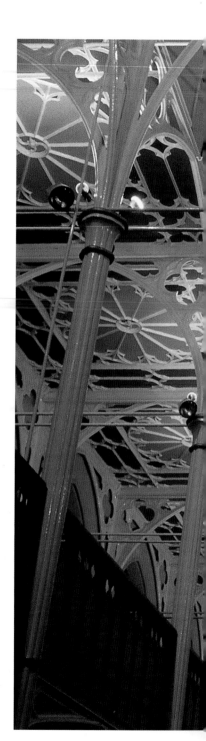

Far too often it has been said that the 19th century's obsession with reviving the styles of the past ignored the progress in using new building technologies. In fact, historical consciousness and new technology often went hand in hand, as the building of St George's, Everton, demonstrated while Britain was still busy defeating Napoleon. This church was the product of an uneasy collaboration between an antiquary and an industrialist. They produced a pioneering building, both in terms of the history of the Gothic Revival and as an enterprising experiment in the use of innovative technology.

Thomas Rickman, designer of the 'Iron Church', was an unlikely architect, let alone early exponent of the use of prefabricated cast-iron structures, which reached its zenith in the celebrated iron and glass Crystal Palace in London by Joseph Paxton (1803–65), erected for the Great Exhibition of 1851. A Quaker, and a failed doctor, accountant and corn factor who was twice declared bankrupt, Rickman took up architecture late in life but had a profound influence on the development of the Gothic Revival. He coined the terms 'Early English', 'Decorated' and 'Perpendicular' to describe the styles of English Gothic architecture in *An Attempt to Discriminate the Styles of Architecture in England* (1817), terms that are still used.

In 1812, having moved to Liverpool to escape his creditors, Rickman met the ironmaster John Cragg, who had made his fortune and was devoting himself to Church and local affairs. Cragg promoted the idea of a new church in Everton and, having been disappointed by one architect, turned to Rickman, then an amateur enthusiast for Gothic architecture. The church he designed is remarkable as a scholarly essay in Gothic in both elevation and plan, when most new churches were classical in style and little more than a galleried box internally.

It is even more remarkable for the extensive use of iron. Although the exterior of the building was faced in stone, the internal columns, the ceilings of nave and aisles and the Gothic tracery in the windows were all cast in iron – at Cragg's foundry.

Although industrial mills with iron columns and beams had been erected by the end of the 18th century, never before had cast iron been used for a complete interior. Before St George's was finished, Rickman and Cragg collaborated on another church in Liverpool, St Michael-in-the-Hamlet (1814–15), in which cast iron was used for pinnacles and door-frames as well. Both churches are light and elegant structures but, because the columns are much thinner than the stone piers in a medieval church, their interiors seem more like Gothic conservatories than places of worship. Pugin, the fanatic for Gothic, later condemned such churches, both for the use of iron and for not being archaeologically accurate in their details. But that, of course, is precisely this church's appeal.

Rickman, in partnership with Henry Hutchinson (1800–31), went on to design other churches and the New Court at St John's College, Cambridge (1826–31), but nothing else he did was quite as thrilling as St George's, Everton.

ST GEORGE'S CHURCH • *EVERTON CEILING DETAIL*

New Palace of Westminster
LONDON, GREAT BRITAIN
1835–60

Charles Barry	A.W.N. Pugin
born London 1795	born London 1812
died London 1860	died Ramsgate 1852

It is easy to take the Houses of Parliament on the River Thames in London for granted: the building is so famous and familiar. But it is an astonishing achievement, both in technical terms and in the consistent splendour of its ornament and decoration. What is properly called the New Palace of Westminster (the old palace was largely destroyed by fire in 1834) is simply the greatest Gothic Revival public building in the world.

Parliament decided the new building should be Gothic or Elizabethan, in the firm belief that architectural style should reflect a nation's history and ideals. Unfortunately, most of the best architects around were comparatively unfamiliar with Gothic detail and several who entered the competition enjoyed the assistance of a brilliant young designer besotted with the Middle Ages, Augustus Pugin. One such was Charles Barry, architect of the Italianate Travellers' Club (*see page 172*), who won the commission.

By the time the Thames had been embanked with a coffer dam and the new building was rising, Barry again needed help with Gothic detail and again turned to Pugin. This was a brave move as by now Pugin was notorious: a zealous Roman Catholic convert and author of *Contrasts* (1836), which reviled most contemporary architecture, and of *The True Principles of Pointed or Christian Architecture* (1841), which argued that classicism was 'pagan' and Gothic alone was Christian. But it was a happy and creative collaboration. The plan and organization were by Barry, who also dealt with the committees and experts, incorporated new technologies such as an elaborate air circulation and heating system, and roofs of iron, while coping with the endless demands for economy. The detail and the interior treatment were by Pugin, who designed furniture and such modern necessities as

gas lamps in a medieval manner. 'All Grecian, sir,' Pugin once famously remarked while passing by on the Thames, 'Tudor details on a classic body.' The plan is almost symmetrical, with the two chambers arranged on a dominant axis, but with Westminster Hall and the skewed axis of old St Stephen's Chapel cleverly integrated, and with a gloriously picturesque exterior silhouette achieved by the placing of the 'vertical features': the clock tower and the Victoria tower. And the detail is fertile. Craftsmen and manufacturers had to be found to make the panelling, furniture, metalwork, stained glass and encaustic tiles: truly it has been said that the Arts and Crafts Movement began here.

Pugin died, worn out and mad, shortly after his masterpiece, the interior of the House of Lords, had been opened. The Commons, by Barry, was destroyed in 1941, to be rebuilt in modern Gothic by Sir Giles Gilbert Scott (1880–1960) after a debate in which Winston Churchill observed, 'We shape our buildings and afterwards our buildings shape us.' The New Palace of Westminster was partly designed for rituals that explain the evolution of democracy in Britain, and the parliament buildings in Ottawa (1859–76; Thomas Fuller, 1822–98, and Chilion Jones, dates unknown) and Budapest (1883–1904; Imre Steindl, 1839–1902) testify to the potency of the association between constitutional government and the Gothic style.

NEW PALACE OF WESTMINSTER • LONDON *HOUSE OF LORDS*

Temple Meads Station
BRISTOL, GREAT BRITAIN
1840–41

Isambard Kingdom Brunel
born Portsea 1806
died London 1859

R.S. Pope
born 1791
died Shirehampton 1884

The Great Western Railway from London to Bristol, opened in its entirety in 1841, was and is the most magnificent of early railway lines. Designed by the Anglo-French engineer Isambard Kingdom Brunel, it was laid out with gentle gradients and generous curves so that record-breaking speeds could be achieved by Daniel Gooch's locomotives running on the unique 'Broad Gauge' track of 2.1 m (7 ft).

The railway was built at a time when the distinction between architecture and engineering was not precise and, when it came to designing bridges and viaducts, the pioneering railway engineers demonstrated a sense of Roman grandeur in response to the heroic scale of the enterprise. Everything about the Great Western reflected the protean genius of its creator, a man who designed Atlantic steam ships and suspension bridges as well as railways. The Wharncliffe Viaduct, the red-brick bridge across the Thames at Maidenhead with the flattest elliptical arches yet constructed, and the sublime entrances to the Box Tunnel, all showed Brunel's attention to detail, while the route he chose displayed great sensitivity to landscape, both rural and urban.

Towards the western end of the line – and even in classical Bath – the Great Western Railway became Tudor-Gothic in the style of both its bridges and buildings, and in Bristol the terminus was designed in the Gothic style out of respect for the medieval city and the nearby 14th-century church of St Mary Redcliffe. Even a man like Brunel, however, could not be expected to display a mastery of Gothic, and in the design of the stone building containing the booking office and a boardroom, flanked by four-centred arches for arriving and departing passengers, he seems to

have enjoyed the assistance of the local architect R.S. Pope, who had recently designed Bristol's Guildhall in the Perpendicular Gothic style.

The train shed, however, was Brunel's own extraordinary creation. To cover two platforms and five tracks, he designed a hammer-beam roof with a span of 22 m (72 ft) – wider than Westminster Hall in the Old Palace of Westminster. The hammer beams are false, however, and the roof is, in fact, a cantilevered structure of timber braced with iron, resting on rows of cast-iron columns running down each side. Pugin believed Gothic construction was ideal for railways, but with his sharp eye for shams, was not impressed. 'The Great Western stations,' he wrote in 1843, 'where any architectural display has been attempted, are mere caricatures of pointed [Gothic] design – mock castellated work, huge tracery, shields without bearings, ugly mouldings, no-meaning projections, and all sorts of unaccountable breaks, to make a design at once costly, and offensive, and full of pretension.'

Today, the Broad Gauge has gone and the tracks have been removed from Brunel's terminus, which has long been bypassed by the through trains from London to the southwest. But, if Pugin's strictures on its hybrid construction had a certain justice, they do not diminish the appeal of this glorious structure of the heroic Railway Age.

TEMPLE MEADS STATION • BRISTOL *J.C. BOURNE'S 1846 ENGRAVING OF BRUNEL'S SHED*

Temple Mill
LEEDS, GREAT BRITAIN
1842–43

Joseph Bonomi junior
born London 1796
died London 1878

James Combe
dates unknown

A textile mill with a façade of an ancient Egyptian temple may seem absurd; it is typical of the early-19th-century cavalier attitude to architectural style satirized by Pugin. But Egyptian architecture, in its severity and grandeur, evoked the aesthetic of the Sublime, inspiring a sense of awe, and nothing could be more Sublime than the huge industrial buildings of northern England. Schinkel, the great Prussian state architect, saw the smoke-belching, multistorey, iron-framed brick mills of Manchester and was at once fascinated and appalled by those 'enormous hulks of buildings'.

The Egyptian Revival was stimulated by Napoleon's military adventures on the Nile, and while it was often used for long-established structures like cemetery gates and masonic temples, the style soon became identified with modernity. It was suitable for big, bold works of engineering: Brunel wanted the pylons of his Clifton suspension bridge to be Egyptian, while Robert Stephenson adopted a similar bare style for his Britannia railway bridge across the Menai Strait.

John Marshall began his flax-spinning business in 1788 and built a succession of steam-powered, iron-framed, fireproof mills in Leeds. Temple Mill was his finest and largest and it was novel in both architectural style and interior arrangement. Marshall wanted an Egyptian façade because the ancient Egyptians made linen from flax. He first consulted the artist David Roberts, who recommended the archaeologist Joseph Bonomi to assist the local architect James Combe. Bonomi had spent a decade measuring and drawing temples in Egypt; later he advised on the Egyptian Court in the Crystal Palace and became curator of Sir John Soane's Museum. In Leeds, he modelled the façade of the mill on the ancient Typhonium at Dendera, while the more elaborate

office block was based on the Temple of Horus at Edfu and the Temple at Antaeopolis. The original chimney was in the form of an obelisk but it cracked in 1852 and had to be replaced.

In the history of the Egyptian Revival, this adaptation of temple architecture to make an industrial building is unique. The mill also, which is behind a very elegant structure, was unusual in being a single storey. Two acres of brick-vaulted ceiling pierced by 66 conical glass skylights are supported on hollow cast-iron columns, modelled with papyrus capitals and stiffened by adjustable wrought-iron tie beams. The brick vaults were covered with plaster and a layer of coal tar, with soil and grass on top – allowing sheep to graze on the roof until one fell through a skylight. Inside, a warm-air heating system and water channels in the floor created the humidity and environmental control necessary for successful flax spinning. The result was praised for 'the convenience of supervision, facility of access to the machines, the power of sustaining uniformity of temperature and moisture, the absence of air currents which are so objectionable in other mills, its simplicity of the driving gear, [and] the excellent ventilation which is so desirable for the health of the workpeople'.

TEMPLE MILL · LEEDS

Bibliothèque Ste-Geneviève
PARIS, FRANCE
1838–51

Henri Labrouste
born Paris 1801
died Fontainebleau 1875

The Bibliothèque Ste-Geneviève, a public library erected by the French government, was the most important work of architecture of its time in France and one which represented the aspirations of the generation of architects touched by Romanticism. It is remarkable for its employment of iron construction combined with masonry, but above all because it is a sophisticated expression of a reaction against the academic approach to classicism characteristic of earlier French architecture.

It was designed by Henri Labrouste who, although a prize-winning student at the Ecole des Beaux-Arts, rejected the pedantic use of the orders in favour of an astylar architecture based on structure, whose meaning came not from the use of traditional forms but from historical and literary references built into its fabric. Later described as Néo-Grec, this was a rationalist architecture in which there was decoration of construction rather than the older desire to construct decoration. The result here was a comparatively plain building that generated intense controversy on its completion.

The site, next to the Panthéon, was long and narrow, and the architect designed a repetitive, two-storey building, nineteen bays by four, with the reading room occupying the whole of the upper floor. The rectangular plan is broken only by a projection at the back containing the staircase. On the ground floor, the understated entrance pierces a plain stone wall whose severity is enhanced by a carved garland between iron paterae (flat rose-like decorations). Above, the articulation is of continuous flat arcades (the expression of deep structural piers internally), with the upper half glazed to illuminate the interior and the lower part filled by panels decorated with incised lettering. Here are 810 names of authors, from Moses to Berzelius, the Swedish chemist who died in 1848 – the Year of Revolutions, during which Labrouste's programme was approved – proclaiming that the library contained the literature of human progress.

Inside, the ground floor vestibule consists of fluted square piers supporting pierced arched iron beams, supporting the (fireproof) floor of the reading room. Above, the library could have been roofed as a single space but Labrouste divided it in two by a row of iron columns running down the centre. This was a spatial division reminiscent both of certain ancient temples and of medieval Gothic halls, and in its emphasis on structural integrity there is a Gothic element in the Néo-Grec. But above their stone pedestals, Labrouste's columns are thin as they are made of cast iron, to make the reading room light and open. These columns then support open iron arches that carry twin barrel vaults running the length of the room.

For some, Labrouste's library was a seminal work; for others, it was too austere, while to some 20th-century commentators, it is an advanced metallic structure compromised by tradition. But Labrouste's masterpiece is rich and complex, full of historical resonances and meanings. Its rational, elegant severity inspired the Boston Public Library (1888–95), designed by McKim, Mead and White.

Cathedral of the Isles

CUMBRAE ISLAND,
GREAT BRITAIN
1849–51

William Butterfield
born London 1814
died London 1900

An architect must know the rules before breaking them; a style must be understood and its grammar learned before interesting things can be done with it. This was the case with the revival of classicism in the Renaissance, and so it was with the Gothic Revival. By the 1840s, largely thanks to Pugin, Gothic architects knew their archaeology and could design 'correct' churches. It was William Butterfield who lifted the revival onto a new plane and showed how to be original and creative in Gothic terms.

This he demonstrated in All Saints, Margaret Street, London (1849–59), built in honest modern red brick, not stone, and decorated inside in patterns of brick, stone, tile and marble, that is, in built-in permanent materials – what the Victorians called 'structural polychromy'. Later, when asked to design Keble College, Oxford (1867–75), this austere and deeply serious artist decided not to compete with the old stone buildings but to build in patterned red brick banded with stone, later irreverently dismissed as the 'streaky bacon style'.

Butterfield has been accused of having a hatred of beauty, but while his urban churches are sometimes very angular, his country buildings can be gentle and harmonious, while always reflecting the idiosyncratic mind of their creator. He designed a complete village at Baldersby, Yorkshire (1855–60), but his most sympathetic and intriguing work is the complex known as the Cathedral of the Isles at Millport on Cumbrae Island off the west coast of Scotland. This was originally the College of the Holy Spirit, founded in 1849 for 'the frequent celebration of Divine Service by a Collegiate Body under circumstances favourable to learning'. The founder was the Earl of Glasgow who, when at Oxford, had been touched by the Tractarian movement which revitalized the Church of England.

The picturesque composition of the grey-stone buildings, raised up on grass terraces, was inspired by Pugin's drawings of ideal Gothic institutions, but Butterfield's architecture was more austere. The church, with its tall spire, dominates, although it is comparatively small inside and has no aisles. The chancel is separated from the nave by an unusual stone screen and the walls are decorated with coloured tiles in a characteristic manner. The other buildings were intended to be residential. The Canon's range is connected to the church by a cloister, while the Choristers' range is detached. There is an emphasis on continuous roof planes, which are broken only by the architect's typical hipped dormer windows. But within his strict language of stone walls and slate roofs, Butterfield indulged in Gothic Mannerism, in the single chimney stack rising from corbels placed either side of a window, and the hood mould above a door placed too high to leave room for a window.

Similar forms can be found in the early buildings of Butterfield's friend and admirer Philip Webb (1831–1915), such as the celebrated Red House at Bexleyheath (1859–60), designed for William Morris and, rightly or wrongly, long regarded as the first flowering of English domestic architecture in the late 19th century.

University Museum

OXFORD, GREAT BRITAIN
1854–60

Benjamin Woodward
born Tullamore 1816
died Lyons 1861

The Oxford Museum is perhaps the most representative building of the Victorian era. It embodies the desire to reconcile the discoveries of natural history with Christian theology, before Darwin's *Origin of Species* (1859) introduced more doubt and uncertainty; it manifests the contemporary enthusiasm for geology in its very fabric, enhanced by naturalistic ornamentation; it emulates an idealized medieval world while extending the use of the Gothic style beyond churches and embracing the new building technology of iron and glass. Flawed and unfinished, it is as beautiful as it is poignant.

A new building to house Oxford University's large natural history collection was proposed by the scientist Henry Acland, who involved his friend, the writer John Ruskin, in the project. The competition held in 1854 was won by the Irish architect Benjamin Woodward. After some controversy, building began in 1855. The models for the exterior were such buildings as the 13th-century Cloth Halls at Ypres, but the detached square laboratory block, with its four prominent chimneys, was modelled on the Abbot's kitchen at the 14th-century abbey in Glastonbury. Behind the main front, the building is essentially a cloistered quadrangle on two floors, with the central court covered by a glass roof on iron columns.

As Ruskin denied that iron structures were architecture, perhaps this metal roof is surprising, but the tall iron arches rising above thin clusters of iron columns harmonize wonderfully with the surrounding masonry arches. Although iron buildings were not new in the 1850s, this glazed scheme was novel in both detail and form; indeed, the original thin wrought-iron columns failed and had to be replaced with cast iron by the manufacturer Frederick Skidmore. Acland later remarked that in the museum, 'a step, but not a final step, has been made towards a harmonious union of the ironwork of the 19th century with refined architecture of the Middle Ages'.

The exterior of the museum is stone, while inside the walls are brick above stone arches. These arcades are part of the didactic scheme, for each of the supporting shafts is made of a different marble, while the capitals are exquisitely carved to represent different plants. Ruskin was an important influence behind all this carving, because for him ornament raised building into architecture and he extolled the 'savageness' or vitality of medieval art. The beauty of nature was a reflection of the divine and 'if we set a simple natural form before [the workman], and tell him to copy it, we are sure to have given him a wholesome and useful piece of education'.

Some of the interior carvings were only completed in 1905, while the front porch was never carried out. The high quality of the original carving on the museum was due to the O'Shea brothers, brought over from Ireland by Woodward. But they were dismissed by the university after carving monkeys and cats around the Gothic windows on the front, work that can still be seen, reflecting the controversy this noble building inspired.

UNIVERSITY MUSEUM • OXFORD *GLAZED COURT*

188

St Pancras Station

LONDON, GREAT BRITAIN
1865–77

George Gilbert Scott

born Gawcott 1811
died London 1878

W.H. Barlow

born London 1812
died Charlton 1902

With its tower and spires and colossal roof overshadowing its neighbour, King's Cross, St Pancras is the most spectacular of British railway stations. During the 19th century, the architect and engineer grew apart, but here they worked together. W.H. Barlow, consulting engineer to the Midland Railway, assisted by R.M. Ordish, had already designed the great train shed when the competition was held for the hotel in front, and the winning architect, George Gilbert Scott, was pleased to find that 'as if by anticipation, its section was a pointed arch'.

The Midland Railway was a late arrival in London and it wanted its terminus to outshine those of its rivals. So Barlow designed a train shed which, with a span of 74 m (243 ft), was the largest in the world at the time. The great iron trusses are integrated into the Gothic-arched brick retaining walls and tied below the railway tracks, the whole being raised up on a basement with iron columns spaced to allow the storage of beer barrels.

The huge train shed, with its expensive single-span roof, was simply an advertisement for the Midland Railway, as was getting a famous architect to design a spectacular Gothic Revival railway hotel in front of it. Scott was already a prolific builder and restorer of churches, who had recently won the competition for the design of the memorial to Prince Albert in Hyde Park, when he was persuaded to enter a limited competition, and the directors evidently did not mind that his design exceeded the brief in both size and cost. It is said that Scott simply reused his rejected Gothic design for the Foreign Office (1862–73, eventually built in the Renaissance style); in fact the plan of the Midland Grand Hotel at St Pancras is quite different but, as Scott admitted, 'having been disappointed, through Lord Palmerston, of my

ardent hope of carrying out my style in the Government offices, I was glad to be able to erect one building in that style in London'.

Scott had written a book to show how Gothic could be used for secular purposes as well as churches and how it could incorporate modern improvements like iron beams and plate glass windows while being full of variety and interest. At St Pancras, his Gothic took hints from both France and Italy and was given 'a certain squareness and horizontality of outline. I combined this with gables, high pitched roofs, and dormers.' The main block is pierced by two large arches, and within each an upper-floor corridor is carried on iron beams. Below the tower is a spectacular staircase, with three flights cantilevered out and leaping across the space below a Gothic vault. The finest materials were used throughout and column capitals were elaborately carved. Some thought that this, in a mere hotel, offended against Pugin's principle of 'propriety', which explains why Scott wrote that 'it is possibly too good for its purpose'.

The hotel closed and the booking hall lost its timber roof in the 1930s, but otherwise St Pancras has survived, as the greatest monument of both the Gothic Revival and the Railway Age.

ST PANCRAS STATION • LONDON *DETAIL OF MIDLAND GRAND HOTEL STAIRCASE*

Victoria Terminus Station
BOMBAY (MUMBAI), INDIA
1878–88

Frederick William Stevens
born Bath 1848
died Bombay 1900

Proponents of the Gothic Revival argued that it was a universal style and that, in its flexibility and honesty, it was suitable for any purpose. Furthermore, with modifications, the Gothic was thought to be appropriate in any climate, and as a result was exported far and wide across the British Empire. The strange consequence is that, because it was spared both bombing during the Second World War and the postwar effects of comprehensive redevelopment programmes, the finest Gothic Revival city in the world is no longer Manchester or Bradford, but Bombay.

In the 1930s, when Victorian architecture was roundly condemned, the writer Robert Byron wrote of 'that architectural Sodom, Bombay'. Today, however, the city glories in a collection of Gothic stone public buildings, all with elaborate decoration and fantastic skylines, and the most spectacular is the Victoria Terminus Station.

Bombay boomed at the height of the Gothic Revival under an energetic Governor General, Sir Bartle Frere, and, because the American Civil War (1861–65) cut off cotton supplies from the South, benefited enormously from the export of Indian cotton. Some of the buildings, like the Law Courts (1871–79) and Secretariat (1865–74), were put up by members of the Royal Engineers, based on plates in the *Builder* and *Building News* of new Gothic designs back home, while the University (1869–78), with its arcades and open spiral staircases, was the work of George Gilbert Scott (at a distance: he sent out the drawings). But one architect made his home in Bombay: Frederick William Stevens, who trained in Bath and at first worked for the Bombay Public Works Department.

Stevens' masterpiece, the Victoria Terminus of the Great Indian Peninsular Railway, was influenced by Scott's St Pancras in London (*see pages 190–91*), but Scott's building was a hotel while Stevens' houses railway offices. And whereas the Midland Grand stood in front of a spectacular train shed, the platforms in Bombay are to the side of Stevens' pile and were covered by a much less interesting structure. Solidly built in local stone and rich in contrasts of colour and materials, the VT building is full of variety and movement, with open arcades on every level to provide shade from the sun. Unlike the Midland Grand, VT is symmetrical, with projecting wings. The skyline is enlivened by pinnacles and a central dome, 'the first applied to a Gothic building on scientific principles'. Scott had long wanted to build a Gothic dome, but it was Stevens who fulfilled this ambition, and his fine Bombay dome anticipated the larger one on the Budapest Parliament (*see page 178*). It is surmounted by a 4.2-m-high (14-ft) figure of Progress by the sculptor Thomas Earp, who also carved Engineering and Commerce on the wings; other carving was carried out by students and staff at the Bombay School of Art.

Stevens gave his Gothic an Indian Saracenic flavour in the Municipal Buildings (1888–93) and in the Church Gate station for the Bombay, Baroda and Central Indian Railway (1894–96), but it is VT which is most impressive – and one of the most appealing Gothic Revival buildings in the world.

VICTORIA TERMINUS STATION • BOMBAY (MUMBAI)

Natural History Museum

LONDON, GREAT BRITAIN
1868–81

Alfred Waterhouse
born Liverpool 1830
died Yattendon 1905

The architect and writer W.R. Lethaby (1857–1931) divided the Victorian Gothic Revivalists into the 'softs' and the 'hards'. Alfred Waterhouse may well seem the hardest of the hards. Although the Gothic was his chosen language of expression and he revelled in its freedom and flexibility, he was unsentimental about the style and hand-crafted ornament, happily using new materials and machine-produced details.

Waterhouse was a brilliant planner – which may reflect his training with Richard Lane (1795–1880), who had studied (unusually for an Englishman) at the Ecole des Beaux-Arts in Paris – and made his name by winning the competition for Manchester Town Hall (1867–77) with a Gothic design. What is, perhaps, strange is that his London masterpiece is Romanesque in style.

Waterhouse's building emerged from the usual muddle of Victorian architectural politics. The competition in 1864 for an independent Natural History Museum was won by Francis Fowke, an engineer promoted by Henry Cole, the dictatorial secretary of the South Kensington Museum who disliked both architects and the Gothic style. But Fowke died in 1865 and Waterhouse was given the job of carrying out his classical design as a sop for being runner-up in another competition, for the Law Courts. He soon produced his own design, but in a round-arched Lombardy Romanesque manner to appease Cole. Ruskin approved of this style, arguing in *The Stones of Venice* (1851–53) that 'its highest glory is, that it has no corruption. It perishes in giving birth to another architecture as noble as itself' – that is, the Gothic.

Work began on Waterhouse's final design in 1873. The building is symmetrical, with galleries placed either side of a dramatic central hall. Many of the galleries are top lit, as required by Professor Richard Owen, the first superintendent of the Museum, while the glazed roof of the hall is supported on curved iron girders which rest on corbels of terracotta. In fact, the whole building is faced in terracotta, inside and out, much of it fixed over an iron frame. Waterhouse admired this ceramic material as it was durable, washable and colourful, and he claimed his building was 'the largest, if not, indeed, the only modern building in which terra-cotta has been extensively used for external façades and interior wall surfaces, including all the varied decoration which this involves'. And, like any great Victorian public building, the Natural History Museum carries a symbolic and didactic scheme of sculptural ornament which needs to be read. At a time when the implications of Darwin's *Origin of Species* were causing concern, the building responded to the contemporary enthusiasm for botany, zoology and geology. Extinct creatures crawl over the eastern half of the façade while living ones are represented on the west ('Man: the greatest beast of all', once stood on the central gable). Inside, sea creatures are depicted on the piers which support the fireproof ceilings of the long, lateral galleries. The building combined a historical style with new technology in a direct and imaginative manner.

NATURAL HISTORY MUSEUM • LONDON *GREAT HALL INTERIOR*

Egyptian Halls
GLASGOW, GREAT BRITAIN
1870–72

Alexander Thomson
born Balfron 1817
died Glasgow 1875

A lexander 'Greek' Thomson was one of two architects of international stature and conspicuous originality produced by Glasgow (the other was Charles Rennie Mackintosh, *see pages 212–13*), and he did more than any other to give the 'Second City' of the British Empire a distinct urban character, designing commercial buildings and warehouses, terraces and tenements, villas and extraordinary churches in his peculiar development of the Greek, touched by Egyptian and other exotic sources.

Yet 'Greek' Thomson never went to Greece, nor even crossed the English Channel. At a time when the 'Battle of the Styles' between Gothic and classical was raging, Thomson decided to uphold the virtues of the unfashionable Greek, maintaining that it was an ideal response to 'eternal laws' and thus the basis for a modern architecture which was able to incorporate new materials like cast iron and plate glass. His finest villa, Holmwood (1857–58), was revolutionary in that it was both Grecian and asymmetrical; it was influenced by Schinkel and yet seems to anticipate the early 'prairie houses' of Frank Lloyd Wright.

Thomson is a paradox, at once a successful commercial architect and a visionary, dreaming of the monuments of the Ancient World and of time and space: 'all who have studied works of art must have been struck by the mysterious power of the horizontal element in carrying the mind away into space, and into speculations upon infinity'. Both sides of the man are evident in the Egyptian Halls, his most extraordinary and elaborate commercial work. Built for the iron founder James Robertson, the grand stone façade is a sort of layer cake with a series of horizontal storeys, each different in treatment, building up to a majestic cornice. On the top storey, the squat Corinthian columns are freestanding, leaving the fenestration behind as a

continuous glazed strip – a feature which some commentators have seen as anticipating the Modern movement but which in fact resulted from Thomson's dislike of ugly collisions between windows and shaped columns. With his belief in trabeation (post-and-lintel construction, as used by the Greeks), Thomson always wanted columns to be seen to be performing a structural purpose.

The exotic character of this façade, with its strong horizontals, shows the influence of the Sublime images of John Martin, the celebrated painter of Old Testament catastrophes, in which fantastical colonnades recede towards infinity under storm-filled skies. Yet behind the façade, Egyptian Halls was iron framed, with fireproof ceilings of iron beams and a concrete infill.

In its heyday, the building was a shopping centre-cum-bazaar, probably inspired by the Egyptian Hall in Piccadilly, London (1811–12; P.F. Robinson, 1776–1858), hosting promenade concerts and exhibitions. (Today, the main doorcase has been destroyed and the magnificent pavement lamps are long gone.) When it opened, a London architectural journal considered it 'probably the architect's most successful effort, and we doubt if its equal, for originality, grandeur of treatment, or imposing effect, could be found in any city, not excepting the metropolis itself'. True.

EGYPTIAN HALLS • GLASGOW *DETAIL OF FAÇADE*

Barclay Free Church

EDINBURGH, GREAT BRITAIN
1862–64

Frederick Thomas Pilkington

born Stamford 1832
died Pinner 1898

The Victorian Age was obsessed by its failure to generate a style of its own, and thoughtful architects saw that part of the problem was knowing too much history. Gothic Revivalists felt too dependent on medieval precedent, despite believing that the style was suitable for all building types. One answer was to adopt ideas from abroad, from France or Italy; another was to exaggerate and distort in a search for originality. Those who chose the last path were called 'rogues' by H.S. Goodhart-Rendel; they were like rogue elephants, 'driven or living apart from the herd, and of savage temper'.

Frederick Thomas Pilkington was such a rogue architect. Born in England, he practised mainly in Scotland but was certainly not part of the High Church avant-garde in the Gothic Revival. Yet it is arguable that he displayed more intelligence and flexibility in adapting Gothic to new purposes than many of the famous 'Goths', for he was almost alone in adjusting the style to unprecedented, un-medieval plans. Most new Gothic churches used a traditional plan, with nave and aisles and chancel as Pugin insisted, although this was scarcely convenient for modern Protestant worship. 'Greek' Thomson challenged the assertion that 'Gothic architecture is the very thing for churches. Instead of being crowded with stone piers, it should be as open as possible. But the mediaevalists never give us such forms.' Yet Pilkington did.

Pilkington built astonishing Presbyterian churches, in Kelso, Irvine and Dundee, each surmounted by a heavy, spiky steeple, but his masterpiece is the Barclay Free Church in Edinburgh, which erupted among the sober stone terraces of Morningside with a huge spire that made it the tallest building in Scotland at the time. The outside of this extraordinary building ripples with polygonal and convex projections; stair turrets and porches collide and the whole is crawling with a sort of fungoid naturalistic ornament – Pilkington had evidently read his Ruskin. Above, spiky gables support roofs with ridges seemingly running in all directions. This is almost organic architecture, and it only makes sense on seeing the interior, for the architect did not even hint at a conventional medieval plan but created a sort of pear-shaped auditorium with curved rows of seats focused on a central pulpit with an organ above.

Coherence is given to the interior by two giant square piers and two dwarf iron columns which support a central rectangular roof structure, but beyond this the outer walls bulge outwards to give the maximum seating capacity on the raked floor and in the (original) three stepped-back tiers of theatre-like curved galleries. It has to be seen to be believed, but the seriousness and practicality underlying this most original expression of Gothic freedom suggests that Pilkington could rise beyond eccentricity to genius. But his sort of rogue Gothic soon went out of fashion: by 1888 the Barclay Church could be dismissed as 'a congregation of elephants, rhinoceroses and hippopotamuses, with their snouts in a manger and their posteriors turned to the golf players in the links'.

Pennsylvania Academy of the Fine Arts

PHILADELPHIA, PENNSYLVANIA,
UNITED STATES
1871–76

Frank Furness

born Philadelphia, Pennsylvania 1839
died Media, Pennsylvania 1912

The ideas of John Ruskin and the English High Victorian 'Goths' soon crossed the Atlantic and achieved the most vigorous and creative expressions in the hands of American architects. Above all, there was Frank Furness of Philadelphia, in whose hands Gothic motifs were stretched and squashed with Mannerist ingenuity. Furness, along with the novelist Mark Twain, belonged to the generation who wished to see an authentic American art, vigorous and pioneering and not dependent on European trends.

Strongly influenced by his father, a Unitarian minister and close friend of the poet Ralph Waldo Emerson, Furness trained in New York in the office of Richard Morris Hunt (1827–95), who had studied in Paris. Furness's hopes to do likewise were thwarted by the outbreak of the Civil War (in which he served in the Pennsylvania Cavalry).

Furness certainly owed a debt to the English Gothic Revival. He delighted in structural polychromy, enjoying the contrasts in colour and texture between red brick and local stone, while revelling in the sheer weight of masonry. He was also interested in generating a vital, organic, naturalistic form of ornament in his buildings. Like the 'rogue' Gothic architects of Britain (see page 198), Furness was a fierce individualist and did not follow the revived interest in European precedents which began to dominate American architecture again after the 1870s. Consequently, he never enjoyed much critical acclaim and far too many of his Philadelphian buildings have been demolished.

Fortunately, his two finest public buildings survive and have been well restored. One is the University of Pennsylvania Library (1888–91); the other the Pennsylvania Academy of the Fine Arts. The building has the heaviness and exaggerated detail typical of Furness, as well as his eccentricity. The exterior revels in the contrast between rough,

rusticated brownstone, smooth sandstone, polished granite and red and black bricks and is enlivened with rich ornament and sculptured panels. The main entrance is divided by a column and shaft that cuts into a segmental arch while all the elevations are full of vigorous invention. The roof is of the French pavilion type, emphasizing that this unique building was the product of both English and French influences. But Furness was open to new ideas and technology: iron girders are exposed inside and even externally along the side elevation, where there are top-lit artists' studios. Such structural honesty was typical of the English 'Goths' and also reflected the ideas of the French architect and theorist, Viollet-le-Duc.

The future pioneer of the skyscraper, Louis Sullivan, worked for Furness while the Academy was rising and recalled him with respect as 'a curious character' who 'made buildings out of his head'. For the influential American architect Robert Venturi (born 1925), he was 'an American-Emersonian, individualist-reformist, naturalist-artist, as one who follows at the same time the sturdy, Continental, functionalist Gothicism of Viollet-le-Duc in France and the exuberant Italianate Gothicism of Ruskin in Britain. And who is also a Mannerist.' Furness was perhaps the most versatile and inventive 'Goth' of them all.

PENNSYLVANIA ACADEMY OF THE FINE ARTS • *PHILADELPHIA DETAIL OF ENTRANCE HALL*

Thomas Crane Library

QUINCY, MASSACHUSETTS, UNITED STATES
1880–82

Henry Hobson Richardson
born St James' Parish, Louisiana 1838
died Boston, Massachusetts 1886

enry Richardson was a big man in every sense. He had more influence than any other American architect of his generation and his distinctive and massive style, at once historical and personal – 'Richardsonian Romanesque' – was much imitated during what Lewis Mumford, the writer and urbanist, called the 'Brown Decades' of the later 19th century. With Richardson, American architecture comes of age.

Richardson trained at the Ecole des Beaux-Arts in Paris during the American Civil War, but his tailor was in London and so he knew the latest work of English Gothic Revival architects as well as being familiar with Ruskin's ideas about ornament, colour and the importance of the integrity of the masonry wall. After his return to the United States in 1865, Richardson's first buildings were Gothic but he soon abandoned the pointed for the round arch, basing his architecture on the Romanesque of southern France and Spain. This is evident, above all, in his first masterpiece, Trinity Church, Boston (1873–77), which revels in the weight and texture of stonework. But in his mature work he tempered his Romanesque style with characteristics he observed as American, using strong horizontal lines in a search for a 'quiet and massive' architecture.

Richardson designed churches and houses, university buildings, a courthouse and a jail *(see pages 208–209)*; in Chicago he built a huge warehouse; in North Easton, Massachusetts, he designed the railway station, town hall, library and a gate lodge made of massive boulders. But perhaps his most sophisticated and sympathetic buildings are his five public libraries in New England. The finest is the Crane Memorial Library at Quincy on the outskirts of Boston, which achieves complete integration of the parts.

Inside, this consists of the main library space with book stacks and a reading room placed axially either side of the entrance hall. These elements are expressed on the exterior, but any exaggerated picturesqueness is suppressed in favour of a unity achieved by the massive, low, long wall of rough granite, relieved by a few courses of brownstone, and by the overall roof, whose plane is broken only by Richardson's 'eyebrow' dormers. The large round entrance arch is not centred on the gable above, and there is a projecting stair turret on one side only. But Richardson's asymmetry always has functional justification. The reading room is lit by a big, simplified mullioned and transomed window, while the book stacks are illuminated by a horizontal band of fenestration, placed high and pushed back from the stone mullions in front – a feature reminiscent of 'Greek' Thomson. Beaux-Arts logic is enlivened with Gothic Revival vigour.

Although the exterior is massive, the interior is surprisingly delicate. All the pine woodwork and furniture was designed by the architect and the balustrades of the upper book-lined alcoves off the main library are as elegant as they are imaginative; the thin pilasters with carved capitals are Byzantine in inspiration. With buildings like the Quincy library, the best American interior architecture overtook the English in general quality and craftsmanship.

THOMAS CRANE LIBRARY • QUINCY

Auditorium Building

CHICAGO, ILLINOIS,
UNITED STATES
1886–89

Dankmar Adler
born Stadt Lengsfeld 1844
died Chicago, Illinois 1900

Louis Sullivan
born Boston, Massachusetts
1856
died Chicago, Illinois 1924

Louis Sullivan has entered the mythology of the Modern movement as a pioneer who preached that 'form follows function'. And his steel-framed tall buildings are certainly clearly structured in terms of a base, a repetitive middle section and a proper termination (rather like a classical column). But, inspired by Ruskin, he also wanted to develop a new form of organic ornament based on earlier precedents and, following Owen Jones (1809–74) in England and Frank Furness in America, he applied a highly personal and elaborate style of low relief decoration to his buildings, inside and out.

Sullivan's best works were designed while he was in partnership with the German-born architect Dankmar Adler, 1881–95, and the largest and most complex was the Auditorium Building. Sullivan had moved to the city of Chicago which, following the devastating fire of 1871, was fast becoming a dynamic focus of architectural and technical innovation. Adler, an expert on acoustics, had designed a temporary theatre for the Chicago Opera Festival, which led to the commission for a permanent building. To make this financially viable, a vast auditorium was to be combined with a hotel and offices. The immense weight of the structure needed huge foundations dug in the waterlogged soil next to Lake Michigan.

H.H. Richardson's last masterpiece, the Marshall Field Wholesale Store (1885–87, demolished), was then rising in Chicago and Sullivan studied Richardson's treatment of windows and massive walls. He eschewed ornament on the ten storeys of the Auditorium Building, organizing the windows in vertical groups, some round arched and some trabeated, from below the cornice. The lower part of the walls was of powerful blocks of rough-hewn granite, the upper part grey sandstone ashlar. The hotel faced the lake. On the south, side elevation, a 17-storey tower announced the entrance to the auditorium itself, a huge space that could seat more than 4,000 people.

This tower is a remarkable structure. It was designed to contain both commercial space and water tanks to supply hydraulic power for the stage scenery. Near the top, under the stepped cornice, is a gallery with unfluted Doric columns, recalling Ledoux (see page 160) and revealing Sullivan's knowledge of the European classical tradition. After the building's completion, the architects moved their office to this floor and here Frank Lloyd Wright worked as chief assistant until he left in 1893.

Adler was responsible for the internal structure and for the successful acoustics of the auditorium, achieved by the use of hollow elliptical arches which also contained ventilation and heating ducts. Sullivan planned the interior volumes and designed the scheme of rich internal ornament, seen at its most sumptuous and beguiling in the gilded relief panels – incorporating electric lights – in the interior of the auditorium.

New technology and traditional masonry, monumental severity and rich ornament, the Sublime and the Beautiful, old Europe and new America are combined in this astonishing creation.

AUDITORIUM BUILDING · CHICAGO *DETAIL SHOWING VIEW OF TOWER*

Fin de Siècle

Richard A. Etlin

In the 19th century, Western architecture underwent an expansion of interests beyond the classicism that had dominated public and institutional buildings during the eighteenth-century 'Age of Enlightenment'. As the last chapter shows, the Romanesque and particularly Gothic architecture of the Middle Ages, neglected and even reviled since the Renaissance, now found favour.

At the same time, a new Romantic sensibility prompted an enthusiasm for the natural world, beginning with the introduction of colour and texture on exterior surfaces and leading to the actual representation of creatures and objects from the natural world. And as the century progressed, a pluralistic appreciation of historical styles even allowed non-Western forms to enter the canon.

However, a two-part crisis also developed in architecture. The rise of the profession of engineering, stimulated by the new building needs of the Industrial Revolution and associated with the new building materials of iron, steel and later concrete, in conjunction with plate glass, challenged the comfortable dominance of the architectural profession. And the cultural imperative of developing an art expressive of the contemporary age made the use of historical styles seem, by the late 19th century, like inauthentic antiquarianism. The response to this crisis assumed three often overlapping directions. Some progressive thinkers

BELOW: Eliel Saarinen, Herman Gesellius and Armas Lingren, Helsinki Railway Station, Helsinki, 1906–14

LEFT: Josef Hoffmann, Palais Stoclet, Brussels, 1905–11

ABOVE: Victor Horta, Van Eetvelde House, Brussels, 1895–98

looked to the domain of glass and iron engineering, ranging from railway sheds to covered markets to World's Fair exhibition buildings, as a source of inspiration for a new architecture expressive of the 'spirit of the age'. Another tendency sought to escape the tyranny of historical revivals of high-style architecture through the vernacular: traditional, local forms of building. These architects were generally influenced by the English Arts and Crafts movement, with its emphasis on handmade decorative objects, natural wood finishes and floral patterns. These three elements of the Arts and Crafts ideal were bound together in a Romantic appreciation of nature, which set the stage for the next development, Art Nouveau, where architects embraced a more extensive and often more exuberant world of plant and animal imagery, as well as evocations of physical forces such as wind and waves, to free themselves of historicism. This dynamic 'new art' first appeared in France and Belgium but soon begain to spread across Europe.

For all three reforming tendencies, the lanterns offered by John Ruskin in *The Seven Lamps of Architecture* (1849) lit the way, guiding the century in its quest for an honest, original architecture. The most important of these seven principles for this period are the lamps of sacrifice, life, power and memory. With the lamp of sacrifice, Ruskin distinguished between mere building and architecture, the latter requiring a sacrifice of effort from the designer who had to add decoration to raise a structure beyond the realm of utility to art. Through the lamp of life, Ruskin articulated what was to become a contemporary obsession with imbuing art with an organic vitality, partaking of the life forces in the natural world. In the lamp of power, Ruskin identified the most potent expressions of nature's energy, which in the previous century had been introduced into aesthetic discourse as the Sublime. Finally, virtually all the reforming architects adhered to the lamp of memory, whereby the past was employed to inform the present, even if in the most audacious and paradoxical ways.

Allegheny County Courthouse and Jail

PITTSBURGH, PENNSYLVANIA,
UNITED STATES
1883–88

Henry Hobson Richardson

born St James' Parish, Louisiana
1838
died Boston, Massachusetts 1886

Henry Hobson Richardson looms large over the late 19th century, and not simply because he was a physically big man, emphasized in the famous photograph showing him covered in a heavy, hooded medieval monk's cape. He solved an intellectual dilemma that had plagued the age, obsessed both by the romance of the Middle Ages and the need to be modern. This Richardson satisfied by creating what was widely recognized as a contemporary version of the Romanesque, a Richardsonian Romanesque, widely appreciated as North America's own authentic, 19th-century style.

The paired structures of the Allegheny County Courthouse and Jail are a masterful interpretation of Richardson's theories and vision. True to the Beaux-Arts principles of his education (see page 202), the front tower of the courthouse serves as a civic marker as it rises above a magnificent Romanesque entrance hall, from where a strongly defined corridor circumnavigates the central courtyard. The tower also served to secure fresh air that was treated according to advanced techniques of heating and ventilating. In a city that had to burn the street lights during the day because of the pollution from its steel factories, Richardson provided a courthouse with ample natural lighting, with all the main rooms illuminated from two sides.

For architecture to capture the public's imagination, it requires a compelling physical presence. Throughout his career, Richardson was successful because he created massive buildings that are emphatically well grounded, marrying a comforting sense of solidity with lively design. They convey a feeling of unchanging endurance and imperturbable calm. With outward sloping walls and tall sheltering roofs, Richardson's architecture is the built equivalent of a reassuring, steadfast friend. The round arches for windows and doors,

along with the delicate Romanesque columnettes, provide a grace to his buildings, whose initial impression is nonetheless one of great power. In the Allegheny Courthouse, the clever functional solution of alternating the courtrooms with the judge's chambers enabled the architect to provide projecting rounded bays for the latter, thereby enhancing the elasticity of the building's mass.

Elasticity is the keynote of Richardson's massive stone façades. At the Allegheny Courthouse and Jail, through the carefully controlled bulge of the rough granite surfaces, Richardson imparts a sense of considerable weight and, paradoxically, a sense of flexing muscles, so that the entire wall seems to be imbued with energy. This dual impression of power and life is reinforced on the courthouse façades by the alternation of wide and narrow layers of stone, the latter creating a cushioning effect that adds to the impression of a living, muscular organism. The jail presents a more sober image, achieved through courses of massive rock-faced stones, with the *voussoirs* (wedged-shaped sections) of the giant arches extending to a length of 2.4 m (8 ft). Today, the mighty walls of these paired civic structures continue to inspire a sense of awe.

ALLEGHENY COUNTY COUNRTHOUSE AND JAIL • PITTSBURGH

Guaranty Building
**BUFFALO, NEW YORK,
UNITED STATES
1894–96**

Louis Sullivan
born Boston, Massachusetts
1856
died Chicago, Illinois 1924

Dankmar Adler
born Stadt Lengsfeld 1844
died Chicago, Illinois 1900

Louis Sullivan is widely acknowledged as the architect who created the vertical look for the American tall office building – quaintly called a 'sky-scraper' at the turn of the century – anticipating the next generation of true skyscrapers, such as the Chrysler Building (1928–30; William Van Alen, 1882–1954) and the Empire State Building (1930–32; Shreve, Lamb and Harman) in New York, which would reach to the clouds.

It was Sullivan who proclaimed and proved that the tall office building 'must be every inch a proud and soaring thing'. No building in his career captured that feeling better than the Guaranty. Although erected in Buffalo, the Guaranty belongs to the Chicago School of multistorey office buildings. This was developed by a pioneering set of architects in the last decades of the 19th century in a Midwest that was free from the pretensions and constraints of the East Coast establishment which, as Henry James' novels amply remind us, looked enviously across the ocean to the aristocratic eminence of the Old World's historical culture. In contrast, the Chicago architects created what was widely recognized as an American style in a building type, the skyscraper, universally deemed symbolic of the American spirit: boldly commercial and fuelled by the ethos of the self-made man. The essential innovations behind the development of these structures were the elevator and, to allow the buildings to grow beyond 10 or 12 storeys, metal-frame construction.

The key to Sullivan's success in giving an enduring look to the tall office building came from his admiration of nature. By studying living organisms, Sullivan coined his famous aphorism, 'form ever follows function'. Departing from the customary practice of making a tall office block

look like a stack of Renaissance palaces, Sullivan applied an organic analogy whereby the form reflected the inner processes of the body. Thus, at the Guaranty, a two-storey base houses ground-level shops and their offices above, which are reached by stairs; then come the identical floors of independent offices, served by the elevator; and the top contains mechanical services. Hence, each change in form marks a change in function.

And nature taught another lesson. Looking to early spring, Sullivan found abundant life. To impart life to a building and make the viewer feel the vitality of natural forces through 'the imperative voice of emotion' was Sullivan's constant goal. At the Guaranty, he turned to the two great styles of Western culture, Greek and Gothic, for the model they presented to the modern age. The building sits on a base that is articulated in the manner of Greek post-and-lintel construction, and so reflects the lines of the actual steel-frame structure in what Sullivan termed the 'logical' manner. Above, he moved into a 'poetical' mode, with thin vertical shafts that rise gracefully in a free adaptation of the Gothic spirit. Sullivan covered these soaring piers with terra-cotta ornamentation that shimmers in the sunlight and so dissolves the solidity of this cluster of vibrant forms, almost vegetable in nature, that ascend effortlessly to the sky.

GUARANTY BUILDING · BUFFALO

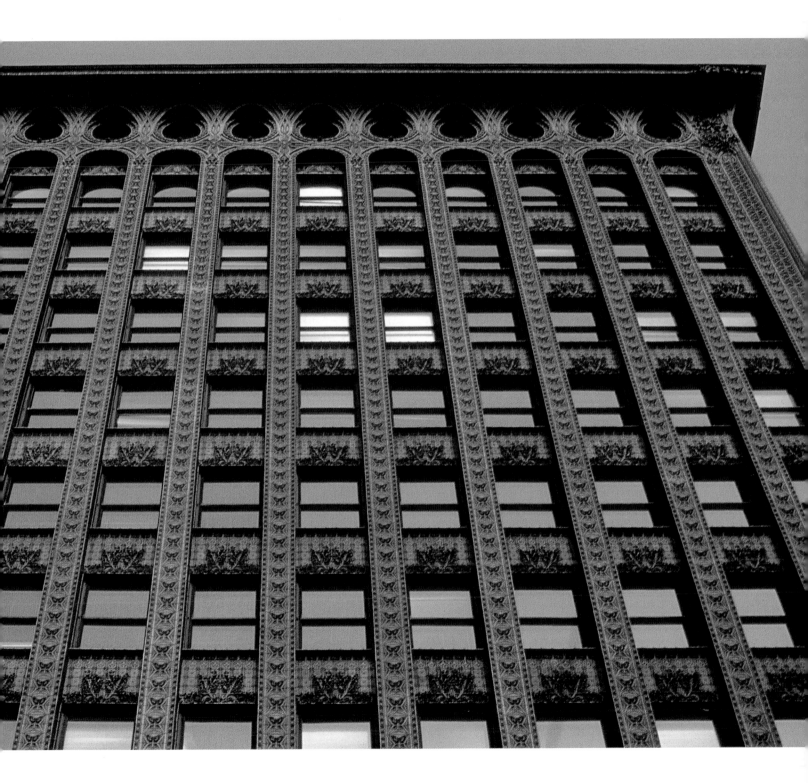

Glasgow School of Art

GLASGOW, GREAT BRITAIN
1896–1910

Charles Rennie Mackintosh

born Glasgow 1868
died London 1928

The architecture and related decorative schemes by Charles Rennie Mackintosh, the leading Art Nouveau architect in Great Britain, illustrate the fruitful fusion of the two approaches used by progressive artists in the late 19th century to break away from what they saw as the stifling constraints of classical form: the creation of a locally based, modern vernacular and the invention of a new art grounded in natural forms.

Along with Mackintosh's Hill House (Helensburgh, 1902–1906), the Glasgow School of Art shows this marriage of outlooks most forcefully. Both buildings combine more or less overt references to the traditional Scottish baronial style, typified by weighty elevations that suggest fortifications, with Art Nouveau features. The art school accomplishes this union with greater subtlety.

The Glasgow School of Art is an ensemble of paradoxes. Massive in form, it is largely open in aspect, thanks to the large glass windows that light the studio spaces. With three bays to the left and four to the right, these are yet symmetrically disposed as wings, all but equal in length, to either side of the central door. This main portal is itself an exercise in balanced asymmetry. Here the heavy wall surface and projecting turret suggest the vernacular Scottish baronial style.

There is a simplicity, even austerity, to the treatment of mass and surface on the façade that finds its counterpart inside in Mackintosh's particular brand of Art Nouveau decor. Here the vertical timbers of the main framing system are slightly tapered forms graced with gently rounded edges. In contrast to the Belgian Art Nouveau architect Victor Horta (1861–1947), famous for his whiplash line with its swirling tendrils, Mackintosh developed an understated Art Nouveau

aesthetic in which the slightest tapering or bending of a line conveys a sense of vibrant life through an intimation of tensile strength. That same line could also be gathered into a cluster of encircling strands to suggest a bud or flower, sometimes reminiscent – as on the studio windows of the school – of the knotted forms of ancient Celtic art.

The library wing, redesigned for the second phase of construction begun in 1906, marries an abstracted reference to the baronial castle with a modern, plastic treatment of surface and mass. Projecting glass volumes, given texture by small panes, are juxtaposed with recessed prismatic volumes of a similar aspect that are set within the wall but isolated from the adjacent surfaces by slots of space. A few years later, German architects of the Expressionist movement would use curvilinear or pyramidally faceted shapes to evoke crystalline forms from mountainous or cavernous settings. Here we find Mackintosh already creating a similarly evocative, poetic effect with straight geometries. The library proper has a double-storey reading room and a mezzanine balcony recessed from the timber frame and detailed in a manner redolent of Japanese construction. The plethora of hanging verticals, including suspended, clustered lighting fixtures, completes the sense of a geometrically crystalline interior world.

GLASGOW SCHOOL OF ART • GLASGOW VIEW SHOWING LIBRARY WING

Castel Béranger
PARIS, FRANCE
1894–98

Hector Guimard
born Lyon 1867
died New York 1942

Now integrated into a continuous urban scheme, the Castel Béranger once dominated its suburban site, surrounded only by low cottages and their gardens. Hector Guimard seems to have been inspired by the local vernacular architecture, characterized by contrasting bands of black and red brick or by *pierre meulière*, a rustic stone much prized in the mid- and late-19th-century Parisian suburbs for the domestic look it imparted. If the neighbourhood was to change scale rapidly, at least the new apartment building would harmonize with, and later recall, the quasi-rural setting.

On the outer walls, Guimard used not only the noble material of ashlar limestone – which had become customary for elegant apartment buildings in France from the mid-century Second Empire onwards – but also different colours of brick – yellow-red, red-orange and white – along with *pierre meulière*. Limestone ashlar dominated the base but the layers of the other materials varied both in width and height, breaking down the scale of the apartment building so that it looks like an ensemble of at least three smaller structures. The *pierre meulière* evokes a modest version of Ruskin's lamp of power, while the variety of colours and textures recalls the lamp of life.

Guimard's interest was piqued by the dynamic lines of Victor Horta's Art Nouveau architecture in Brussels. After a visit and a meeting with the Belgian architect, Guimard returned to Paris to alter the designs for the decorative details of Castel Béranger, from the metal parapets of the balconies and the metal gate and glazed ceramics of the entrance to the interior floor mosaics, stained-glass doors and windows, wall coverings, ceiling brackets, columns, fireplace mantels, and even ovens. Guimard used the new material of glass bricks in a coloured arrangement along a

stairwell and the new ceramic glazes developed by the chemist Alexandre Bigot. Just as Horta used exposed iron structural members of modest size on his elegant town houses, thereby introducing an engineering form into the world of high art, so Guimard employed an exposed and even more substantial iron beam, placed at eye level, above the one shop incorporated into the ground floor.

Designed and built in an era when Art Nouveau architects were campaigning for everyday life to be infused in all of its aspects with art, the Castel Béranger was honoured by the City of Paris for having beautified the street with its splendid façade. So important was the ideal of surrounding oneself with an ambience that captured the flavour of the modern age that Guimard installed his office in the building and the Neo-Impressionist painter Paul Signac took an apartment there. This is the equivalent of the gesture of the 18th-century revolutionary philosopher and writer Thomas Paine who chose to live in a Parisian apartment building decorated in the then new, austere Directoire style. It is a reminder that revolution is not limited to the domain of politics, but, at moments of radical cultural fervour, the character of the very setting of daily life acquires a new urgency.

Saint-Jean de Montmartre

PARIS, FRANCE
1894–1904

Anatole de Baudot
born Saarebourg 1834
died Paris 1915

A natole de Baudot was the pre-eminent disciple of the great architectural theoretician Viollet-le-Duc, and Saint-Jean de Montmartre realizes the challenge posed by the master to design a modern architecture inspired by the Gothic but using modern structural methods. In Viollet-le-Duc's time, this meant iron; at the close of the 19th century, for Anatole de Baudot, the material was reinforced concrete.

Saint-Jean de Montmartre was built using an experimental technique patented by the engineer Paul Cottancin called *ciment armé*, comprising cement arches reinforced with iron wire, used in conjunction with walls and piers of *brique armé*, where perforated brick is strengthened with iron wire and bonded with cement. The Cottancin technique yielded a lofty, light-filled interior with elegantly thin piers and rhythmically disposed interlocking, airy arches which repeat in the manner of a musical basso continuo. But the city authorities, fearful about the thinness of the piers, delayed completion of the church for several years.

The interior has a lyricism that confounds any attempt to explain the structural system in a simplistically logical way. The principal piers soar upwards to arch gracefully across the ceiling in interlocking patterns of breathtaking audacity; the ceiling slides down onto the side walls that then dissolve into interlocking arches, which, in turn, become suspended in space before they too dissolve into dramatically thin pillars that descend onto the top of a range of daringly thin and tantalizingly flat suspended arches. Here the visitor finds a version of Ruskin's lamp of life where, through synaesthesia, the faculty of sight evokes that of hearing, because the whole display is the visual equivalent of organ music.

Taking advantage of the drop in the land, De Baudot stacked the principal hall of worship upon a lower chapel. Both exhibit the eminently modern aesthetic of architectural space-making as volume, a concept that the Dutch architect Hendrik Berlage (1856–1934) was exploring at the same time in his seminal Amsterdam Exchange (1897–1903) and that Le Corbusier would immortalize two decades later in his essay, 'Three Reminders to Professional Architects. Part I: Volume', which would become an important chapter in the highly influential treatise, *Vers une architecture* (1923, *Towards a New Architecture*). This volumetric emphasis is also evident on the exterior of Saint-Jean de Montmartre. Built, however, at the turn of the 20th century rather than during the pioneering phase of the subsequent avant-garde Modernist movement, De Baudot's church reflects the contemporary interest in ornamental effects. The orange-red glazed-brick façades are further enriched with rows of small, rounded and colourfully glazed ceramics, executed according to Bigot's new method (*see page 214*), which impart a jewel-like quality to the towering mass. On sunny days, the façades glow with a warmth that seems to come from within. At the top, solidity dissolves into an arabesque of interlocking arches, similar to those that form the major visual theme inside.

Apartment building, Rue Franklin

PARIS, FRANCE
1903–04

Auguste Perret
born Brussels 1874
died Paris 1954

Gustave Perret
born Brussels 1876
died Paris 1952

The Perret brothers' apartment building on Rue Franklin in Paris is one of the first examples of residential architecture to be erected with an exposed concrete structure, clearly proclaiming the modern nature of its construction. The architects unashamedly made aesthetic use of a means of building that had previously been assigned to the culturally inferior domain of engineering.

Daring is everywhere: in the remarkably thin structural elements – 20-cm-thick (8-in) façade walls and 15-cm-thick (6-in) floors; in the large plate-glass window of the architects' ground-floor office; and in the paired six-storey cantilevered bays that are suspended dramatically over the pavement, while appearing at the upper level as a thin, freestanding frame. Like Louis Sullivan (see pages 210–11), the Perret brothers applied Ruskin's lamp of memory by abstracting the lessons of the Greek and the Gothic, but here the same form is given two readings: a trabeated reinforced concrete frame that evokes the former, classical style; or a skeletal structure with large glass surfaces and recessed, non-structural infill panels that evokes the latter, medieval. The duality unites in a single point of focus – a delicate Gothic pendant rendered with Greek detailing – that hovers directly over the heads of passers-by.

Equal to the designers' daring was their ingenuity. The site was a difficult one, which would have left insufficient room for dwellings had the legal light and air requirements been satisfied by incorporating a traditional interior courtyard. The Perret brothers, however, pushed the front façade inwards in an angled manner that satisfied the law while providing all the rooms of each apartment with a frontal aspect facing the park opposite. Thanks to a precipitous drop of the land, this also gave a splendid view over Paris and across the Seine to the Eiffel Tower, that symbol of modern technology and French engineering daring.

Yet the Rue Franklin apartment building was not only a functional and engineering achievement. It was fully a work of art, conceived according to the parameters of Ruskin's lamp of sacrifice, suitably revised to allow for mass-produced decorative forms. Here art beautifies all exterior surfaces, which are covered with a variety of textured ornamentation so that the building offers the refined sensuousness of restrained elegance. Glazed ceramics executed by Bigot (see page 214) are everywhere: smooth tiles protect the concrete frame itself; recessed exterior wall panels carry patterns of clustered chestnut leaves; fields of small raised beads cover other, narrower interstices. The delicate rectangles of the wire parapets in front of the French windows, as well as similar forms inside serving in lieu of traditional stair-hall balusters, complement these variegated ceramics, as does the stair hall's glass-brick wall whose prismatic surfaces fracture the light into a shimmering form that is decorative in its own right. For the Perret brothers, the entire building was a moulding and modelling of the earth, 'béton riche sur béton pauvre', literally, 'rich cement over poor cement'; that is, ceramic art on top of cement, or architecture covering engineering.

Secession Building

VIENNA, AUSTRIA
1897–98

Joseph Maria Olbrich

born Troppau 1867
died Düsseldorf 1908

The motto that graces the portal of the Secession Building – 'To the Time its Art, To Art its Freedom' – can be understood not only as the rallying cry of the group of progressive artists who 'seceded' from the Austrian academy in 1897, but also of all the architects discussed in this chapter. And like Charles Rennie Mackintosh in his Glasgow School of Art *(see pages 212–13)*, Joseph Maria Olbrich in the Secession Building explores a version of Art Nouveau that eschews the wild fantasies of Victor Horta's whiplash line in favour of a more restrained appeal to natural imagery.

Laurel bushes, rendered in low relief, appear to grow up the edges of the façade that frames the exhibition building's entrance, which they surround as well. The laurel re-emerges as a gilded metal globe which crowns the ensemble of simple massive blocks, whose plain walls emphasize the qualities of surface and volume that became the hallmarks of the 20th-century Modernist aesthetic. Behind the entrance pavilion, huge glass pyramidal skylights rise over the gallery spaces to create a vibrant composition of powerful forms.

In contrast with the expansive impact of the majestic façade, minute details send a shudder up the spine: the delicate modelling of the cornices; the raised and incised geometric patterns on the pylons that frame the gilt globe; the snake-like hair of the Three Muses over the entrance, and the comparable writhing linear forms – half vegetable, half reptilian – that emerge from under the cornice of the central, raised block. In the same way that small diamonds have a particular lustre or perfume seems most potent when it comes in a small flask, this thin and restrained ornament acquires a power over the imagination, enhanced by the contrast with the larger unadorned, flat surfaces. (The entrance doors, with their small, bevelled glass panes, reinforce this effect.) Herein lies one of the secrets not only of this work but of all the architecture of the Viennese Secession.

The pyramids and pylons, which evoke the architecture and hence the world of ancient Egypt – long a visual metaphor for eternity – recall Ruskin's thoughts on the lamp of memory, that in architecture, 'decorations are consequently animated by a metaphorical or historical meaning'. Olbrich supplies both qualities through overall massing and ornamentation: the large gilded globe appears as the rising sun passing over the paired pylons, symbolizing mountains, to renew the world. Composed of laurel leaves, the symbol of victory, this shimmering globe proclaims the arrival of a new era, bringing with it the victory of the new art.

In the foyer, a dynamic volumetric structure, delineated by dramatic natural lighting, recalls that great emblem of Viennese architecture, the nearby Karlskirche by Fischer von Erlach *(see pages 138–39)*, rendering the lamp of memory in a local manner. The pylons and central globe of the façade can be seen as modern versions of the freestanding columns and dome of von Erlach's 18th-century church; there the iconography was also about the timeless and universal.

Karlsplatz Station
VIENNA, AUSTRIA
1894–1901

Otto Wagner
born Penzig 1841
died Vienna 1918

Otto Wagner's twin pavilions for the Karlsplatz Station wielded great polemical force at the beginning of the 20th century, when there was a fascination with modes of transport and travel. At that time, architects and critics talked about the 'representative' building types of each age, traditionally conceived as monumental works such as churches and palaces, but by then associated with new functional forms.

And so we find Auguste Perret in 1905 designing a reinforced-concrete garage in Paris with his customary modern rendition of Greek and Gothic lessons, including a mechanized version of the medieval cathedral's rose window. Similarly, Otto Wagner conceived his Karlsplatz entrance to Vienna's metropolitan railway as a modern abstraction of the revered Karlskirche (see pages 138–39). Ruskin's lamp of memory provided powerful symbols that avant-garde architects could use to celebrate the mechanistic 'spirit of the age'.

Yet, unlike the functionalist architects of the 1920s, these forerunners insisted on dressing up mere engineering with art. Wagner followed the same principles as Perret who, in the Rue Franklin apartment building, distinguished between the structure and non-load-bearing infill walls by the articulation of surfaces and through differentiated cladding (see pages 218–19). Wagner's use of thin marble panels to cover the Karlsplatz Station owes much to the linguistic theories and historical analyses of the influential German architect Gottfried Semper (1803–79), which gave rise to the Secession's fondness for infill walls as decorative cladding. The Karlsplatz Station provides a modern rendition of this notion by creating a metaphor for metal construction: the thin slabs of marble are held in place by a visible, external iron frame that echoes the true structural members embedded within the wall. These exposed metal pieces are detailed to resemble taut straps, which in an earlier age would have been rope, thin pieces of wood or leather, and so suggest a richly tactile effect rather than the cold neutrality of iron.

The art critic Adrian Stokes has written of the imaginative force obtained by juxtaposing the rough and the smooth, the paired tactile qualities that dominate the station's exterior. The white marble panels are largely as smooth as ice. Their upper reaches are decorated with stencilled, abstract floral motifs that complement this elegant finish. However, at the bottom of each panel, a closely stippled finish hints at the traditional rustication of the ground floor in Renaissance architecture. Below each panel sits a textured granite slab with a somewhat further raised surface and an incrementally coarser rustication. Held in place by metal strapping and detailed with two layers of light rustication, these stones are raised off the ground and are not overbearing. Like the marble surfaces above, they belong to the exquisitely wrought world of modern architectural cladding placed on a modern iron-frame structure. At the Karlsplatz Station, Wagner created an architectural equivalent to famous Viennese pastry. This is neither an idle achievement nor a frivolous compliment: the sensuous delight of such architecture was the key feature of the age.

KARLSPLATZ STATION • VIENNA DETAIL

Goldman and Salatsch Store

VIENNA, AUSTRIA
1910–11

Adolf Loos
born Brno 1870
died Vienna 1933

O n Vienna's Michaelerplatz, dominated by the grandiose 18th-century Baroque façade of the imperial palace, the Hofburg, rises Adolf Loos' Goldman and Salatsch Store. Built as a gentleman's outfitters, today it has become a bank, and the dark-stained wooden interior with gilt accents is now filled with precious art objects where once elegant gloves and finely tailored shirts were stacked.

Compared with the monumental, classicizing façades typical of the 19th-century Ringstrasse district, the smooth surfaces of Loos' building, dominated from a distance by the unadorned simplicity of the whitewashed residential section, present a striking contrast: historicism and modernity starkly juxtaposed. And yet we should not allow either Loos' rejection of a facile historicism or his seemingly shocking association of ornament with crime in an essay of 1908 to blind us to the manifest sensuous pleasures afforded by the Goldman and Salatsch Store.

Rejecting the curvilinear surface decoration of Art Nouveau, Loos sought an ornamentation integral to the material itself. Just as I have praised Otto Wagner for creating in the Karlsplatz Station an architectural equivalent to Viennese pastry, so I maintain that Loos' building is the equivalent to Vienna's famous Sachertorte, that luscious chocolate cake with a hint of orange essence which adds a certain *je ne sais quoi* to the palate. The first two storeys are covered with richly veined polished marble, saturated with swirling patterns of deep greyish green, alternating with contrasting whites; in the centre rise four freestanding columns of the same rich material. Such sensuousness is unmatched even in this era of sumptuous surface treatments.

Windows with small square panes of bevelled glass – similar to those of the doors in Olbrich's Secession Building, but faceted and isolated in a manner reminiscent of Mackintosh's library wing of the Glasgow School of Art (see *pages 212–13 and 220–21*) – complement the marble surfaces and so intensify the seductive effect. Even the entrance porch presents a dazzling display, the canopy shimmering with sparkling reflections, comparable to those that pass through the small prismatic glass surfaces set all around the base of the façade. One visit to this building will convince you that my gastronomical analogy is fully apt.

Yet it is not simply through patisserie that Loos' building belongs to Vienna. The chocolate-coloured interior, with its restrained gilding, echoes the late-18th- and 19th-century shops still to be found in the area; a Neoclassical apothecary's shop shows a similar understated use of columns. To find the historical precedent – and reference – to Loos' richly veined polychromatic columns one would have to turn, once again, to that recurrent inspiration, the Karlskirche (see *pages 138–39*). Although the marble columns and pilasters inside the church exhibit a broader colour spectrum, typical of the Viennese Rococo, they appear relatively subdued when compared with the colour saturation of Loos' late Secession style.

Apartment building, Rue Vavin
PARIS, FRANCE
1912–14

Henri Sauvage
born Rouen 1873
died Paris 1932

Charles Sarazin
born Bourges 1873
died Le Canadel 1950

When this stepped apartment building was completed, the popular French periodical *L'Illustration* wondered whether it signalled a 'revolution in the art of building?'. Henri Sauvage certainly envisaged entire neighbourhoods of these terraced structures, which would provide more light both to the street and to the apartments than traditional designs. Unfortunately for enthusiasts of this new urbanism, only one more example was erected, about a decade later, but both still thrive today.

The first building is located in a wealthy district near the Jardin du Luxembourg; the second provides low-cost workers' housing and is furnished with an indoor municipal swimming pool, an ideal use of the deep interior space at the base of the pyramidal block. Like the Cranston tea-rooms (1897–c.1911) which Charles Rennie Mackintosh designed to provide a social space for workers as an alternative to the pub, this pool was to serve a similar purpose, along with the added benefits derived from exercise.

Physical fitness was an important theme in the progressives' programme for modern life; the terraced building on the Rue Vavin was originally called '*une maison à gradins sportive*', an athletic house with terraces. The architects had hoped to provide these apartments with private gymnasiums to complement the sunning terraces where children could play outdoors, away from the noisy, dusty and dangerous city streets. The terraces are 2.25 m (almost 7½ ft) deep and run as long as 18 m (59 ft). Complete privacy from neighbours on the upper floors is assured by the diagonal projection of the parapet walls, which double as planters to bring pleasure both to those living in the building and to people on the street. Pedestrians are also treated to the decorated underside of these tilting

parapets, a delicate pattern of glazed blue tiles punctuating the white-tile surface. Both apartment buildings are covered with white glazed tiles, a radical transposition of a utilitarian material, usually found in underground stations, bathrooms and kitchens, into the world of architecture and, in the case of the Rue Vavin building, into the architecture of the upper classes. These tiles were intended to serve both actual and symbolic purposes of hygiene. The architects often called their workers' housing schemes 'hygienic habitation'. Exercise and hygiene were paired concepts for the more socially orientated proponents of Art Nouveau, along with the goal of a 'democratic art', achieved by investing all areas of life, from the home to the street, with beauty.

Sauvage had begun his career by using the sweeping curvilinear lines of Belgian and French Art Nouveau. Then, towards 1909, in his early sketches for terraced apartment buildings, he experimented with a modern vernacular aesthetic. By the time he designed the building on Rue Vavin, he was working within the elegantly restrained idiom of the Viennese Secession. Whereas the Art Nouveau architecture of Horta and Guimard today looks like a period piece, Sauvage's Rue Vavin building exudes an enduring timeless quality.

APARTMENT BUILDING, RUE VAVIN · PARIS *DETAIL*

Casa Battló
BARCELONA, SPAIN
1904–06

Antoni Gaudí
born Reus 1852
died Barcelona 1926

Waves and bones, flowers and reptiles, Catalonia and Spain, the Holy Family and the devil: Antoni Gaudí's Casa Battló abounds with contrasts that engage both sensuously and intellectually. Called the great irrationalist, Gaudí emerges as the most rational architect of all in an age obsessed with nature. Among the giants of the day, he alone posed the questions: what are the underlying mechanisms and forces in the natural world that guide the flow of water, the patterns of waves, the shape of bones, and how can they be applied to an architecture that shares in this organic logic?

Remodelling an ordinary apartment building now called the Casa Battló, Gaudí transformed the interiors of the *piano nobile* apartment so that walls flow gracefully into ceilings, as if tides shaped all the surfaces. Outside, sinuous stone carvings reach across the bottom three floors to combine the nautical theme with an anatomy lesson of twisted bone-like shapes, provided in turn with joints evocative of buds and flowers. The rest of the façade appears to have been sprayed with multicoloured glazed ceramic discs of varying sizes, interspersed among broken pieces of glazed tile.

The tall roof is covered with reptilian glazed tiles and is pierced by a tower crowned with a form that combines a cross with a budding plant. The imagery of the roof is echoed by the devil-like iron masks on the balcony parapets to the three floors below. But decorative initials reveal that the tower is actually dedicated to the Holy Family. The whole façade embodies a movement in two directions: from above, the devil alights on the roof and sends down his minions; from below, the world of nature with its forces of purity and goodness rises up, ending in the rounded tower, the incarnation of evil speared on the symbol of Christianity. This is a recurrent theme in Gaudí's architecture and is likely to have a politico-cultural significance; in transforming the legend of St George and the dragon, the tower represents a renascent Catalonia throwing off the yoke of an oppressive Spain.

This dynamic oppositional movement runs throughout Casa Battló, resulting in a sensuous interplay of effects. The roof tiles display a rainbow of colours that move across the spectrum from one side of the building to the other, creating an iridescent quality. Conversely, the bulbous ridge tiles, along the upper seam of the roof, work through the colours of the rainbow the other way.

Inside, a glazed-tile central courtyard is covered with a glass roof to keep out the rain, producing an ambiguity between outside and in. Again, there is a reverse colour shift. Looking up from the courtyard, one sees what appears to be a continuous wall of predominantly glazed white tiles enlivened by blue accents. But on ascending the stairs, it is clear that the wall gradually changes colour, with the blue tiles – and hence the colour saturation – becoming more dominant the higher you go. At the top, visitors find themselves in a totally different tonal world, enveloped in a progressively darkening blue environment. One feels, quite magically, high in the sky.

CASA BATTLO • BARCELONA *DETAIL*

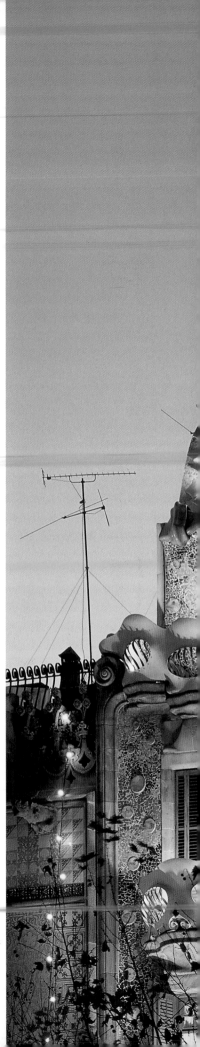

Gamble House
PASADENA, CALIFORNIA, UNITED STATES
1907–08

Charles Greene
born Brighton, Ohio 1868
died Carmel, California
1957

Henry Greene
born Brighton, Ohio 1870
died Pasadena, California
1954

The Gamble House is the Californian equivalent of Frank Lloyd Wright's Prairie Houses: low, with horizontal lines and spreading roofs to give a sense of shelter, a massive fireplace for additional psychological comfort, and integral furniture and decoration. The Greene brothers created a West Coast vernacular bungalow whose stained-wood interiors reveal the influence of the English Arts and Crafts movement.

Yet no amount of labels can convey the magic and even mystery of a home whose large and rambling size never overwhelms. The primary secret to the Gamble House's intimacy is that it is detailed like a giant piece of hand-wrought wooden furniture. Each of its timbers has rounded edges and ends; on the inside, there is extensive use of exposed ceiling beams, an elaborate living-room truss frames the fireplace inglenook and all the wood is hand-polished to a rich glow. Scattered throughout are small suspended lamps, with deeply saturated coloured glass, which emit a pale glow into the soothingly dim rooms. The crowning achievement of this ensemble of coloured glass and polished woods, and the most powerful sensory experience of the house, is in the entrance hall: the broad front wall, including the generously wide doors, comprises yellow stained glass that glows with a rich golden hue. From this luminous background a gnarled tree of leaded glass rises upwards and reaches across the panels in an Oriental style, as if the entire wall were an unfolded silk screen. These natural forms are abstracted in a geometricized fashion as small, interlocking wooden pieces that serve in lieu of balusters for the stair rail.

This Oriental influence was typical of much modern Western art in the late 19th and early 20th centuries. It recurs in the roofs and sleeping balconies, which take inspiration from Japanese timber construction, and where overlapping members create a richly textured pattern, heightened by the rows of wooden shingles covering the façades. The multiplicity of these roofs, rising to different levels but also in close proximity, as well as their gently sloping pitch and their extension beyond the boundaries of the walls, which open at several of the corners into sleeping porches, contribute strongly to the sense of an expansive but nonetheless sheltering home. The effect is similar to that of Frank Lloyd Wright's Robie House in Chicago (1909), where there is an analogous fracturing of the massing and the building envelope. Yet, whereas Wright was constrained to erect his masterpiece of the Prairie Style on a restricted urban street corner, the Greene brothers had the luxury of a suburban location with a magnificent view from the sleeping porches to the Pasadena hills.

Stepping-stone paths, also of Oriental inspiration, lead from the garden to the house, whose rear patio has a complementary flowing shape. The garden paving combines bricks and tiles in ways that not only create texture but also demarcate a progressive movement from nature into the domain of the house. Grass steps and low, stepped, planted walls enhance this effect.

GAMBLE HOUSE · *PASADENA DETAIL*

First Church of Christ Scientist

BERKELEY, CALIFORNIA,
UNITED STATES
1910

Bernard Maybeck

born New York, New York
1862
died Berkeley, California
1957

Bernard Maybeck was a leading architect in California who developed a regional vernacular style of shingle-covered bungalows. His First Church of Christ Scientist combines his vernacular interests with his Parisian Beaux-Arts training, resulting in a work of public dignity and homely charm. With its layered and cascading rooflines, the church can be seen as an institutional echo of the Gamble House (see pages 230–31).

Maybeck applied the craftsman aesthetic, the American version of the British Arts and Crafts movement, to transform industrial materials into appealing objects. For example, he used factory sash windows but inserted additional, thinner glazing bars to break down the scale into an intimately textured surface, and then filled the metal framework with small panes of handmade glass in warm flesh tones. The multiplicity of glazing bars heightens the rich texturing of the surface, and the overall effect is a modern version of the medieval stained-glass church wall.

Maybeck also took the banal industrial material of asbestos and made a crafted covering for the exterior surfaces of the church, consisting of grey asbestos panels decorated around the edges with small red diamond-shaped asbestos 'fasteners'. With such imaginative uses, Maybeck was able to tame and domesticate the new industrial materials, which at the same time lent a contemporary aura to his building.

The conscious marriage of ancient and modern is evident throughout the church. Massive concrete piers that have classical fluting and medievalized, historiated capitals (decorated with figures) are ubiquitous. Outside, a wisteria-covered pergola is supported by these freestanding piers and slightly finer, octagonal concrete posts, the

complete structure creating a striking transitional zone that wraps around the church and forms a connection with the projecting roofs and deep entrance portico. Inside, the robust piers support giant wooden trusses that span the sanctuary. The trusses have exaggerated gilded Gothic tracery. Several of these members rise gently to form an arch over the centre of the Greek-cross plan. The whole composition suggests a Gothic interpretation of a Byzantine space, realized with industrial techniques and materials, and rendered with historicizing details. Large hanging bowls of hammered steel pierced with Gothic trefoils and small, perforated cylindrical lamps contribute further medieval accents to this eclectic ensemble.

Maybeck repeatedly juxtaposed the tiny and the large. The capitals of the huge piers feature small arches carried by miniature columnettes that have straight or alternating spiral fluting. Just above, but still below the enormous brackets from which the giant trusses rise, is a row of small diamonds that recall the diamond 'fasteners' on the exterior walls. Shadows cast within the fluting of the piers to either side of the pulpit create a line of downward-facing triangular wedges. Worshippers are left to complete the ascending, upper half of the diamond in their minds as their thoughts and eyes are directed towards the heavens.

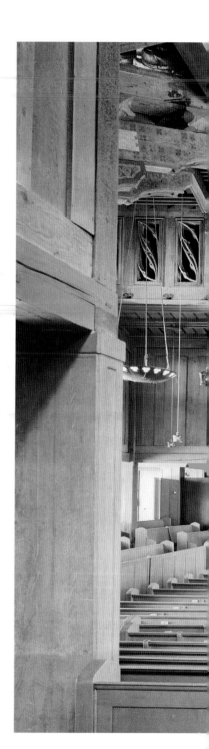

FIRST CHURCH OF CHRIST SCIENTIST • *BERKELEY INTERIOR*

233

Taliesin
SPRING GREEN, WISCONSIN, UNITED STATES
1911, 1915

Frank Lloyd Wright
born Richland Center, Wisconsin
1867
died Taliesin West, Arizona 1959

No architect in the Western world has demonstrated a deeper feeling of spiritual intimacy with the earth than Frank Lloyd Wright. After more than a decade of designing Prairie Houses that echoed the landscape of the American Midwest plains and were firmly bonded with the ground, Wright left his Chicago-area home (and family) to begin a new life with the wife of a client in the part of Wisconsin where his Welsh ancestors had settled and where he had been raised. Here he created a new home and studio called Taliesin, after the Welsh term for 'shining brow'.

Originally built in 1911, Taliesin was damaged by fire in 1914 and rebuilt by late 1915, in Wright's words, as 'a more reposeful and a finer one'. Like the architect's earlier home in Oak Park, Illinois (1889 onwards), Taliesin was a living laboratory of architectural and landscape experimentation.

Taliesin was built on a hill, not at the top but nestled into the rising land near the summit, overlooking a lush, rolling landscape of fields, hills and copses of trees. Here Wright employed all the signature elements of his Prairie Houses (*see page 230*) along with one major change: in keeping with the desire to create a building at one with nature, Wright used rough-hewn blocks of the local sedimentary stone, creating walls with dramatically jutting courses. The result is a feeling of mass and power that would find its counterpart decades later in the similar walls of Wright's other nature masterpiece, Falling Water (*see pages 266–67*). Wright made these buildings look rather like geometricized natural outcrops, rising out of the earth one stone course at a time. The desire to achieve this effect had haunted Wright since the time of his early Prairie Houses, when he had used various techniques ranging from horizontal board and batten work to brick walls with jutting courses

or deeply raked horizontal mortar joints, to impart a sense of mounting layers. Such minute attention to the detailing of mostly suburban dwellings bore fruit in the rural sites of Taliesin and Falling Water, where the architect felt free truly to adopt a rustic approach to his walls and chimney stacks.

These walls and chimneys formed the central focal point in an architecture that renders homage to the fecundity of nature. At Falling Water, nature's plenty is expressed through the waterfall over which the house sits. There, the massive chimney stack rises on – and conveys the sense of being rooted into – the jutting bedrock left exposed in the living-room floor. At Taliesin, abundance is symbolized by the hilltop around which the house wraps. A flight of stone steps built into the hillside completes the architectural pilgrimage, ascending to the gently rising summit, sheltered by two oaks that allow private communion with nature, which appears to be swelling upwards from deep within the earth. Wright's mentor, the 'lieber Meister' Louis Sullivan, had rendered Ruskin's lamp of life through soaring vertical forms (*see pages 210–11*); the apprentice, as a mature architect building his own home, created a calmer rendition of the same theme by working with the earth itself.

Cranbrook School for Boys

BLOOMFIELD HILLS,
MICHIGAN, UNITED STATES
1924–30

Eliel Saarinen
born Rantasalmi 1873
died Cranbrook Hills, Michigan
1950

A campus, Thomas Jefferson once said, should be an 'Academical Village', a prescription that he applied in the Neoclassical manner to his early-19th-century University of Virginia *(see pages 166–67)*. Yet if we wished to find a true village feeling at a campus, we would have to turn to Eliel Saarinen's Cranbrook School for Boys. From the first sight of the school, everything conspires to make you feel at home.

The low brick buildings convey nobility while also exuding a sense of warmth through their detailing, including the minute attention to the crafted texturing of the brick walls. Vistas of moderate size through portals, columns on a human scale, and repetitions of gabled rooflines all combine with a richly variegated paving pattern to create a strong sense of place making. A small tower provides one of several focal points, others including the chapel and a fountain. A sense of human proportion is so pervasive in this modest complex of buildings that it even extends to the very plan, gently inflected away from a strict alignment, like the asymmetrical features on a typical face. Here is the picturesque incarnate, a modern rendition of a vaguely medieval-feeling vernacular, yet more genuine than the recent Tudor Gothic revival of a campus such as Princeton University (1897–1903, 1906–11; various architects), where the undeniable charm issues more from a Walter Scott fantasy than from a sense of 20th-century forms.

Eliel Saarinen's Cranbrook School for Boys is contemporaneous with Walter Gropius's Bauhaus *(see pages 246–47)*. What a striking juxtaposition of two radically alternative visions of modernity! Saarinen would not give in to the rising influence of the Modernist industrial aesthetic that dominated the avant-garde of the 1920s. He followed the Cranbrook School for Boys with the adjacent campus of the Kingswood School for Girls (1929–30), where he combined his vernacular approach with hints of the new Art Deco style, whose features he had helped to create with his epoch-making Helsinki Railway Station (1904–14) in his native Finland.

As we close this chapter on Art Nouveau and its attendant interest in nature and vernacular traditions, let us indulge in a fantasy and imagine that the Museum of Modern Art in New York had been a building like those at Cranbrook rather than the 1939 Modernist edifice by Edward Durrell Stone (1902–78) and Philip Goodwin (1885–1958). In keeping with Saarinen's vision of modernity, the Symbolist windmills and abstracted treescapes by Piet Mondrian (c.1910) might have been exhibited as the height of the modernist accomplishment rather than Mondrian's 1920s complete abstractions with their black-line grids and primary colour fields, which correspond so well to the hospital and factory aesthetic of the Bauhaus. The lesson of Mondrian's semi-abstract landscapes and their comparable architectural style is the enduring importance of an artistic and metaphysical dialogue with the polarities of nature and abstraction, the matter-of-fact and its psychic energy, and human artefacts and the trace of the hand. As we enter the age of disembodied cyberspace, we must keep such issues in mind.

Modernism before 1945

Alan Powers

Almost a hundred years after it first appeared, the world is still unravelling the complexity of the type of architecture called 'Modern'. Certain lines of definition seem clear: this architecture was a reaction against the use of historical styles in favour of a new aesthetic based on the discoveries of Modern art in the first years of the 20th century and looked forward to a brave new world made possible by scientific advances.

Beguiled by the wonders of scientific invention, it believed in the capacity of new technology, including glass, steel and reinforced concrete, to achieve unprecedented forms of building which would require no 'expression' other than that of being themselves. And finally, it tended to define itself in terms of the effect it hoped to have on society, providing improved facilities for housing, recreation and work at a lower cost than before and, in a more subtle way, working to make political changes governed by new ideologies. In

practice, Modern architecture, or, as many architects involved preferred to call it, The New Building (in German, Das Neues Bauen), achieved all these things, even though it included many contradictions. Some of the great Modernist buildings were luxury villas for the rich, like the Villa Savoye by Le Corbusier or the Tugendhat House by Mies van der Rohe. It aimed for a timeless,

BELOW: Erik Gunnar Asplund, Paradise Restaurant, 1930. From the 1930 Stockholm Exhibition

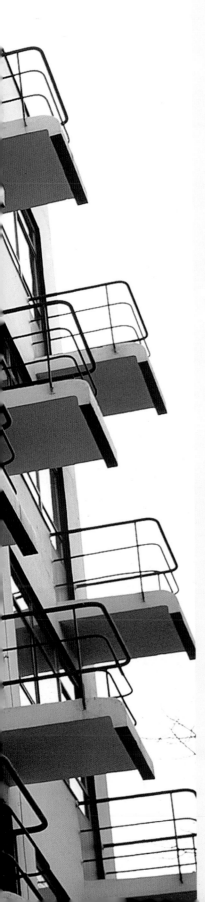

LEFT: Walter Gropius, the Bauhaus, Dessau, 1925–26. Balconies on dormitory tower

ABOVE: Walter Gropius, Fagus Factory, Alfeld, 1911–12

Platonic truth at a time, between the wars, when economics and politics were exceptionally turbulent and provided none of the conditions of stability for gradual development that this architecture required. Many people therefore see Modernism as an unfinished project.

The result of such drastic interruptions as the rise of Nazism in Germany, a power that would not tolerate Modern architecture, and the termination of the movement in Russia by Stalin in 1932, is that many Modern buildings now seem like prototypes for a future that is yet to come. Most architects in the last 50 years have looked to this brief but fertile period for inspiration, but in their own changed conditions they run the risk of creating pastiches of Modernism rather than capturing the original spirit of innovation. The political message of Modernism has been distorted, both by the way international corporations adopted the architecture of glass and steel, making it faceless and repellent, and by architects and critics who intolerantly rejected non-Modernist forms as tainted by political reaction.

The original Modernist buildings have qualities of mystery and magic that, if they were appreciated at the time of their construction, tended to be concealed beneath severely rational and materialistic explanations. For years after their construction, many Modern buildings seemed to be just obsolete and decaying masses of concrete, but even in this condition they inspire awe and affection – many of the famous examples illustrated here have been lovingly restored. Nothing replaces the experience of actually visiting these buildings, many of which are open to the public either as museums or, better still, because they still serve their original function. Their sense of scale is often deceptive but delightful; they may be larger or smaller than they look in photographs. Usually they seem more intimate and human. To stress their three-dimensional character may sound like a truism, for all structures are three-dimensional, but these buildings were particularly designed to excite a more vivid sense of space and the magic still works magificently.

Schindler-Chase House

Rudolph Schindler
born Vienna 1887
died Los Angeles 1953

T here is often something messianic about Modernism. It promises a land flowing with milk and honey, an escape from the mundane problems of life. In the Schindler-Chase House in Hollywood, these dreams almost came true. The equable climate of California was a perfect setting for the new kind of lightweight, open architecture that expressed simplicity and freedom of lifestyle.

Rudolph Schindler came to California in 1920, ending a journey that was begun in Vienna, where he studied architecture during a time of great artistic and intellectual excitement. Among his mentors there were Otto Wagner, the city architect, and Adolf Loos, one of Modernism's most original theorists (see pages 222–25). Schindler also discovered the work of Frank Lloyd Wright through the great portfolio of his designs published in Berlin in 1912. In 1914, Schindler went to work in Chicago, and three years later entered Wright's office, moving to Los Angeles to supervise work on the Aline Barnsdall ('Hollyhock') House.

In 1921–22, Schindler and his American wife Pauline built a house in King's Road, Hollywood. It was designed to be shared with the engineer Clyde Chase and his wife, with separate bedroom suites but shared living rooms and kitchen. Schindler was influenced by the open-air health practices of Dr Phillip Lovell, and the single-storey house is built for ease of movement between inside and out. Each household had a patio with an outdoor fireplace, and the rooftop included outdoor 'sleeping baskets' or porches over each entrance, which took the place of bedrooms.

The walls are built of concrete, using the 'tilt slab' principle, developed in California, of casting each slab on site and raising it into position. This imposed a modular system on the plan. The concrete is untreated both inside and outside; the wooden roof structure is similarly lacking in any kind of extra lining or decoration. The idea that in modern architecture 'what you see is what you get' has seldom been more completely realized.

The appeal of the Schindler House is not only in its unusual human story. The interior is the most striking and memorable feature. Most of the original furniture and fittings made for the house have survived and are both simple and beautiful. The light coming into the space from clerestory windows (in the upper part of the walls) and narrow slits between the concrete slabs flatters the roughness of the concrete and timber and creates a striking contrast with the reflective copper hood over the living-room fireplace. The effect is close to that of a traditional Japanese house, although it has a dynamism and improvised, experimental quality of its own.

The dream of paradise represented by the Schindler House did not work out. The shared kitchen did not run smoothly, and the 'sleeping baskets' took too optimistic a view of the warmth of the summer nights. The Schindlers divorced but Pauline lived in the house until her death in 1979, after which it was rescued by the Friends of the Schindler House and is now open to the public.

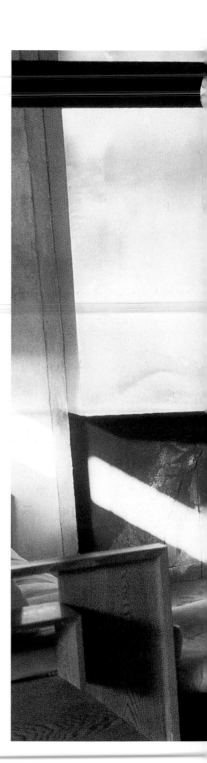

Schröder-Schräder House

UTRECHT, THE NETHERLANDS
1924

Gerrit Thomas Rietveld

born Utrecht 1888
died Utrecht 1964

Certain houses and interiors from the 1920s and 1930s are still astonishingly unconventional in ways that no subsequent efforts have surpassed. One of these is a small house in a suburb of Utrecht, built in 1924 for a widow and her children in the difficult but hopeful years after the First World War. Mrs Truus Schröder-Schräder gave the credit for the design of her house to Gerrit Rietveld, but she was involved in its conception and lived there until her death in 1984 (it is now open to the public).

The house originally stood overlooking open country at the edge of the town, attached to the end of a terrace of conventional brick houses. The exterior is composed of horizontal and vertical lines and planes, using a palette of white, grey, black and primary colours. It is a tiny object, even in a country notable for its intimate scale, but it has an alluring and even slightly cheeky quality. A short path leads to the front door and a small dark hallway; the main living floor is above. This upper floor is one continuous space, going around the stairway which forms a cubicle-like box in the centre. This openness, with windows on three sides, is one of the intended effects of the house, but the space can also be divided with hinged and folding wooden partitions to make three or four separate rooms. The small space is full of controlled incident, with the same primary colours as the exterior applied to surfaces of furniture – all designed by Rietveld, including his famous red, blue and yellow chair (1923).

There are few examples of Modern interior design where appearance and function are so well matched. The materials are simple and inexpensive, and the furniture and fittings, which are an integral part of the space, are similarly of the simplest kind of jointed construction and

painted finish. The result is an artistic unity that also expresses and serves a concept of an improved lifestyle, uncluttered by status objects or sentimental associations. The design is directed towards the outside world, through the broad windows, and so to the simple pleasures of life.

This attempt to strip away unnecessary layers and get down to a more basic reality was typical of Modernism as a whole but most strongly found in the Netherlands, where it made a continuity with older religious and moral beliefs. What is new and delightful in the Schröder-Schräder House is the sense of fun that comes with it, the sliding walls that make and unmake rooms, the bright colours. It is more like a seaside holiday than everyday life. The house was designed for young children, and Rietveld continued to make special furniture and equipment for children.

Rietveld began his career as a furniture designer, then devised shop interiors, but this house was his first building. He was attached to the movement named after the magazine *De Stijl* (The Style), first published in 1917, which linked the abstract paintings of Mondrian with sculpture and design. The Schröder-Schräder House is the only building which fully illustrates the principles of this influential movement.

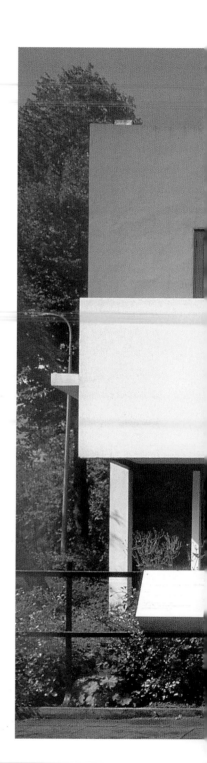

SCHRODER-SCHRADER HOUSE • UTRECHT

Grossseidlung Britz

BERLIN, GERMANY
1925–31

Bruno Taut

born Königsberg
(now Kaliningrad) 1880
died Istanbul 1938

A principle of Modern architecture was that it should make the benefits of new technology and artistic vision available to people of all classes, not only those who could afford one-off houses. Increasing industrialization in Europe in the late 19th century had only led to overcrowded cities and barrack-like housing blocks. Before the First World War, architects and social thinkers were impressed by the English Garden City Movement which showed how efficient transport let workers live close to the city with the advantages of the countryside – a garden to grow vegetables and recreational space.

The Germans were among those most impressed by Garden Cities. The architect Bruno Taut built housing in Berlin suburbs before 1914 in the simplified classical style popular at the time. Part visionary thinker and part practical builder, he became an adviser to the GEHAG housing association in Berlin. This was formed from existing smaller associations in 1924 when, following defeat in the First World War and a period of rampant inflation, Germany was able to begin constructing a new future.

Taut was thus responsible for 10,000 new dwellings in Berlin in 1924–32, concentrated in a few large housing estates. Despite their size, these developments are amazingly human in feeling. The Grossseidlung Britz (or 'Big housing estate at Britz') lies to the southeast of the city. The buildings consist mostly of three-storey blocks of flats, some of which have pitched roofs and look relatively traditional. Behind these are terraces of single-family houses with long gardens, not unlike the terrace houses of London and other English cities. The housing is composed to make interesting street pictures, with occasional curves and set-backs. The centre of the estate is marked by a great curved formation of housing known as the Hufeisen (Horseshoe), surrounding a park and lake and designed by Taut as a continuous terrace, similar in its grandeur and relationship to nature to the terraces of a hundred years earlier in Regent's Park, London by John Nash. The Hufeisen provides a landmark and orientation point and many of the roads lead towards it; the shops for the estate were situated on the main road in front and form a ceremonial gateway.

In the 1980s the original colours designed by Taut were restored to the exteriors, helping to create an effect of contrast against the greenery of the gardens and roadside trees. The walls are subdued shades of red, blue and yellow, and in one area dusty blue balconies are set against an apricot background. Window frames and doors are picked out in brighter colours. Taut felt that these colours were not just decoration – they would transform people's lives. As the architect wrote in 1931, 'Colour has the capacity to diminish or augment the distance between housing, to influence the proportion of buildings by making them appear larger or smaller, and to place them in relationship with nature and other elements. One must work with colour in a logical manner, as if it were another material.'

GROSSSEIDLUNG · BERLIN *AERIAL VIEW*

The Bauhaus
DESSAU, GERMANY
1925–26

Walter Gropius
born Berlin 1883
died Boston, Massachusetts 1969

Walter Gropius, a key figure of Modern architecture, was as much concerned with education as design. These interests met with the construction of the Bauhaus (House of Building) as a purpose-built home for the school Gropius created in Weimar in 1919. By the mid-1920s, the school had a reputation for its innovative curriculum, uniting fine art, craft, design and, from 1926, architecture, and was producing versatile designers with a creative attitude to materials and abstract forms. The new building gave physical expression to the interdisciplinary ethos of the institution.

The Bauhaus stands to the south of the city centre in Dessau in what was originally open ground. It included new premises for an existing technical school, a workshop block, lecture theatre, dining hall, student dormitory and administrative offices, the last housed in the bridge that forms one of the most arresting features of the design. The resulting plan is a pinwheel, with arms going off in different directions, centred on the main entrance. It is a beautifully scaled building, impressive without being overly dominant, and has generous stairs and circulation spaces. As in much of Gropius's work, it recalls the classical and patrician values of the 18th century, translated into a democratic and technologically updated form. Gropius created a neutral but sympathetic background for human activity and, unlike many Modern buildings which look their best when empty, the Bauhaus needs people and activity. The idea of architectural reticence was also a political principle, avoiding monumentality and an individual viewpoint. This can produce dull buildings, but the Bauhaus shows the concept at a time of urgency and freshness.

The glazed walls of the workshop block, carried right around a corner and revealing the reinforced concrete structure of columns and floor slabs, are the most memorable aspect of the Bauhaus. The balconies on the dormitory tower proved equally photogenic, and there are many pictures of students hanging precariously off them.

The building suffered some disfiguring alterations under the Nazi regime following the forced closure of the school in 1932 and its short-lived move to Berlin. After the war, Dessau became part of East Germany, but the building was well maintained and features such as the plain sans serif lettering, typical of the Bauhaus typographic style, were restored.

Gropius's purpose was to humanize technology. He was a charismatic and influential leader, but a closer inspection of his life shows interesting contradictions between the rational and the romantic sides of his personality, the latter being prominent in his tempestuous affair with Alma Mahler, the wife of the composer. He had no skill in drawing, but a tremendous ability to absorb information from building plans. Gropius left Germany in 1934 and, after a period in England, settled in the United States and became Head of the Graduate School of Design at Harvard. The Bauhaus building remains the greatest monument to his work as a teacher and as an architect.

Tughendhat House

BRNO, CZECH REPUBLIC
1928–30

Ludwig Mies van der Rohe
born Aachen 1886
died Chicago 1969

Modern architecture stretched across central Europe before the rise of Hitler. Brno was the historic capital of Moravia, which became part of Czechoslovakia after the First World War. The town had a lively school of Modern architects, but, in 1928, Fritz and Grete Tughendhat chose the German architect Ludwig Mies van der Rohe to build them a house. They admired the simplicity and directness of his work.

The couple wanted to shed the trappings of bourgeois existence. Grete recalled, 'I always wanted a Modern house with generous spaces and clear, simple forms. My husband for his own part retained a horror of the doilies and knickknacks that overflowed every room of the houses of his childhood.' Simple though it looks, their house is undoubtedly a luxury dwelling, showing how Modern architecture when properly built is never a cheap substitute for traditional styles.

The house is on the top of a steep hill. Entered from the back, it presents a single storey to the road but drops down two further levels to a sloping garden, with stepped terraces at the sides which give the house an anchorage in the hillside. From below, the dominant impression is of a single continuous line of windows. These belong to the large living room which is the most famous feature of the house.

The idea of open-plan living seems simple enough, but it is actually rather difficult to make a large domestic space into a comfortable place to sit, eat or work. The solution was to provide screen walls that made divisions without completely enclosing any of the spaces. One of these walls is a pinkish marble, with the grain 'book matched' so that a symmetrical pattern is formed from two faces of a single block, an ancient technique found in Roman and Byzantine architecture. The high polish reflects the light and so at certain angles solidity is dissolved. The cross-shaped columns supporting the roof and upper storey are steel, finished with chrome, so that these too are highly reflective and play optical tricks.

Coming into the room from the entrance hall above, there is an oblique view to the town, over tree tops. The marble wall acts as a baffle to the right, and to the left a curved wall of veneered wood conceals the dining area. As with most of the best Modern buildings, the absolute sense of rightness of scale in relation to the context is breathtaking. The room oscillates between feelings of large and small. And the technical achievement is remarkable, with the use of huge, and sliding, sheets of glass. No detail is left to chance, and, now restored and freed from Communist-imposed isolation, the building is a direct, and not just photographic, inspiration to architects.

Mies was the third and final director of the Bauhaus from 1930 to 1932, against a background of the rise of Nazism. He moved to the United States in 1937 and settled in Chicago, where he became a successful practitioner as well as a revered teacher (see pages 270–71). Tall and laconic, he would come to life around midnight after much brandy and many cigars.

TUGHENDHAT HOUSE • BRNO

Maison de Verre
PARIS, FRANCE
1928–32

Pierre Chareau
born Le Havre 1883
died New York 1950

Bernard Bijvoet
born Amsterdam 1889
died Haarlem 1979

Tucked out of sight in the smart 7th arrondissement of Paris, the Maison de Verre remained relatively unknown for at least 30 years after its completion and does not figure in many of the standard histories of Modern architecture. But since the 1960s it has become for many the most important Modern building of the interwar period and the principal precursor of the High Tech style of the late 20th century.

The Maison de Verre (House of Glass) was designed by Pierre Chareau in collaboration with the Dutch architect Bernard Bijvoet for Dr Jean Dalsace and his wife Annie. The couple already had an apartment designed in 1919 by Chareau, who was more of a furniture and interior designer than an architect, having trained with the English firm of Waring and Gillow at their Paris workshops. The Maison de Verre was a new departure for all concerned. Mme Dalsace's father bought the property and the plan was to build a new structure, but there was an elderly tenant on the top floor who exercised her right to remain. Chareau therefore devised a new building to be inserted into the space beneath the recalcitrant resident, leaving her part of the structure undisturbed.

The design of the building was influenced by several requirements. The ground floor was used by Dr Dalsace for his medical practice, so visitors to the family ascended a broad, open-tread staircase inside a glass stairwell and arrived in a magnificent double-height living space, intended for musical parties. Mme Dalsace would stand at the head of these stairs to receive her guests, silhouetted against the light. A retractable stair led to the bedrooms above. The clients wanted plenty of light but Chareau felt that the effect of large areas of plate glass would be ugly so he used

'Nevada' lenses (glass bricks), a relatively new product in France at the time. The front façade is composed of panels of 24 blocks each, held in a grid of steel, with a window-cleaning ladder running along a track, while the garden elevation has sections of clear glass mixed with glass blocks. Small hinged panels provided ventilation.

Inside, there is a remarkable sense of space, and the dislocated and mysterious quality that comes from seeing light coming in without being able to see out. Floodlights produced a similar effect at night. The practical qualities of the house as a 'machine for living in' are emphasized almost to excess, with doors moving on tracks, panels opening on hinges and built-in furniture suspended from the ceiling. The floors are laid with specially made thick white rubber tiles with a grid of studs, the first of their kind, much imitated in later years. The materials, including steel, bronze and aluminium, are displayed with pride. The principal craftsman, Louis Dalbert, played a major role in bringing Chareau's scheme to completion – and so the paradox that the perfection of machine art required a high level of traditional craft skill. The other paradox is that the machine-like quality of such design, often feared as dehumanizing, acquired pathos with the passage of time, like a plan for a future world that never happened.

MAISON DE VERRE • PARIS *STUDY*

Rusakov Club
MOSCOW, RUSSIA
1927–28

Konstantin Melnikov
born Moscow 1890
died Moscow 1974

O n one of the main approach roads into Moscow from the northeast stands the most dramatic of several workers' clubs which were typical of architecture in the newly created Soviet Union in the 1920s. Designed by Konstantin Melnikov, it was built for the Union of Municipal Employees in 1927–28, at a moment when Russian Modernism was able to realize some of the dreams that had sprung into existence with the revolution of 1917 but had been hindered by a lack of resources.

Melnikov designed the Soviet Pavilion at the Paris Exhibition of 1925, an ingenious building in its form and construction which showed the world how the revolutionary politics of Russia had produced an architecture to match, which also had personality and charm. In 1927–29, he designed an extraordinary cylindrical house for himself in Moscow where he continued to live, enjoying a revival of fame in his later years.

The Rusakov Club consists largely of a theatre with a 1,200-seat auditorium. The three dramatic projections on the street façade contain the upper galleries of the auditorium, divided by stairtowers, and originally carried inscriptions like billboards. These galleries can also be divided off from the main auditorium and used separately. The projections represent a kind of legible function that is a primary characteristic of architecture, usually overlaid and confused during periods of cultural stability, and then retrieved and reinterpreted at times of revolution. (Something similar happened to architectural form during the French Revolution, when architects sought to discover an underlying reality in the familiar language of classicism.)

It was exactly this type of dramatization and clarity of function that was distinctive to Russian Modernism, or Constructivism. Geometry, which

was seen as an objective and scientific foundation for architectural culture, took on an almost mystical significance as it appeared to defy gravity and the normal conventions of load and support. If it is true to say that most Modernist buildings aspire to a condition of weightlessness, then the Russian examples worked hardest to become airborne, inventing in the process many original architectural forms.

Constructivism was in many ways the most radical architectural movement of the 1920s and immediately influenced the avant-garde in several countries. Le Corbusier in particular was inspired by its fragmentation of building volume, while Gropius's Bauhaus (see pages 246–47) probably owes its asymmetrical dynamism to Russian influence. The design of public housing in Europe has been permanently affected by the awesome scale of blocks like the Narkomfin flats in Moscow, 1928–29, by Moisei Ginzburg (1893–1946). But in 1932, Stalin's policy of Socialist Realism led to a long-lasting return to architectural conservatism.

The projecting chamfered shapes on the façade of the Rusakov Club inspired James Stirling (1926–92) and James Gowan (born 1923) in the design of their famous Engineering Faculty Building at Leicester University, Great Britain, in 1959.

RUSAKOV CLUB • MOSCOW

Paimio Sanatorium
PAIMIO, FINLAND
1929–33

Alvar Aalto
born Kuortane 1898
died Helsinki 1976

The prevalence of tuberculosis in the early 20th century is hard to conceive. A disease that did not respect class barriers, its causes were little understood and cures, prior to antibiotics, were environmental rather than strictly medical. In 1901 fresh air and sunlight were demonstrated to have a positive effect – at the very time when the hygienic, structural clarity of Modernist architecture swept away Art Nouveau, with its unhealthy interest in the soft organic insides of things.

The architectural type of the sanatorium, which specialized in long-stay patients with tuberculosis, was established in the years before the First World War. Long tiered ward-blocks were angled towards the sun, all with deep balconies and fold-back windows so that beds could be pushed out or the fresh air let in. Certain key aspects of Modern architecture – large windows and dominant horizontal lines – were therefore established independently of architectural theory.

Among the sanatoria designed between the wars, Paimio has pride of place for the beauty of its setting in pine woods and for its thin-profiled ward-block, standing like a crisp wafer of concrete. But there is more to its importance than striking architectural imagery against a pretty background. Alvar Aalto felt that the patients might want to socialize, so he made a series of balconies forming a discrete element at the end of the ward-wing, facing south, while the rooms themselves are angled towards the rising sun. In the original design this block was twice as long and half as high as in the actual building; the revision adds compactness, drama and better rooftop views.

Aalto was born in Finland and, despite an international career, drew his inspiration from Finnish mythology, with its worship of nature. He created novel building forms, responding to a sense of place and occasion, which have had a lasting influence on other architects.

The plan of Paimio is like the spread fingers of a hand, with staff and administration blocks branching off. The arrangement allows for two welcoming arms to extend into a three-sided courtyard at the entrance, while the front door is covered by a projecting concrete canopy of a whimsically wavy shape. The chimney of the boilerhouse was given a specially characterful expression. Such apparent freedom of design was deftly calculated. The interiors are not elaborate, but the yellow stairs and blue skirtings give an air of subdued jollity. Outside, sun blinds are in green and orange on the dining-hall block. At this time Aalto had just begun to design the bent plywood furniture for which he is still well known, and he made a special reclining chair for the patients of Paimio which was supposed to assist in the right kind of breathing.

So often, 'Functionalist' architecture in the 1920s ignored or drastically reinvented the needs of the human being. Aalto remained sensitive, above all, to the needs of the sanatorium's patients, and even if not all of his ideas worked in practice, his compassion was evident and sincere.

Villa Savoye
POISSY, FRANCE
1929–31

Le Corbusier (Charles-Edouard Jeanneret)
born La Chaux-de-Fonds 1887
died Rocquebrune-Cap-Martin 1965

If one work had to stand for the whole of Modern architecture it would probably be the Villa Savoye. In some ways this would be quite unrepresentative, since this luxury villa, serving no great social or industrial function, used technology only as a way to make an image of architecture as fragile as a film set. Yet on aesthetic grounds it surpasses most other buildings of its type and has become a Modernist pilgrimage site.

The villa came at the end of a series of similar projects by Le Corbusier. In it he believed he had found a synthesis between the severe classic grid that is one of the inspirations of Modernism, and a free-flowing romantic style which represented the other aspect of his complex personality. The villa has been compared to Palladio's Villa Rotonda at Vicenza (1565–67). Both are designed to respond to a location with views on all four sides, with the main living accommodation raised off the ground. Le Corbusier was devoted to the past but believed he could make poetry out of the conditions of modern life. While the Villa Savoye is intended to evoke Virgilian simplicity, its design idea begins with the car journey of 30 km (19 miles) from Paris which finishes with a scrunch of gravel under the 'piloti' – the concrete columns which support the upper floor, creating a porte cochère – as the car follows the tight curve of the entrance hall.

Inside, a light but somewhat disorientating space opens up. Straight ahead is a ramp which leads away into space; to its left, a wash basin stands between the pillars, practical but also a little dream-like; a spiral staircase rises on the left, providing 'backstairs' access. Ascending the ramp, one turns a corner and looks out to the left over a large roof terrace, enclosed by the same pure square of wall that defines the shape of the whole villa; a table fixed by the perimeter encourages a contemplative pause. The single main living room of the villa is seen through floor-to-ceiling sliding glass doors, and beyond, a further strip of window opens onto another view. Also on this floor is the main bedroom with its open-plan bathroom, which includes a built-in blue-tiled recliner where Madame Savoye could rest after taking exercise. Further mystery remains, however, for the ramp continues upwards from the roof terrace to a higher level, where curved walls make a sky-garden sun trap, concealing the view apart from a window opening. This superstructure represents the remains of an early scheme for the house that would have placed madame's bed meaningfully at the furthest point on the *promenade architecturale* (architectural promenade) that began in Paris and continued upwards from the door of the villa.

Like many Modernist buildings, the Villa Savoye was only partly an attempt to satisfy the needs of a client. It was an experiment in the poetic potential of movement that Le Corbusier hoped to implement on a grander scale in public buildings. He dreamed the future on a vast scale, realizing some of his ambitions in the 1950s in the government buildings at Chandigarh, the new capital of the Punjab in India. However, there remains a dichotomy between the inspiration of his built work and the frequently damaging impact of his theoretical ideas in the hands of imitators.

Pavillon Suisse
PARIS, FRANCE
1930–32

Le Corbusier (Charles-Edouard Jeanneret)
born La Chaux-de-Fonds 1887
died Rocquebrune-Cap-Martin 1965

The Cité Universitaire in Paris is a collection of student hostels commissioned by different countries. The Swiss hostel, the Pavillon Suisse, was designed by Le Corbusier and his cousin and partner, Pierre Jeanneret (1896–1966). Although resident in Paris, both architects were of Swiss nationality, but the commissioning body knew they would not get a building in the style of a Swiss chalet, as some wanted.

The architects had to contend with significant problems: a tight budget and a site with large underground caves which required the use of piles (sunken supports) driven deep into the ground to carry the four-storey residential block, itself raised off the ground by a whole storey. The structure above ground level was constructed on a steel frame, with artificial stone cladding on the sides and ends. A blank curved wall stands forward from the main block, containing the stairs and shared facilities, while beneath it a larger, single-storey building houses the entrance and common room. All seems simple and obvious, but each element represents a new departure in Le Corbusier's design vocabulary, from the wall of rough stone which greets the visitor, to the sculptured form of the piloti, or supports, beneath the slab block of rooms, which left the ground-floor level open. As is typical of Le Corbusier's buildings, the roof terrace was given a different treatment, with a solarium for the residents and two staff flats with terraces.

As was so often the case, Le Corbusier created as many practical difficulties with his design as he solved, notably in the excessive heat generated by the south-facing, all-glass façade which had to be modified. Nonetheless, the Pavillon Suisse was one of the most inspirational buildings for architects in the 1930s and long

afterwards, partly, perhaps, because it was easy to visit, unlike some other key Modernist works. While earlier Modernist buildings, including Le Corbusier's own, tended to suggest a world of alien machinery, the Pavillon Suisse was romantic in its forms and materials, without ceasing to be practical in its planning. The common room was decorated with photographic enlargements of biological forms, giving the clue to a new phase in Le Corbusier's understanding and appreciation of nature, which is manifested in the dialogue, on the plan, between the straight and curved walls. These were later replaced by Le Corbusier's own murals. The use of building materials on the outside suggests the collages made by Cubist painters some 20 years earlier.

Most of the slab blocks with connected podium buildings that have been derived from the Pavillon Suisse lack the building's specific relationship to its site, which enjoyed an open outlook to the south over the students' playing fields. The space beneath the piloti frames the distant view, while the slab block overhead is small enough to prevent the covered space becoming dark and dismal.

Le Corbusier had first set out his blueprint for the future in *Vers une architecture* (1923, *Towards a New Architecture*). The Pavillon Suisse reflects the growing complexity of his vision.

PAVILLON SUISSE • PARIS

City Hall Extension
GOTHENBURG, SWEDEN
1934–37

Erik Gunnar Asplund
born Stockholm 1885
died Stockholm 1940

In the 1920s, most Modern architects believed that their mission was to change the world by creating forms that were entirely new. By the 1930s, Modern architecture was often more mature and worldly-wise, more relaxed and less dogmatic. In 1913 Swedish architect Erik Gunnar Asplund won a competition to extend the 17th-century Baroque town hall in Gothenburg, Sweden's main western-facing port. This was at the beginning of his career, but the work was only completed shortly before Asplund's death – giving him plenty of time to think and change his mind.

The first design involved a complete rebuilding of the original structure, to create a unified brick façade. By the 1920s, Asplund was involved in a revival of Neoclassicism and a series of alterations to the project reflect this phase of his career. Then in 1929–30 he, like many other leading Swedish architects, felt a compelling urge to adopt the Modern style which was already well established in Germany, The Netherlands, Czechoslovakia and elsewhere in northern Europe. Asplund managed to make it his own, retaining in his Modern work a sense of highly finished and considered detail, wit and a feeling of architectural occasion.

When work finally began on the extension in 1934, Asplund relished the opportunity to have a whole wall of windows facing the internal courtyard and flooding light into what, in an earlier scheme, seemed like a tomb-like classical atrium. Although the extension contains two magistrates' courts on the upper floor, it would be hard to imagine a less authoritarian mood. The staircase ascending to the courts almost floats its way up a gradual ascent, while the lift rises in a glass lift-shaft, one of the first of its kind. Another stairway curves gracefully up at the far end of the atrium, disappearing through the ceiling to reach the offices above.

The waiting area on the broad balcony overlooking the courtyard has low-slung wicker chairs, indoor plants and a specially woven rug, based on 'paragraph' signs from documents. The lights, which hang on slender wires, were also specifically commissioned, and even the drinking-water fountain is a unique object. Inside the curved walls of the courtrooms the atmosphere is orderly but not intimidating, with seats of three different kinds designed for the building.

Externally, Asplund kept changing his mind about how to respond to the building he was adding to. Having tried virtually every variation in a classical style, he finished with a simplified square grid, with the windows pushed to the edges in order to maintain a Modernist sense of dynamism. The solution is an unhappy compromise, showing how, in spite of certain points of contact, the architectural language of Modernism cannot be merged with that of classicism and has greater difficulty creating simple but satisfying façades for buildings. Internally, however, there is no contest and Asplund's light-filled spaces epitomize the potential for architecture to change society for the better, which was one of Modernism's most important beliefs and the hardest to achieve.

CITY HALL EXTENSION • GOTHENBURG *ATRIUM*

Casa del Fascio

COMO, ITALY

1932–36

Giuseppe Terragni

born Meda 1904

died Como 1943

This austere building, like a white grid extended around four sides of a square, is the most representative example of Modern architecture in Italy between the wars. This was the period of Mussolini's rise to power and his increasingly dominant position as a dictator. Unlike the Nazis in Germany, the Italian Fascists did not prohibit the adoption of Modern architecture, and so the young architect Giuseppe Terragni was proud to be asked to design a headquarters for the party in his home town of Como, a historic city beautifully sited beside a lake ringed with mountains.

Terragni believed, along with many other patriots, that Fascism would offer a better future for Italy, unencumbered by the corruption and bureaucracy associated with the old Liberal regime. In the end their hopes were dashed, but the Casa del Fascio represents an aspiration to accessibility and transparency in local administration which remains a valid social ideal. As Terragni wrote, 'Here is the Mussolinian concept that Fascism is a glasshouse into which everyone can peer, giving rise to the architectural interpretation that is the complement of that metaphor; no encumbrance...no obstacle, between the political hierarchy and the people.'

Much of the volume of the building is occupied by a central atrium, reached through rows of glass doors which could be opened automatically and simultaneously, to allow a crowd of the faithful to run out into the piazza. Around the atrium are committee rooms and offices, reached from the surrounding galleries, like many traditional Italian urban buildings. The Casa del Fascio also uses claddings of marble and travertine to cover its concrete frame, giving the geometric grids of its façades a quality of sharp definition in the light. These grids follow a proportional system of classical derivation, but the orderliness of the composition is relieved by unexpected variations in rooms and their placement so that the dominant Rationalism (preferred in Italy as a description for Modernism) never becomes obsessive.

Terragni introduced Modern architecture into Italy in 1927 with a group of friends. They were inspired by the works of Le Corbusier and Walter Gropius, among others, but also felt a sense of cultural continuity with their Italian roots, which is apparent in this, Terragni's most famous building, and has caused it to grow in reputation in later years. The complex undercurrents in Rationalism, including the conflict between technological modernity and a culture which valued tradition and national identity, give this building and some of its contemporaries a special kind of emotional charge.

Terragni only became disillusioned with Fascism after the war had begun, but then the shock probably caused his early death. His later projects expand the dimension of meaning in Modern architecture, which was missing from most of the more overtly classical buildings which Mussolini favoured as he tried to revive the Roman Empire. These possibilities of expression without explicit iconography have inspired later architects, such as the American Peter Eisenman (born 1932).

CASA DEL FASCIO • COMO

**De La Warr
Pavilion**
BEXHILL-ON-SEA,
GREAT BRITAIN
1934–35

Eric Mendelsohn
born Allenstein 1887
died San Francisco,
California 1953

Serge Chermayeff
born Grozny 1900
died Cape Cod,
Massachusetts 1996

Modern architecture can appear as a stern and forbidding way of viewing the world, with its veto on ornament and decoration and its private language of abstract form. British people in the 1930s could appreciate it as a kind of medicine for a sick society, but were only given occasional opportunities to appreciate its tonic qualities. The De La Warr Pavilion was just such a balm.

The De La Warr Pavilion at Bexhill-on-Sea, a largely Victorian resort on the south coast, was one of the most popular and successful examples of a Modern public building of the 1930s intended for pleasure and recreation. It was a brave decision by the town council to run a competition for a new theatre and restaurant complex in 1933, just as Britain was emerging from the Depression, and to keep to the assessor's decision to build the design by the famous German architect Eric Mendelsohn (whose birthplace is now in Poland). Mendelsohn had escaped from Nazi Germany and formed a partnership with Serge Chermayeff, a younger designer of Russian origin but British nationality.

The pavilion has a simple plan, based around an entrance from the land side which leads directly to a great spiral staircase. Going up the broad treads with their gentle ascent, it is hard to know whether to look out to the sea and sky or inwards to enjoy the architectural effect of the uncoiling spiral. This is the dramatic moment of the building and the principal feature of the south-facing seaward side of the building. To the left, looking from the sea, there is a large, almost windowless box which contains the theatre with its flytower and backstage access. To the right, two storeys extend in a long ribbon with balconies and continuous windows. The ground floor was the original restaurant and the upper floor the public library.

Mendelsohn was interested in dynamic composition in architecture and liked to listen to certain pieces of music (often J.S. Bach's Brandenburg Concertos) over and over again when working on his design sketches. Chermayeff's role was largely in the interior fitting-out, which survives best inside the theatre, an elegant interior with its wooden acoustic ceiling pierced with circular holes and rows of unstuffy canvas-seated chairs. He also commissioned a mural-scale painting of shells and nautical paraphernalia from the artist Edward Wadsworth, which originally hung at the far end of the restaurant next to the dance floor and is still a prized possession inside the building.

The critic and historian John Summerson wrote at the time of its opening that 'Two qualities may be held to account for [its] success. One is the "openness" of the building; one has a sense of walking within enclosed space rather than within a structure. The other is the exquisite finish of the design, so far as structural details and equipment are concerned.' These are qualities which postwar Modern architecture often lacked but which have once more become desired.

The De La Warr Pavilion was altered inside in the postwar years but a programme of restoration and careful adaptation began in the 1990s, an expression of local pride in a building which has helped to put Bexhill on the cultural map.

DE LA WARR PAVILION • BEXHILL-ON-SEA

Falling Water

BEAR RUN, PENNSYLVANIA, UNITED STATES
1934–37

Frank Lloyd Wright

born Richland Center, Wisconsin 1867
died Taliesin West, Arizona 1959

Modern architecture in its 'classic' period between the wars is full of paradoxes. In some ways, it appears as the antithesis of nature with its exclusion of ornament and its celebration of machinery. At least half the time it promoted the idea of everyday life in the modern city, but the other half is about escape, fantasy, holiday and the simple life in contact with nature.

Falling Water, designed by Frank Lloyd Wright at the beginning of the third phase of his career, is a prime example of the second category. The client, Edgar Kaufmann, ran a department store in Pittsburgh where Wright made him an office in 1937, with its own furniture (now in the Victoria and Albert Museum, London). Kaufmann owned an extensive wilderness property at Bear Run, with a campsite for his employees. He and his family liked to sit on a particular rock in the middle of the stream above a waterfall, and after visiting the site Wright decided that the house should stand on this very spot. Where other architects might have detracted from the wildness of the setting with their designs, Wright harmonized with it, showing the depth of his understanding of the interaction between man and nature. Kaufmann's son wrote, 'When Wright came to the site he appreciated the powerful sound of the falls, the vitality of the young forest, the dramatic rock ledges and boulders: these were elements to be interwoven with the serenely soaring spaces of his structure. But Wright's insight penetrated more deeply. He understood that people were creatures of nature, hence an architecture that conformed to nature would conform to what was basic in people.'

This belief, widely expressed in American 19th-century thought, is at odds with the sense of alienation in our own time which requires that

nature and culture exist in separate spheres, if it allows nature any separate form of existence at all. Wright's way of achieving interaction included the use of local stone for the giant central chimney stack, the softening of the edges of his concrete cantilevered balconies, and the eruption of the natural rock in front of the main fireplace of the large open-plan living room. While the view of the house up the gorge is one of the famous images of Modern architecture, the design is equally about the experience of views out, framing and selecting details from the woodlands around. As Edgar Kaufmann Junior said, 'Sociability and privacy are both available, as are the comforts of home and the adventures of the seasons. So people are cosseted into relaxing, into exploring the enjoyment of life refreshed in nature.'

Falling Water, which is open to the public, was important in launching Wright on the immensely fertile final phase of his long career, his many commissions including the Solomon R. Guggenheim Museum, New York (1942–60). His work retained its formal inventiveness in the use of space and relationship to site, while coming into tune with the 1950s' taste for colour and decoration. This creative freedom and spontaneity remained undiminished; as Wright said to an audience of students in London in 1951, 'I don't design any more, I just shake 'em out of my sleeve.'

Johnson Wax Factory

RACINE, WISCONSIN, UNITED STATES
1936–50

Frank Lloyd Wright
born Richland Center, Wisconsin 1867
died Taliesin West, Arizona 1959

Frank Lloyd Wright is sometimes dismissed as an impractical dreamer, however magnificent the imagery of his architecture. At least half a generation older than most of the famous Modern architects working between the wars, his designs embody a romanticism which he believed was grounded in the nature of the universe. The administration building (1936–39) and laboratories (1943–50) for S.C. Johnson and Son (still makers of cleaning products) showed how the activity of going to work could be made into something mysterious and exciting through imaginative architecture.

The site, in the small industrial town of Racine, north of Chicago, is unappealing, so Wright designed a building that turns in on itself, ignoring the views outside. Spread over a large area, his group of structures is like a small city, crowned by the tower housing laboratories. Although never easy to use, the tower justifies itself as a symbolic marker. The main administration building, with its bands of bright red brick and ribbons of glazing, looks like a fortress or piece of machinery, but is welcoming rather than threatening. The building opens, on a formal, symmetrical axis, from a covered driveway into a foyer, and then into the double-height 'great workroom'. Here managers and secretaries worked in an open-plan space, ringed by a gallery, in a forest of concrete columns.

These columns create the identity of the Johnson building. They were one of Wright's most practically and aesthetically successful translations of natural form into architecture. He called them 'dendriform' (tree-like), and with their broad crowning pads, based on the capabilities of reinforced concrete, they create a sense of space different to classical columns. As Wright said in 1939, 'There is no feeling of weight when you are inside, mass has vanished, no sense of being enclosed either as you have not been cut off from outdoor light or a sense of sky anywhere.' The workroom has been likened to being underwater, looking up to the surface with its lily pads, for the spaces between the columns are the main source of light, diffused through Wright's invention of glass tubes laid in formation like a flattened groin vault.

The architectural language of curved corners extends throughout the building and into the desks and chairs that Wright designed specially for the offices. The colour scheme is all in warm russets and browns, with cream paint for the columns, so that it is both restful and stimulating, counteracting the underwater impression with what Wright felt were the typical colours of the Midwest.

One remarkable aspect of the Johnson building is the scale. It looks much bigger in photographs than it is in real life, so that the thrill of the architecture is balanced by an almost domestic accessibility. The columns, for example, rise from a circular brass shoe that is hardly more than a hand's breadth across – a detail that gives to Modern architecture the kind of relationship that classicism has to the human body, even though many of the classical presumptions about load and support are turned upside down.

JOHNSON WAX FACTORY • RACINE

Modernism after 1945

Peter Blundell Jones

In terms of architecture, the period 1945–90 can be divided into two halves. Before 1970 a widespread Modernist orthodoxy prevailed, known as the International Style. Believed by architects, taught in architectural schools and widely accepted by the public, it proposed a break with history and tradition.

Scientifically based and universal in application, the new architecture was supposed to mark the dawn of the technological age. Embracing the machine, it was to signify nothing more than its own identity and means of production. It began optimistically, but by the end of the 1960s had become tired and bureaucratic. The idea of form following function had become thoughtless utilitarianism and only bare construction was expressed. Prefabricated system building swept the world, but seldom proved cheaper than traditional methods and made all places alike. Around 1970 a reaction began to emerge. The oppressive quality of large mechanized developments and the destruction of old cities were regretted, as was the negation of history. Pleas to re-engage with the question of meaning brought a new obsession with the building's role as a symbol. The conception of buildings as self-contained objects was recognized as destructive of the city and new attention was given to context, to streets and squares. Pre-Modern architectural history was reopened, and even modern history began to be rewritten.

BELOW: Jan Duiker, sanitorium, Zonnestraal, 1926.
An early and dramatic example of a concrete frame contrasted with a glass skin

LEFT: Norman Foster, Willis Faber Dumas Building, Ipswich, 1975.
Technological developments at last allowed sheer glass walls
without mullions

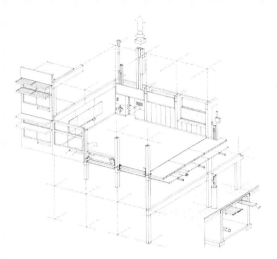

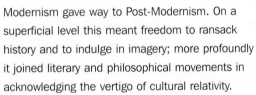

ABOVE: Günter Behnisch and Partners, component system devised
for Ulm technical college, 1963

ABOVE: Günter Behnisch and Partners, school at Bad Rappenau, 1991.
Typical of Behnisch's later work, the building eschews repetition of
components in favour of a response to local conditions

Modernism gave way to Post-Modernism. On a superficial level this meant freedom to ransack history and to indulge in imagery; more profoundly it joined literary and philosophical movements in acknowledging the vertigo of cultural relativity.

Post-Modernism was strong on irony and experiment, but liberation gave way to pluralist chaos. Since it seemed to have failed as science, architecture was re-declared an art with predictably self-indulgent results. Some proponents of the classical revival even sought a return to 19th-century building methods. More seriously, political changes deprived architecture of its former public programmes, their built image declining in the West with the wane of welfare systems. No wonder the Deconstructivist movement of the 1980s, which proposed the fragmentation of the architectural vocabulary, was supposed to reflect the anguish of homelessness! Commerce and the media increasingly exploited the effect of the image, and design became synonymous with fashion, detaching style from substance and promoting print and screen over the world of everyday life.

Looking back from the new millennium, we still struggle to comprehend where we stand. No longer dominated by the view now denigrated as the 'Modernist Project', 20th-century architecture instead offers great diversity, and with hindsight we see that it was there from the start. The changes caused by new technologies and social forms were so drastic that we are still digesting them, and much architecture at the century's end stands as footnotes to the bold visions proposed at its beginning. Examples in this chapter start with the generation of Modernist pioneers but show ideas already running far beyond the International Style orthodoxy. Later examples are by architects who emerged after 1945 and launched the critique of Modernism. Stirling's Staatsgalerie and Piano and Rogers' Centre Pompidou are included as seminal works of Post-Modernism and High-Tech respectively; while Kroll's Mémé represents participation. But good architecture is about getting several ideas to interact, and the following projects actually encapsulate a remarkable diversity of concerns.

New National Gallery
BERLIN, GERMANY
1963–68

Ludwig Mies van der Rohe
born Aachen 1886
died Chicago, Illinois 1969

A key figure in 20th-century architecture, Ludwig Mies van der Rohe was principal among German architects who transferred the Modern movement to the United States. He was the inventor of the glass-sided office block, and also the original minimalist with his famous declarations 'less is more' and 'God is in the details'. Mies proved more suited than other Modernists for transfer across the world, perhaps because of his interest in general types and repeatable design solutions.

He held that buildings should follow the discipline of construction and assembly, with straight sides and standard bays, using steel as it comes from the mill on a Rational (precise and controlled) system. This was coupled with the parallel belief that modern buildings change function frequently and so should not be planned too specifically. They should rather be of a generalized type, convertible to any purpose, with wide structural spans to allow flexibility. This philosophy led to buildings elegant as pristine objects, but aloof both from the places where they stood and the activities they contained. Mies's was an ideal universal architecture, the epitome of the International Style. Rectangular glass blocks across the world nod back at his Lakeshore Drive Apartments in Chicago (1949–51) and Seagram Building in New York (1956–59).

Towards the end of Mies's life the Germans were embarrassed that they possessed no major building by this world master, so gave him the task of West Berlin's new art gallery and a large budget. Mies revisited a favourite unbuilt project: the headquarters for Bacardi in Cuba from 1958, changing the construction from concrete to steel. Ideal in its double symmetry, it consisted of a great square roof slab, coffered underneath and carried on eight columns, two for each side. The glazed enclosure just contains the entrance and a temporary exhibition space, but it stands on a great raised podium. Containing basement rooms, this houses the entire permanent collection, open to the outside world only via a rear court. Poor daylighting and ill-defined routes detract from the building's performance as a gallery, but it is a powerful monument. The tapered cruciform columns and pin-joint capitals echo Doric columns, while the canal-side setting and the exquisite proportions echo the Altes Museum by Schinkel (*see pages 168–69*).

The podium allows cool contemplation of the city, its space measured out by the gridded floor and coffered roof, proof of an eternal geometry. Every detail is lovingly resolved. In its essential uniqueness this building contradicts Mies's claims about serial production, while the tapered columns, the change from concrete to steel, and the need to correct a 10-cm (4-in) structural deflection in the roofplate to keep it straight, contradict his claims about pursuing the logic of construction. Finally, one realizes too that the flexibility is not really about adaptation but about the creation of an ideal Platonic perfection. The building could be filmed by a time-lapse camera over centuries: days and seasons come and go, activities change, people scramble like ants. The building alone remains the fixed point.

Philharmonie Concert Hall
BERLIN, GERMANY
1956–63

Hans Scharoun
born Bremen 1893
died Berlin 1972

Hans Scharoun was one of the younger German Modernist pioneers of the 1920s and had just established himself in Berlin as a housing architect when Hitler came to power in 1933. Remaining in Germany during the Third Reich, he put his creative energy into a remarkable series of private houses which are conventional on the outside, due to Nazi planning restrictions, but have complex flowing spaces within.

The departure from geometrical conventions in these interiors, particularly the use of acute and obtuse angles in the plan, was unprecedented and later proved influential, particularly on 1990s Deconstructivism. After the Second World War, Scharoun briefly became City Architect of Berlin but lost the post before his ideas could be realized. As the German economy recovered he put his energies into a brilliant and widely published series of competition designs, becoming the leader of the Organic Tradition in German Architecture. Based on the theories of his mentor Hugo Häring (1882–1958), this meant making each work unique to its site and brief, in opposition to the prevailing mood for general-purpose buildings. In a complete reversal of the total detachment of Mies (see page 272), the Organic meant total engagement.

Following the brilliant but unbuilt competition designs for the Kassel Theatre and the National Theatre, Mannheim in 1952 and 1953, Scharoun finally realized his idea for a community building in the Philharmonie, home of the famous Berlin Philharmonic Orchestra under Herbert von Karajan. He had observed that whenever music is played in the street people gather around the musicians in a circle, so in his theatre the audience surrounds the central orchestra in an auditorium divided into terraces, each level having its own entrance. This produces an effect of extraordinary 'togetherness' as opposed to the usual division of 'producers' and 'consumers'. The complex geometry responded to the demands of acoustics, circulation and sightlines, but it also produced an 'aperspective' space, elusive in size and shape, which generates an appropriately ethereal atmosphere.

The surrounding foyer, which the architect-engineer Frei Otto (born 1925) called 'the room of a thousand angles', is a wonderful foil to the unity of the hall. Cascades of stairs and landings link all levels, modelled around the natural flow of people and designed to entice and draw them on, to experience the progression through space. The detailed design and accompanying art works display a degree of harmony and collaborative success that marked the peak of Scharoun's career. The one failure of the hall is its poor relationship with its context, but it was built on a wasteland and none of Scharoun's general plans for the area was properly carried out. This is a tragedy, for he was the most contextually minded of Modernists and had his own theory of *Stadtlandschaft* (city landscape). The hall interior, however, became *the* new concert-hall type of the 20th century and is much imitated. None of the progeny has yet challenged the parent for spatial complexity or musical atmosphere.

Philharmonie Concert Hall, plan at floor level

Säynätsalo Town Hall
SAYNATSALO, FINLAND
1949–52

Alvar Aalto
born Kuortane 1898
died Helsinki 1976

The dominant figure of Finnish Modernism, Alvar Aalto shared with Frank Lloyd Wright world leadership of the Organic Tradition; of architecture built in specific response to place and activity. Aalto never wavered in his faith in Functionalism but understood it in a broad and qualitative sense, and when Modernism wavered he remarked that it had simply not penetrated deeply enough into psychological and spiritual realms.

Born a decade later than the leading Modernists, Aalto produced his first important works in the late 1920s, but he quickly became a world figure with the Paimio Sanatorium (see pages 254–55) and the Viipuri Library (1928–35). At the latter, the invention of a new kind of rooflight to aid reading proved the worth of the functional approach and also heralded a concern with inventive daylighting which remained unrivalled among 20th-century architects. Perhaps this is due to the profound effect of light on Finland: its absence during the winter, while in summer the sun circles the sky. Villa Mairea (1937–39), with its sophisticated use of natural materials, showed Aalto breaking with the cubic conventions of the International Style to absorb a wider range of influences. Its clients were the Gullichsens, manufacturers of a range of Aalto-designed laminated timber furniture that remains in production and is world famous.

Growing up in a small country undergoing its industrial revolution gave Aalto great advantages, for he was able to control the construction of his buildings down to the smallest detail and to design objects such as lamp fittings for mass production which set new standards. Stylistically, he drew not only on the influence of Modernists further south and west but also on Scandinavian Neoclassicism and the local indigenous architecture.

Säynätsalo is a small industrial town on an island in Lake Päjänne. It was established in 1945 and Aalto won the competition to design the town hall in 1949. The programme of offices and a small council chamber was slender but he added shops, a library and dwellings to swell it, grouping all the parts around a small raised courtyard which is both a memory of the Finnish farmyard and the classical agora (a civic public space). Into this courtyard climb urban and rural steps, the former paved and orthogonal, the latter grassed and following irregular contours which spread across an angled gash in the plan. The urban steps lead to a glass-roofed entrance shared between the library in the front block and the administration offices behind, and the main internal passage follows the court around like a cloister. The massing of the building spirals up into a tower-like culmination above the urban steps which, appropriately enough, contains the council chamber. Its stair winds up the side, lit by a clerestory window, and the chamber's monopitch roof is supported internally on exposed timbers, using an impressive fanning form which is both a real structure and a rhetorical gesture. The scale of the building is domestic yet it achieves an extraordinary civic presence, and the architect's skill covers an unusually wide range, equally inspired from site plan to fine detail.

SAYNATSALO TOWN HALL • SAYNATSALO *VIEW SHOWING COUNCIL CHAMBER (RIGHT)*

Sydney Opera House

SYDNEY, AUSTRALIA
1956–66, completed 1973

Jørn Utzon
born Copenhagen 1918

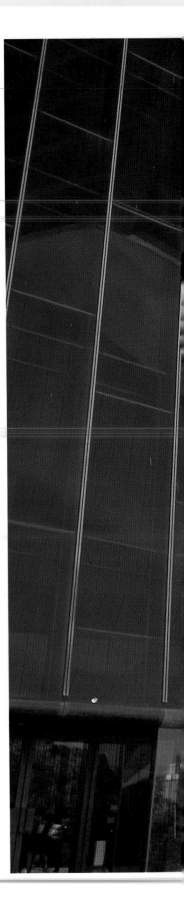

No 20th-century building has been more successful in the sheer power of its image than the Sydney Opera House. Appearing endlessly on travel posters and in film location shots, it epitomizes the new, progressive, post-colonial Australia, despite the fact that Jørn Utzon, the architect, was Danish. The photographed image of the whole structure has had a thousand times more cultural impact than the actual theatres, where plays and operas are performed.

The seldom-seen interior is actually functionally flawed and visually a disappointing compromise. During the construction of this difficult, technically innovative work, budgets were exceeded, nerve lost, one of the leading contractors died at a crucial point, and the architect was undermined to the point of resignation. Current work to remake the interior more in line with Utzon's original plans will hopefully repair some of the damage.

But for the rest of the world it is the exterior that matters: why has it been so successful? Certainly the site is spectacular and prominent, right on the edge of Sydney harbour with the bridge as backdrop. The unique form of the building is striking and original, helped by its rather uncertain scale, while the imagery, purporting to recall sails, has just the right level of ambiguity. A technical headstand was required by the architect-engineer Ove Arup (1895–1988) to achieve the structural shells, which meant considerable innovation in this area also. The most revealing explanation of the building, however, comes from the architect himself in a seminal essay of 1962, *Platforms and Plateaus*. In visits to South America in the 1940s, Utzon had been impressed by the ceremonial platforms erected by the Incas and Mayas which lift you with great flights of steps out of the jungle and give a view of 80 km (50 miles). These artificial, geometric hills were architecture at its most powerful, yet in essence nothing more than a manipulation of the ground plane. Fascinated by this concept, Utzon explored it in project after project until he realized it at Sydney.

The essential form is a great platform with steps rising onto a flat podium, into which the seating ranks of the two main theatres are carved and under which ancillary elements are absorbed. This could have worked as a pair of outdoor theatres but shelter was needed. A horizontal roof would repeat the ground plane, spoiling the clarity of the concept, so Utzon explored roof forms whose shapes contrasted as much as possible with the platform. Hence the curved shells which Arup post-rationalized as segments of a sphere for ease of calculation and construction. This modification from the original form did not lessen their impact. Legend has it that Utzon won the 1956 competition for the building at the last moment with a few sketches due to the intervention of one of the judges, which perpetuates the idea of a sudden stroke of genius, but he had worked long and hard on a redefinition of architecture as ground works and sky works, and this is what gives the Sydney Opera House seminal importance.

SYDNEY OPERA HOUSE • SYDNEY *DETAIL*

St Peter's, Klippan
KLIPPAN, SWEDEN
1963

Sigurd Lewerentz
born Bjärtra 1885
died Lund 1975

The Swedish architect Sigurd Lewerentz was the precise contemporary of the better-known Gunnar Asplund (see pages 260–61) and his partner in the design of the famous Enskede (Woodland) Cemetery just outside Stockholm (1915 onwards), where in 1922–25 Lewerentz contributed the severely Neoclassical Chapel of the Resurrection. In the 1930s he took a leading role in Swedish Modernism.

After early successes, Lewerentz lapsed into comparative obscurity, only recovering his international reputation with two late churches: St Mark's, Björkhagen of 1960 and St Peter's, Klippan of 1963. These are characteristic of the movement known as the New Brutalism: as a reaction against the white cubic abstraction of early Modernism came a rediscovery of the nature of materials and of the possibility that a building's identity might be derived from the stuff of its construction, often the roughest form of concrete used with expressive drama. In Scandinavia this tendency had started early, prefigured in the rough and raw indigenous architecture highlighted by the National Romantic Movement, which Lewerentz had witnessed at the turn of the 20th century as a student.

St Peter's was Lewerentz's last great work. Intimate and dark, the square-planned church at its heart was based on the idea of *circonstantes* – gathering together in a circle of prayer – suggesting a return to the intimate Early Christianity of the Catacombs. The church is surrounded by a narrow street bounded by parish offices and social rooms in an L-shaped formation. Relatively mute in plan, the scheme nonetheless allows strong articulation of each part through fenestration and roofing.

Not a hint of Lewerentz's earlier classicism is to be seen: all is asymmetrical and there is an obsession with materials that puts the rest of the

Brutalist movement in the shade. Brick is everywhere, as walls, floors, even roofs. The traditional language of the vault is radically reinterpreted. Used only for the hierarchically important church and chapel, vaults are suspended between steel joists which seem to float above the supporting beams on narrow props, the whole structure carried on a single T-shaped steel column which, cross-like and rusty, becomes a symbol of suffering. All bricks are used uncut, with wide and irregular joints and a play of different bonding patterns throughout the building. After years spent as designer and manufacturer of some of the best metal window frames in Sweden, Lewerentz decided to do without frames altogether. Instead, a brick-lined hole was made in the thick brick wall, and sealed double-glazed units – then a new technology – were clamped to the outside face. From within only a brick edge is seen; from without the surfaces are almost mirrors. Doors, too, are bolted to the outside, their laminated construction and expansion joints laid bare, the surface grain left rough without and sanded smooth within. Handrails and drainpipes were left raw-welded instead of being tidied up by grinding off. The rules of conventional 'good practice' were everywhere challenged as, at the end of a long life in architecture, Lewerentz seemed to question the very basis of construction.

Kimbell Art Museum

FORT WORTH, TEXAS, UNITED STATES
1966–72

Louis Kahn
born Saarama, Estonia 1901
died New York 1974

With his Beaux-Arts training, Louis Kahn was one of the most formal and geometrical architects of the 20th century, working with the square, the circle and the rectangle to produce such monumental works as the Assembly Building in Dhaka, Bangladesh (1962–87). He is also admired by architects for his great sensitivity to materials, and his most frequently quoted phrase tells of asking a brick what it wants to be. But Kahn's main contribution to the development of architecture was his division of buildings into served and serving spaces.

Born into an age without electricity, Modernist masters like Mies always treated services as an afterthought: in Berlin's New National Gallery (*see pages 272–73*), they are completely hidden away. But Kahn showed how they could become the very stuff of a building's order and organization, which paved the way for such innovative works as Centre Pompidou (*see pages 290–91*).

The Kimbell Art Museum is one of Kahn's most perfect and accomplished works. The starting point was a daylighting device to reduce the harsh southern sun to levels appropriate for valuable paintings. Taking the archaic form of the vault, Kahn built it in concrete with a glazed slit at the apex. A perforated metal reflector beneath reflects most of the light back onto the grey underside of the vault, from which it is reflected again onto the paintings. The light seems natural and varies with outside conditions, so as clouds pass across the sun, their shadow races through. A natural structural form supported by its own four legs, the vault could be repeated with variations right through the building: minus its slit, it covers the lecture hall; minus the infill between its concrete legs, it becomes an external portico; left out, it allows an internal court to be included.

As served spaces, the vaults are linked by narrower serving spaces, their floors and ceilings dedicated to air-conditioning, electricity supply and drainage. Staircases too, when needed, occupy these intermediate serving bays, whose presence is underlined by travertine flooring as opposed to the wood used elsewhere. The whole building thus takes on an A-B-A-B-A rhythm in the east-west direction, while in the north-south direction there are three long spans of vaults, again with narrow gaps between. The ratio of span between the two directions of 5:1 is unprecedented and gives rise to a memorable gallery space, measured out by the length of the vaults while also flowing freely across them. The way the vaults run counter to the direction of entry is also effective in controlling the right-angled turn made on entering.

Materials are used fastidiously and detailing is impeccable, but particularly successful is the contrast between the exquisitely wrought cast concrete, whose rhythmic holes show the discipline of the shuttering bolts (which secured the mould, or formwork), and the expensive slabs of travertine infilling the vault ends. In this wonderful late work, Kahn brought together all his architectural interests in the happiest and most convincing way.

Protestant Chapel, Dachau Concentration Camp

DACHAU, GERMANY
1964–67

Helmut Striffler
born Ludwigshafen 1927

Helmut Striffler belongs to the generation of architects who trained immediately after the Second World War and came into their own in the 1960s. He made his reputation by winning the competition for the Protestant Memorial Chapel at Dachau in 1964. He has built many fine works since, mostly in and around the city of Mannheim, but nothing exceeding the chapel in power and originality.

Preserved as a museum, the former Nazi concentration camp includes reconstructed huts where the inmates slept in bunks three deep, the remains of very utilitarian-looking cremation ovens, and harrowing displays in the former guard buildings about medical experiments carried out there. The chapel was needed as a place of prayer for Protestant visitors – there are other chapels for Jews and Catholics. On a pragmatic level the brief was simple, consisting of the chapel proper, a less formal community room, an office and services. Much more difficult was the question of what kind of architecture could possibly be appropriate. It had to be a religious place, yet exist within the accursed territory of the camp. It needed to be fitting to the setting yet completely detached from the utilitarian pattern of barrack-like structures, fences and watchtowers.

Striffler felt that recourse to known forms of religious architecture was impossible. Only the inside could welcome people in a normal way: the outside had to be harder, more ambiguous, even, in a way, anti-architecture (*nicht-Architektur*). It should not try to relate to the other buildings nor should it participate in the discipline of their hierarchical order. Drawing on his wartime experience, Striffler conceived the idea of a 'protective furrow for the outcast' dug into the mother earth. Here visitors would be able

temporarily to escape the horror of the camp. The military order was denied by asymmetrical placing and free planning, and the building became a combination of a wall and a route.

The wall stands sheer and hard, its board-marked concrete (imprinted by the timbers of the mould) contrasting with a sea of pebbles, as arid as a dry river bed. The route invites visitors down broad and gentle steps and funnels them into a sunken court which provides daylight for both chapel and community room. As you enter you pass sculptural panels and an elaborate gate: the staging of the threshold is everything. The ground plane closes protectively over you, outside views are closed by kinks in the wall, and you enter another world. Views from chapel and community room take in the sky but no camp. There is a chance for prayer and tranquil contemplation before rising again into the hardness of the camp via the narrower, less-elaborated exit route. The materials are of their time but could hardly be more appropriate, for the now stained concrete is grim and tough, windowless and protective like a bunker, yet sculptural too. The downward route treated with such ceremonial care is a brilliant touch: it denies the expected hierarchy of the altar and the usual celebration of God triumphant, for here God had no place, save in the secret recesses of the victims' hearts.

Magistero
URBINO, ITALY
1968–79

Giancarlo De Carlo
born Genoa 1919

The ideology of Modern architecture was dominated by the organization CIAM (Congrès Internationaux d'Architecture Moderne; International Congresses of Modern Architecture), started in 1928 and led by Le Corbusier and the architectural historian Sigfried Giedion. It emphasized functional zoning and rational urban planning. By the late 1950s it had become moribund and a group of young architects, appointed to prepare the tenth congress, broke away and called themselves Team X (10).

In some of the earliest and toughest criticism of Modernist assumptions, Team X questioned issues such as the takeover of the machine, the negation of the user, the loss of place and local character, and the negation of history. Two key members were the Dutchman Aldo van Eyck (*see pages 288–89*) and the Italian Giancarlo De Carlo. De Carlo's contribution revolved particularly around the question of the traditional city, its preservation and its reinterpretation for modern life. He stressed the need for a deep understanding of the place and a 'reading of the territory'. The best example of his practice is the city of Urbino, for which he produced the master plan, restored historic buildings and contributed many new ones. The pressing need and problem was that a university had to be accommodated whose student numbers equalled the population of the city itself. De Carlo set up a dual strategy, slipping teaching faculties into redundant fabric within the old city while building new residential colleges on the outskirts.

The Magistero is the university's Faculty of Education, incorporating its largest and most important lecture halls. De Carlo chose to place it in a redundant convent within the old walled city, keeping most of the perimeter walls and a corner chapel intact but rebuilding the interior of the block. He restored or rebuilt accommodation along the edges while inserting two new figures into the void: a great semicircular theatre and a smaller circular courtyard. The theatre is the meeting place for the university. It echoes classical precedent and gives a note of centrality that resounds through the building. Used in its entirety, with 1,500 seats, for major occasions such as graduation and inaugural lectures, it can be subdivided for everyday teaching into several rooms at various levels by means of sliding and folding partitions.

The theatre's many parts are commonly top-lit by a conical glass roof light, and bridge-like passages cross to the central upper rooms so the full volume can be appreciated as a whole. The rooflight folds around an open terrace which also registers the building's presence in the city skyline. The small courtyard provides daylight for offices and for the unusual foyer spaces which make up the rest of the plan. Perfectly integrated into the old town, this large building is entered through an old and modest façade but opens into a surprisingly rich and varied set of inner spaces. The old convent has been given a new purpose, the university is able to bring fresh life and commerce to the city, and the dialogue between old and new makes for a rich and interesting architecture.

Section of the Magistero

Orphanage
**AMSTERDAM,
THE NETHERLANDS
1957–60**

Aldo van Eyck
born Driebergen 1918
died Amsterdam 1999

Aldo van Eyck was a leading member of Team X, a group which started the critique of Modern architecture in the late 1950s *(see page 286)*. He complained that the Modernists had concentrated excessively on those things that had changed in human existence rather than those that had remained the same, and in consequence architecture had become increasingly mechanistic, universal and placeless.

To counter these tendencies, he used his studies in anthropology to inform his work, particularly a visit to the Dogon people of Mali, who impressed him with their symbol-laden architecture. Implicitly criticizing the title of Sigfried Giedion's magnum opus *Space, Time and Architecture* (1941), he said 'whatever time and space mean, place and occasion mean more, for space in the image of man is place, and time in the image of man is occasion'. Architecture's primary role, he claimed, was 'to welcome people's homecoming', and to do this it needed to be specific. This involved close attention to how people use space and give it meaning. In later years van Eyck deplored the superficial styles and architectural games of Post-Modernism, to the point of declaring, 'I'm just a hard-boiled Functionalist'.

The orphanage, located on the edge of central Amsterdam, is van Eyck's masterpiece, bringing together all his main ideas. At a time when such institutions were housed in a single monolithic slab, he broke it into separate low pavilions like houses in a village, each occupied by a family-like group of orphans under a 'parent'. The aerial view reveals the courtyards between units and the upper-storey parts under large vaults which contain bedrooms. These 'houses' are connected by an internal 'street', entered from the central courtyard. Bridged protectively by the slab of the administration block, the court's outer entrance is further protected by a string of trees, showing van Eyck's concern with thresholds.

Aside from the articulation of family groups, a strong rhythm is given by the smaller vaults above cells about 3.5 m (11½ ft) square from which the whole ground floor is formed. This modular approach combines ideas about spatial organization with ideas about construction. Spatially, it sets a very small scale for the building, which is further accentuated by setting most of the vertical dimensions to the child's scale. The multiplicity of little 'houses' supports van Eyck's conviction that the orphanage is 'both a city-like house and a house-like city'. From a constructive viewpoint, the intention was to create an open-ended system of repeated parts, mainly in pre-cast concrete, sometimes inside and sometimes outside, with various kinds of infill. In the late 1950s mass production and prefabrication seemed inevitable, and van Eyck sought to show how such a system could be humanized through variation. The building was much admired for its child-friendly detail, sympathetic atmosphere and vivid internal colour scheme. It seemed the epitome of a humane welfare state, but it did not remain an orphanage. Single parenthood became acceptable and adoption was promoted. The building is now the Berlage Institute, a school of architecture.

Centre Pompidou
PARIS, FRANCE
1971–78

| Renzo Piano | Richard Rogers |
| born Genoa 1937 | born Florence 1933 |

Winning the competition for the Centre Pompidou launched the careers of two world-famous architects. Rogers went on to become one of the leaders of the British High-Tech movement (along with Norman Foster *[see pages 328–29]*), while Piano generated an equally successful practice in his native Italy and beyond, developing a sophisticated architecture marrying form and fabric *(see pages 318–19)*.

Centre Pompidou, a multifaceted cultural institution, realized for the first time on a large scale an idea that had been under discussion for a decade. Prefigured in the space-age and colourful Pop visions of the 1960s English group Archigram (Peter Cook, born 1936, and others) and in projects such as the Fun Palace (1961) by Cedric Price (born 1934), it was theoretically underpinned by the writings of Reyner Banham. The theory was that buildings change function in unpredictable ways and should therefore be made as flexible as possible. For ease of mass production and ready extendibility they should be assembled from a standard kit of parts. Structural spans should be very wide to allow for future subdivision, and services should be stuck on around the outside where they would be easily accessible for alteration or replacement. Even the circulation of people was treated this way, consisting of escalators in glass tubes hung on the front. Since it eliminated all specificity to place and programme, this strategy reduced architecture to a structural framework accompanied by a set of services, and these became the objects of architectural rhetoric. The huge trusses were lovingly jointed and the service runs were elegantly applied and painted bright colours. The scale was breathtaking and the form a huge surprise: the nearest precedent was an oil refinery, resulting in the nickname 'Pompidolium'.

Because of the design strategy, somewhat temporary looking enclosures had to be built within the main framework to accommodate permanent features such as the libraries and gallery. Direct daylighting of the paintings, a priority in other galleries such as Louis Kahn's Kimbell (*see pages 282–83*) and Piano's later Menil (1981–86), could obviously not be managed, so as an art museum it proved less than ideal. But the square next to it became one of the hot-spots of Paris, filled with entertainers, and the escalator-ride to view Paris rivalled even the Eiffel Tower as a tourist attraction.

Visitor numbers broke all records and the building seemed a huge success, but paradoxically not for the efficacy of the original concept. It was never extended, the kit of parts was not reused, and it did not become the standard model for arts centres elsewhere. Its potential flexibility has never been properly exploited and the late-1990s refit imposed changes against the original concept, particularly an interior stair which short-circuits the escalators on the façade, much to the architects' disdain. Despite their efforts, it had not proved flexible enough to satisfy the changes needed only 25 years on, and its popularity is due more to its unprecedented image. It works as a monument to Georges Pompidou, but it also displays a powerful mid-20th-century idea about architecture as a servicing framework; here it is unrivalled.

CENTRE POMPIDOU · PARIS *DETAIL OF REAR SIDE*

Mémé Residential Building, Louvain University

LOUVAIN, BELGIUM
1968–72

Lucien Kroll
born Brussels 1927

Among the few direct architectural outcomes of the student movement of 1968, Kroll's Maison Médicale (Mémé) for the University of Louvain is the most famous. The university had built a huge and repetitive teaching hospital and was about to use the same method for an adjacent hostel for medical students. The students rebelled and order was only restored when Kroll – their choice – was appointed as architect.

Known as a pioneer of participation, Kroll had promised the students a role in deciding their accommodation. He established a group design process, setting the young architects in his office to work simultaneously on different parts of the complex. In consultation with the users, they gradually put together a model. It was allowed to develop freely in response to stated requirements, both in terms of general organization and at the scale of the individual room. The relationships between building parts had to be explored and negotiated, quite the opposite of the usual master-plan which sets the small scale at the mercy of the large. From time to time the architects were obliged to exchange roles so that they did not get too possessive of any particular part.

As it was the late 1960s and the height of system building, Kroll felt obliged for economic reasons to adopt a modular system and standard components, but he explored how such systems might be used without their mechanistic discipline taking over. To avoid the limitations imposed on the construction grid by large prefabricated units, he took the narrow gauge of 100 mm (4 in) as the minimum dimension and, in the interest of variety, tried to use the whole range of the component catalogue. Materials and sizes were therefore ruthlessly mixed. Rather than imposing a design

solution according to known formulae or a chosen aesthetic stance, Kroll had embarked on a voyage of discovery of unpredictable outcome. Even mistakes were retained as part of the history of the process. He intended to mimic in modern form the rich pattern of vernacular building in old towns and villages, where the complex and changing needs of the inhabitants over the years had given rise to a similar kind of free expression.

The buildings seemed shockingly anarchic and subversive, especially in contrast with the hospital next door. Relations between Kroll and the authorities soured as the radical nature of the method became understood. Critics argued that the specific and idiosyncratic design of residential rooms was inappropriate since the inhabitants on whose wishes it was based soon moved on, but Kroll replied that the key issue was simply to achieve variety, to make the rooms different. Lining people up in identical rooms implies a military discipline: it is like putting them in uniform.

In all his projects, Kroll has combated blind mechanization and authoritarianism. The most politically aware of architects, he still fights for a humane, egalitarian and ecological architecture. Through its polemical stance, the Mémé exposed the hidden political forces underlying architectural projects, and that is its historical importance.

Olympic Park
MUNICH, GERMANY
1967–72

Günter Behnisch
and Partners

Günter Behnisch
born Dresden 1922

Günter Behnisch is a key figure in contemporary German architecture as the figurehead of the Organic Tradition *(see pages 274–75)*. He studied architecture in Stuttgart in the late 1940s and set up his first partnership in 1952. Since then he has run a lively and constantly evolving office, concentrating particularly on social buildings such as schools and old people's homes. The work is of high quality and surprisingly diverse, perhaps because of the unusual working method.

Behnisch seldom draws himself, preferring to steer the work as manager and critic, employing young talent often fresh out of architectural school. In the early 1960s his office was a pioneer in the design of prefabricated building systems, but it soon became disillusioned by this technically dominated approach. Instead of pursuing the standardized and repeatable, it turned towards what Behnisch called *Situationsarchitektur*, that is, architecture rooted in a particular place and situation. Winning the competition for the Munich Olympic Park marked for the Behnisch office the turning point away from the tyranny of system building.

Planned at the tail-end of the liberal 1960s for the games of 1972, the Olympic Park represented the postwar Federal Republic to the rest of the world at a time of optimism and prosperity. In contrast to the previous German Olympics – in Hitler's Berlin of 1936 – the atmosphere needed to be free and egalitarian, the buildings unmonumental. The site lay to the north of Munich where huge hills of wartime rubble had been dumped, which, along with the natural gravel layer beneath, could be moulded into a new landscape. Axial arrangements were avoided, a central lake was created around an existing stream, and the seating of the large arenas was

absorbed into the hillsides like classical theatres. Most of the architecture thus took the form of ground works, a great sleight of hand being needed to house all the technical and emergency services and provide adequate fire-escape routes for such large numbers. But the beautifully reshaped landscape, designed with the help of Günther Grzimek, won through to dominate the complex.

The arenas needed roofs but box-like buildings would have threatened the concept, so Behnisch proposed the largest cable-net structures ever erected. These were developed by the engineer Jörg Schlaich with Frei Otto, the leading pioneer in the field of tensile structures, acting as adviser. Much innovative technology had to be developed, but the huge roofs were completed on time and stole the show. They still dominate photographs because the manipulations of the ground are so easily taken for granted as 'natural'. After the Olympics the park became a permanent and popular recreational facility for the people of Munich. For the Behnisch office the Olympics project brought international recognition and paved the way for such prestigious works as the Frankfurt Post Museum (1990), the Parliament building in Bonn (1993) and the Berlin Arts Academy (due to be completed in 2002).

Neue Staatsgalerie

STUTTGART, GERMANY
1978–84

James Stirling

born Glasgow 1926
died London 1992

James Stirling was a dominant if controversial figure in British architecture from the 1960s to the 1980s. He achieved fame with two buildings designed in partnership with James Gowan: Ham Common Flats (1958), influenced by Le Corbusier, and Leicester University's Engineering Faculty Building (1959–63). With its rugged forms, red brickwork and cascades of glass, this broke with precedent to an extraordinary degree.

The building's rationale was a ruthless articulation of internal functions, but it also drew on arcane sources such as northern industrial buildings and the work of the Constructivist Konstantin Melnikov (see pages 252–53). Stirling repeated the same vocabulary to critical acclaim in the History Faculty at Cambridge (1965–68) and the Florey Building, Queen's College, Oxford (1966–71), but both suffered technical faults and user complaints which discouraged potential clients, causing him to seek work abroad. At the same time he was becoming famous in architectural circles for seductively drawn projects with great formal appeal.

The 1970s saw a growing cynicism about Modernist ideology, particularly the idea that direct expression of function and 'honest' use of materials was sufficient. Instead, fresh attention was given to questions of image and meaning, while it became acceptable once again to trawl history books for ideas. Known as Post-Modernism, this phase suited both Stirling's playful formal skill and his sceptical and humorous bravura. His Clore Gallery extension at London's Tate Britain (1980–87) and Neue Staatsgalerie at Stuttgart were among its most brilliant examples.

The Stuttgart building drew on a vocabulary worked up through a series of competition designs for German galleries. It combined without a qualm classical columns, rotundas, wavy glass canopies, Corbusian ramps, Egyptian cornices, and lifts and ducts painted in bright colours. Its stone walls were not solid but cladding, a fact gleefully exposed in a basement opening where stones appear to have fallen out. There was a pedestrian right of way across the site, and this Stirling chose to take as his main theme. Incorporated as a *promenade architecturale*, it rises up a double ramp past the entrance, travels up further ramps, through the main wall, around the edge of the central rotunda with a view to the court below, and so on and out to the upper street. The dominance of this external public route subordinates the internal ones and upsets the hierarchy of the building's axes, while it also makes the rather ordinary white-box art galleries around the edge feel peripheral. All this was seen as cleverly ironic: the gallery *belongs* to the general public and it is fitting that they *should* see it without entering; the art is not much good anyway and the gallery *is* a big sculpture in itself.

Architectural historians competed to spot the sources and found a playful version of Schinkel's Altes Museum (see pages 168–69) in the plan. They congratulated Stirling: Sir John Summerson proclaimed him *Vitruvius Ludens* (playful Vitruvius). When it opened, the gallery seemed to be the most lauded and widely published building on earth. It was much imitated, but now nobody builds like that: it is a period piece of the 1980s.

NEUE STAATSGALERIE • *STUTTGART VIEW SHOWING WALKWAY*

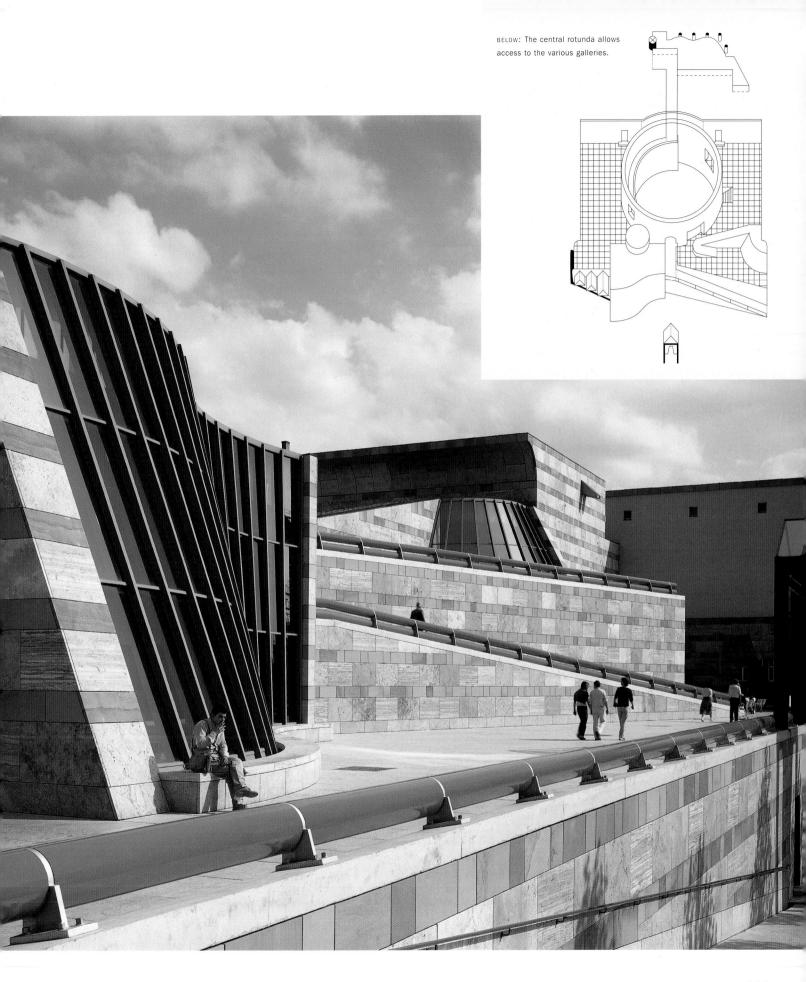

BELOW: The central rotunda allows access to the various galleries.

Waisenhaus
EICHSTATT, GERMANY
1989

Karljosef Schattner
born Magdeburg 1924

The powerful technology of the 20th century has made it too easy to destroy and rebuild, obliterating all memory of previous occupation. Shells and bombs in the Second World War wreaked havoc on European cities, but in many places the replanning that followed was even worse, providing for increased traffic with huge ring roads and tearing down whole districts for 'comprehensive redevelopment'.

In the 1970s and 1980s these drastic changes were widely regretted and conservation became the watchword. Old buildings were protected and there was pressure to build new work 'in keeping' with the old. This raised new problems, for building methods and user requirements had changed too much to allow simple reproduction of old patterns. Instead, new buildings were produced with phoney old faces, diluting the authentic and confusing the historical record. But if imitation of the old by the new is not the answer, what should the relation be between the two? Karljosef Schattner spent a long career pondering this problem while designing new buildings and converting old ones as Diocesan Architect for the small town of Eichstätt in Germany. The Waisenhaus is a key example.

Waisenhaus means orphanage. A curious old building on the main street of the town, this structure began life in the 15th century as two Renaissance houses placed side by side. These were converted into an orphanage in the 18th century, one house accommodating boys, the other girls. A chapel was added in the space between and the gabled fronts were united by a new Baroque façade with a central entrance. Closed as an orphanage in the 1920s, it had been used sporadically for other purposes, and after long neglect was considered ready for demolition.

But Schattner saw its potential and suggested converting it into Departments of Psychology and Journalism for Eichstätt's Catholic University.

Faithfully restoring the Baroque façade and repairing such elegant rooms and ceilings as remained, Schattner rediscovered 15th-century wall paintings under the 18th-century plaster and left them on view. The rotten rear 19th-century elevation was demolished to reveal the original back walls of the houses and Schattner built his own abstract new façade as a screen beyond them. He removed the chapel to rediscover the void between the two original buildings, turning it into a top-lit hall space with a new main stair built as a slender independent structure. He also added a stack of new washrooms. Fastidiously made in steel, glass and cut stone with panels of stucco lustro (subtly coloured render), the new work is wonderfully detailed, drawing on the example of the Italian Carlo Scarpa (1906–78) who showed a remarkable sensitivity to materials. Schattner's close working relationship with local firms was rewarded with high quality at affordable prices.

The Waisenhaus throws the building's three layers of history into relief: walking around one is confronted by bits of Renaissance house, bits of Baroque, and the flowing space of Modernism. They complement each other beautifully.

WAISENHAUS • EICHSTATT INTERIOR AND FAÇADE

Münster City Library

MUNSTER, GERMANY
1985–93

Bolles Wilson and Partner

Julia Bolles
born Münster 1948

Peter Wilson
born Melbourne 1950

Marking the end of this period is a key work by younger architects. The Australian Peter Wilson and his German partner Julia Bolles met at the Architectural Association, London, in the 1970s where they studied and then taught, part of a talented group nurtured by the chairman Alvin Boyarsky, which also included such well-known figures as Rem Koolhaas (born 1944) and Zaha Hadid *(see pages 310–11).*

The Münster City Library was their first major job, won in a competition in Bolles' home town where they now have their office. Its formal inventiveness certainly reflects the liberation of the 1970s but also the intense revival of interest at that time in the nature of cities, for although the building can be read in a sculptural way it is profoundly contextual in intention.

Wartime bombs had left an irregular hole in the city-centre fabric which was being used as a car park, but there was a need to knit the area together again. The most prominent local monument was a church spire to the west, and the architects conceived the idea of making a new pedestrian alley on its axis. Initially intended to divide the library from a museum included in the competition brief, it finally became the division between reference and lending libraries. The two halves are linked at basement level and by a high-level bridge. The part to the north completes an existing urban block, looking into an enclosed court, while the crescent-shaped block to the south completes the street pattern while acknowledging the object-like car showroom opposite, a building from the 1950s. Marked by a café and raised piazza, the main entrance is at the northwest corner where the streets meet. All the main staircases within the building run next to the alleyway and windows open onto it, visually combining movement inside and out to animate the path. The linear form of the north block lends itself to open galleries while the deeper south block offers a calmer atmosphere for browsing stacks and reading at tables. And while the outer wall is sheer and high with deliberately undifferentiated windows, the pedestrian street is small in scale. Its sides lean outwards to increase light, their roof-like surfaces clad in copper. Supported inside by prominent, visible curved timber ribs – again roof rather than wall materials – their vulnerability emphasizes the importance of this crack through the building.

Just how contextual the library is can be understood by imagining it transplanted to another location, lacking the specific connections on which it depends. But for all its sensitivity in plan and massing, it makes few concessions to surrounding buildings in terms of style. Instead it brings to the situation its own rather hybrid vocabulary which seems more reminiscent of the work of Organic Modernists such as Aalto, Asplund and Scharoun than of earlier architects. There is a good deal of interplay between the exposure of materials and surfaces in some places and the contrary intention elsewhere of suppression under abstract render and paint. The intense relationship between architecture and abstract painting discovered in the 1920s is here re-explored.

Plan for Münster City Library

MUNSTER CITY LIBRARY • MUNSTER

The End of the Millennium

Diane Ghirardo

In 1990, two styles dominated debates in the world of architecture: Post-Modernism (*see page 270*) and Deconstructivism, both of them reactions to the dominance of Modernism since the end of the Second World War. Deconstructivists, led by Peter Eisenman (born 1932), offered an aesthetic that was loosely linked to a philosophical movement called Deconstructivism which emphasized the inherent arbitrariness of meaning.

Associating with the political radicalism and aesthetics of early 20th-century Russian Constructivism, 1990s Deconstructivists also claimed an avant-garde, radical position, even though their designs amounted to nothing more than formal exercises. After the Deconstructivist exhibition at New York's Museum of Modern Art in 1988, the movement faded away to an emphasis on personal, idiosyncratic expression.

Although challenged by these two movements, Modernism remained a strong current during the 1990s, with the Psychology Faculty for the University of Padua (1994–98) by Gino Valle (born 1923) illustrating the richness that is possible within a fundamentally Modernist sensibility, and

BELOW: Gino Valle, Faculty of Psychology, Padua, 1994–98. View of south elevation

LEFT: Machado and Silvetti Archtects, construction mock-up of the Getty Villa, Malibu, due to be completed in 2003

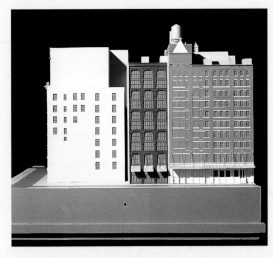

ABOVE: Model for Aldo Rossi's Scholastic Building, New York, 1996–2000, Mercer Street elevation

projects by talented and thoughtful architects such as Charles Correa (born 1930) artfully blending Modernism with local traditions.

After an early association with the work of the Deconstructivists, the recent designs of Rem Koolhaas (born 1944), such as that for the Seattle Public Library (1999), reveal a Modernist foundation joined to an intense search for a way of expressing the fusion of old and new demands – in the context of the library, this is highlighted by the new central role of computers in users' research. In architecture in general, meanwhile, the trend towards the internationalization of practice has been greatly facilitated by the growing use of computer technology in design, which also conditions a building's programme and is often responsible for its appearance (most notably in the work of Frank Gehry).

The style battles of the 1970s and 1980s disappeared during the 1990s as architecture came increasingly to be seen as a very personal expression of the architect, or as an individually tailored response to the demands of a specific project in which questions of style depended less on fashion than on the context, the commission, the preferences of the client and, increasingly, on issues of sustainability. Energy-efficient buildings composed of renewable materials have become a concern of ever more architects, as in Foster's Reichstag and the Bryant House by Auburn University Rural Studio, but there is still a long way to go before sustainability dominates design.

Liberation from the tyranny of fashion and signature forms and materials has allowed architects great flexibility in design, and is what unifies the diverse projects that illustrate the 1990s here. Aldo Rossi's design for the Scholastic Building in New York (1996–2000), for example, tucked between two radically different structures, blends the rhythms of the adjacent grid systems into a spirited, original elevation on Broadway while fashioning an entirely different scheme of superimposed arcades for the more industrial area to the rear. The Boston-based team of the Argentinian Rodolfo Machado and Jorge Silvetti (both born 1942) also illustrates how to bring dignity, richness and a thoughtful design to buildings as different as a car park at Princeton University (1990–91) and the renovation and alteration of the Getty Museum, Malibu (1994–1999, 2000–2003) without resorting to a stylistic bag of tricks.

The buildings I have chosen to represent the 1990s illustrate the decade's diverse aesthetics; they stand out because of the simplicity, beauty, warmth and elegance with which they resolve problems – characteristics that are among the many reasons why we appreciate a building.

Bonnefanten Museum

MAASTRICHT,
THE NETHERLANDS
1990–94

Aldo Rossi

born Milan 1931
died Milan 1997

P lans, sections, elevations, photographs: these are the conventions by which we have come to understand a work of architecture today. However informative they might be, they can never tell the entire story, for architecture fundamentally entails synthesizing concept and execution; its success lies in experience. Rossi's Bonnefanten Museum in Maastricht reminds me of this most powerfully.

Set between the river and a brick warehouse-museum, the Bonnefanten rises with elemental simplicity on the site of demolished ceramics factories, its wings opening to the river and to the city. In many respects, the design and execution of the museum are an artful collage of ideas, motifs, details and materials devised by Rossi over the years in drawings and projects; the green I-beams so elegantly deployed as lintels at the Casa Aurora in Turin (1984–87), for example, here form piers and window frames. Rossi's architecture defies simple stylistic labels, being neither Modernist nor Post-Modernist but driven by architecture's tectonic majesty and its power to evoke history and memory. After years spent writing for the architectural magazine *Casabella*, Rossi displayed his talents in a stunning design for the San Cataldo Cemetery in Modena (1971 onwards), where monumental masses fused with archaic elements and Modernist details. From the 1970s onwards, Rossi's architecture and drawings, which blended established forms with a personal interpretation, electrified a worldwide audience.

The Bonnefanten Museum's collection includes old masters, archaeological artefacts and decorative and minor arts. Rossi set the smaller objects in cupboards with glazed, four-light doors, similar to furniture found in a domestic setting, rather than standard museum display cases. By contrast with the massive, complicated and often redundant rhetoric of many recent museums, the Bonnefanten is the essence of simplicity, its heart and soul centred on a spectacular staircase. This is the feature that haunted me after my first visit: the sheer, uninterrupted brick walls framing untreated wooden steps, the sense of being drawn up to the museum's heart, the celebration of material sensuousness so characteristic of Rossi's architecture in Japan, Paris and Germany, and, where finances permitted, in Italy. Illuminated from above by a glazed skylight-arcade, the stairwell is washed by different qualities of light: the raking light of midsummer that fades the bricks to dusty rose, the diffuse and faint shadows of the short days of winter – all the characteristics so common to 17th-century Dutch painting, gathered and summarized in this exhilarating space, the backbone and core of the museum.

In building this stairwell, Rossi has referred to the 16th-century Italian *scala santa* (holy staircase), traditionally found on pilgrimage routes, where each stage is marked by its own devotions. The inspiring Bonnefanten stairs pull skywards to the light like a *scala santa*, but on the descent they focus attention on the architecture – the end panel with its stack of windows and the unadorned brick walls – in a remarkable dialogue between memory and presence, movement and stasis.

Putnam Lake House

Mahar Adjmi

Morris Adjmi
born New Orleans, Louisiana
1959

Lisa Mahar
born Gainesville, Florida 1965

A significant weakness of much architecture can be self-consciousness, where a building is burdened by the architect's belief that they are creating 'art'. When architects recognize the limits of their craft, but craft those limits adroitly, the result can be thrilling. In the case of the Putnam Lake House, Lisa Mahar and Morris Adjmi understood that the forested hills set above the diminutive lake, with their seasonal display of chromatic changes, were the true strengths of the run-down little house, and that the house's renovation could be best served by letting the location take command.

A 12-year partnership with Aldo Rossi (see pages 304–305) honed Adjmi's skills in design and reinforced his belief in the value of simplicity, one shared by his partner Lisa Mahar, a photographer as well as an architect. And, despite the architects' previous experience of designing massive buildings, the Putnam Lake House reveals their refreshing ability to design small.

Just an hour by car north of Manhattan, Putnam County is dotted with small lakes, each lined with summer houses of various ages and in different states of decay. Set close to the shore in a hollow descending steeply from the road, Putnam Lake House was uninhabited for some time before it was restored and was little more than a cramped, musty summer cottage with three tiny bedrooms, an awkward kitchen facing the hollow, a small living room and one bathroom. Only a generous front porch relieved the oppression of the interior. The renovation added two bathrooms and enlarged the existing one, and provided a new master-bedroom suite and study and a generous kitchen. Such an expansion is not uncommon among summer houses in this region, but the design managed to transform the Putnam Lake House with breathtaking elegance and simplicity.

Two new wings, one for the master suite and one for the kitchen, form the core of the design. Facing the lake, the entire ground floor has floor-to-ceiling glass doors. In the kitchen, additional glass doors lead to the rear hollow, allowing the room to serve as a breezeway during the summer and to be flooded with light in the winter. This is the house's year-round heart, the gathering spot for meals, for conversation, for quiet contemplation of the lake and the forested hills beyond. Leaving the low ceilings of the entrance and the living room, one enters on the diagonal into the kitchen, which suddenly expands laterally (the glazed walls of doors) and vertically to a steeply pitched, 4.25-m-high (14-ft) ceiling: a delightful shift of scale and space enhanced by the pale yellow walls that merge into the clapboard ceilings.

From a tight, two-storey box the architects crafted an expansive tripartite structure, while maintaining the overall scale, materials and structural system of the area. In other hands, the house could have turned into a monster mansion, typical of new houses on the Pacific Coast, but Mahar and Adjmi manipulated the scale to achieve generous dimensions without overwhelming size – a marvellous feat too rarely accomplished.

Nexus World Kashii
FUKUOKA, JAPAN
1989–91

Mark Mack
born Judenberg 1949

Fukuoka in Japan has been a centre of architectural interest since the 1980s, with major projects by Aldo Rossi (Hotel Il Palazzo, 1985–87) and, more recently, the Fukuoka mall (1997–99) by the Californian architect Jon Jerde (born 1940). On a piece of land reclaimed from Hakata Bay, the Nexus Corporation developed a new town with a Master Plan by Arata Isozaki (born 1931) and housing by talented designers from around the world, including Rem Koolhaas, Steven Holl (born 1947) and Mark Mack.

Each architect was allocated a plot along the edge of the site on the bay, with Mack receiving the difficult corner section. His design not only deftly resolved the problem of turning the corner in what was becoming a dense urban district, it also offered a remarkable solution to the monotonous repetition of living units in apartment buildings. Shops on the ground floor and Mack's decision to carve out the actual corner and turn it over to the landscape architect Martha Schwartz (born 1950) enrich the sophistication of the project and, with the extraordinary design of the apartments, make it a suitable solution far beyond Japan.

Mack brought to the Nexus project more than 15 years' experience of designing housing in the Californian wine country, Texas and Europe, together with an architectural education in his native Austria that advocated construction over theory. His architectural projects, therefore, exhibit not only a rich amalgam of ideas from Europe and the United States but also an attentiveness to construction and materials often absent among contemporary architects. One of the best illustrations of this intriguing combination was the Holt House in Corpus Christi, Texas (1981–83), where stately classicism was crafted in travertine and marble on the Gulf of Mexico.

The exterior of the Nexus apartment conceals Mack's enormous inventiveness in plan and section even as it yields a thrilling diversity. The scheme consists of two building blocks, one slotted under the other, each marked by distinct materials, colours and articulation. The southern, six-storey wing is ordered by a grey concrete grid with yellow infill, while the four-storey wing to the north is bright red stucco. Projecting balconies of different sizes, some concrete and some concrete and wood, on the red wing, and a symphony of solids, voids and different types of windows and colours of window frames on the grey wing, hide 29 apartments, no two of which are the same. On the higher wing, the window and porch sequences are never repeated; each form signals a different floor plan behind. Moreover, most of the apartments spread across two levels, locking and interlocking within two apparently distinct building slabs with an elegance that belies their complexity.

Mack's reputation also rests on his interiors, where he adopts a palette of ash panels stained in different colours and stucco walls of mottled ochre or russet to create a relaxing environment. Here, these elements are orchestrated with varied windows and mullions in tonal harmonies that recall the interconnections of the apartment plans.

NEXUS WORLD KASHII • FUKUOKA

Vitra Fire Station
WEIL AM RHEIN, GERMANY
1989–93

Zaha Hadid
born Baghdad 1950

Its sharp planes rake the landscape, at once jutting boldly into space and into history. Zaha Hadid's small building for the German furniture-maker Vitra is only one among several by renowned architects (including Frank Gehry, Tadao Ando, Eva Jirična, born 1939, and Nicholas Grimshaw, born 1939) who have been engaged to rebuild the company's campus (initially after a devastating fire), but the Fire Station stands out.

The first line of defence against a future fire, the Fire Station is also Hadid's first building. After winning the competition for (but not building) a golf club, The Peak, in Hong Kong (1983), Hadid worked on competitions and drawings until she secured this commission. In the meantime, she achieved worldwide recognition for her Deconstructivist drawings of buildings with raking planes of such unusual geometries that they seemed to defy construction. The Vitra Fire Station holds the distinction of being the first building by this already world-famous architect.

For pure exuberance of forms the structure knows no peers, either at Vitra (despite its distinguished company) or elsewhere. Hadid is known for her exploding parallelograms, masses and planes, but until the Fire Station it was unclear how she would actually put them together in a building. Fortunately the programme allowed her the freedom to collate her signature shapes in such a way that many of the functions, like the changing room, occur in the interstices between the dramatic planes. Elsewhere, spaces interlock but snake through slabs and surfaces cunningly torqued or split open to the light. Most internal walls are exposed concrete, while the exterior concrete slabs, in the tradition of Louis Kahn (see pages 282–83), are punctured by bolt holes – but

these boldly cantilevered and slanted planes are far from the serenity of Kahn's forms. Hadid skilfully handles two other essential elements: the site and the details. It is something of a surprise to discover that a dedicated formalist like Hadid is able to combine genius in sculptural form with such a sure sense of urban design – because the huge campus resembles a small town – beautifully resolving an awkward, sharp entrance while giving visual definition to the disparate buildings behind a long wall which is angled to hug the street.

Hadid mapped and remapped the practical needs of the whole site, using their increasingly complex geometries as the basis for the Fire Station's design. The mappings remain abstract and arbitrary, but Hadid convincingly frames the urban scheme using a partially walled precinct behind her building. And for anyone who has gazed with irritation at awkward fittings, Hadid's resolute refusal to clutter up the structure with light fixtures, skirting boards or doorframes is a wonder: surfaces are sleek and slide effortlessly, following the flow of space without interruption from necessary but often jarring fixtures. Ingenious strips set in ceilings or floors illuminate the planes with haloes of glowing light, and even the flashing on the roof is tucked deftly out of sight. Zaha Hadid's Fire Station was certainly worth the wait.

Offices and Art School, Museum of Fine Arts

HOUSTON, TEXAS, UNITED STATES
1991–94

Carlos Jiménez
born San Jose 1959

In a career lasting less than 20 years, the Costa Rican Carlos Jiménez has managed to garner an international reputation as Houston's best-known and most representative architect. That he has accomplished this primarily on the basis of some 30 houses, most of them in Houston, and only three larger-scale projects is astonishing, and is a testimony to the extraordinary quality of his design.

But perhaps the best evidence to justify his position is the Central Administration and Junior School Building for the Museum of Fine Arts, which stands on Houston's museum campus alongside works by major architects such as the Museum of Fine Arts by Ludwig Mies van der Rohe (1958–74; *see pages 248–49 and 272–73*), the Museum of Contemporary Arts (1968–72) by Gunnar Birkerts (born 1925), and the new wing of the Museum of Fine Arts (1994–2000) by Rafael Moneo.

Jiménez's L-shaped project occupies a block on the campus's northern edge. A three-storey wing on Montrose Boulevard houses administrative offices; the diagonal entrance to the lobby, clad with aluminium panels, marks the junction; while the art school's two-storey wing is disposed at a right angle to admit northern light to the studios. With glass bricks framing the rear entrance, white walls and a lift shaft sheathed in white marble with a glass staircase wrapped around it, the lobby becomes a luminous interlude between the two wings. Tucking the car park behind a building is a much-used urban strategy in Houston, but Jiménez's decision to do this is impressed with his commitment to urbanism in the equitable treatment of the parking and street façades. In front of the latter, Jiménez retained several old oak trees, while newly planted oaks and magnolias shade the parking lot and rear entrances.

Each office in the administration wing enjoys a window overlooking the trees, and long narrow windows above the doors allow light to spill into the interior cubicles. Such generosity with views and light is typical of Jiménez's belief that every space and every activity merits the same thoughtful treatment.

In a city that has celebrated reflective glass skyscrapers since the 1980s, and a campus dominated by Mies van der Rohe's steel girders, Jiménez took the bold step of fabricating the structure with limestone facing, anodized aluminium panels at the Montrose Boulevard entrance, galvanized-steel roofing panels, and wall units of glass bricks or insulated glass. Points of contact between different materials, such as stone, frame and window, are held flush, so that only contrasting textures interrupt the wall surfaces; rhythm, instead, is achieved through the composition and form of the different parts of the building. And, unlike so many projects, even the roof received thoughtful attention; instead of the typical flat surface that collects rain water, Jiménez designed a shallow steel vault. One of Jiménez's achievements was to create a minimalist aesthetic which is crisp without being monotonous, lean without being stark. His attention to minute details during construction paid dividends: the building is a superbly constructed and detailed work.

BELOW: original section by Carlos Jiménez.

Faculty of Economics, Utrecht Polytechnic
UTRECHT, THE NETHERLANDS
1991–95

Mecanoo

Francine Houben
partner in charge
born Sittard 1955

Dutch architecture of the 20th century was characterized by fine craftsmanship, inventiveness, and an emphasis on social and cultural commitments, particularly in housing. These are all features of the Faculty of Economics designed by the architects of Mecanoo (formed in 1984). Although their designs are fresh and striking, they do not aim for the cutting edge or to be avant-garde; rather, there is a historical resonance in their buildings: architectural traditions are transformed in innovative ways.

A good illustration of their approach can be found in the plan of the faculty. One of the principal movements in Dutch architecture, as seen in the work of architects such as Aldo van Eyck (*see pages 288–89*) and Herman Hertzberger (born 1932), was to integrate anthropological studies of human behaviour with architecture and planning, interlocking the relative notions of house/city, space/building in tightly organic units. Rather than imitating the style of their illustrious predecessors, Mecanoo re-examined some of the African sources that van Eyck and Hertzberger had studied and refashioned them for the faculty building.

Although the Economics department consists of 5,000 students and 400 faculty members, it actually breaks down into smaller units, each with its own identity. Shared facilities – the library, restaurant, computer facilities and meeting rooms – form separate boxes unified behind a wall of glass along the northern side, while the tutorial rooms, elevated and punctuated by concrete piers, occupy a wing running through the middle of the site. The administrative offices line the perimeter along a canal, and the remaining wings grouped around courtyards accommodate the clusters of academics' rooms. Benches and areas for informal gatherings are scattered throughout the complex.

Mecanoo endowed each part of the scheme with a distinctive character. The ramps leading to the tutorial rooms are suspended from the ceiling as if they are weightless, while the rooms are robust boxes jutting out over the atrium, connected to the glass skin of the elevation by steel beams and vertical stays. Each courtyard expresses a different mood, one being dense with bamboo within steel-mesh-clad and plywood walls, while another is a Zen court, with boulders, gravel and two small trees, framed by cedar latticework and okumen (an exotic wood) panels used in rhythmic patterns. And each façade is a distinct entity with a unique architectural personality; alternating bands of glass and steel panels adorn two wings overlooking the canal, which are adjacent to a Modernist glass façade pulled over a steel grid.

The Faculty of Economics is so specific to its site and programme that it is difficult to imitate; other than in terms of the attention given to the overall scheme and to the detail and the high-quality construction, it is unlike any other building by Mecanoo. This uniqueness is the hallmark of their work and is what makes it so interesting; each commission is understood to present new problems that cannot be resolved with a tool kit of emblematic design elements.

Supreme Court of Israel

JERUSALEM, ISRAEL
1986–92

Ada Karmi-Melamede
born Tel Aviv 1936

Rem Karmi
born Jerusalem 1931

In an era when architects design relatively uncontroversial public buildings such as museums, concert halls and shopping malls, the Supreme Court of Israel stands out not only as an extraordinary building but as a unique government body that celebrates a city and its history. The architects wanted to give shape to an inclusive cultural identity, create a sense of permanence and inspire hope in social order and harmony.

Although Jerusalem is an ancient city, the waves of conquests, destruction and reconstruction, not to mention the diverse heritage of 20th-century immigrants, have left the idea of an indigenous architectural tradition open – uncomfortably so, in a city deeply divided among several religious groups who claim Jerusalem as a sacred city, and the state of Israel, which claims it as the capital. The Israeli architects who won the international competition in 1986, sister and brother Ada Karmi-Melamede and Rem Karmi, created a design based on a close analysis of the site, the city and the patterns of relationships embedded in them. Above all, the Supreme Court building is animated by a conviction that, to survive the tensions of competing factions, a society must be governed by laws that mediate among the differing interests.

The site occupies the junction of three major axes, one connecting the Knesset (parliament) and the Israel Museum, another the Hebrew University and two major parks, and a third which leads from the eastern part of Jerusalem, the Old City, to a new area of government buildings, of which one is the Supreme Court. Although the dominant style is Modernist (most typical of the work of Karmi-Melamede, who studied architecture at Columbia University and has an international reputation), the architects infused it with archaic features such as apses and vaults. They were inspired by four settings or buildings in Jerusalem dating from the 1st century AD to the 1930s, representing different secular and religious influences, from which they drew liberally to give historical depth to the design without directly imitating any specific work. The building was new but it had to reflect the continuity of the old justice system.

In antiquity, judges held their sessions at city gates, which were the only openings in the city's walls. This became the inspiration for two major walls in the building: the rough stone wall that encloses the library, judges' chambers, courtrooms and the car park, and another stone wall that curves through the complex on the east–west axis, delimiting the foyer of the courtrooms. The stones, drawn from quarries throughout Israel, also symbolize the Supreme Court's aspiration to unity.

As the needs of judges and visitors (including witnesses) are paramount in the building's function, the architects brought visitors in on the street level, while judges' chambers occupy an upper level and prisoners enter from the basement. Passageways and halls are generous, especially the great foyer, which is illuminated by skylights and lined with benches and chairs to ease the waiting. Top lighting throughout the Supreme Court, including in the vast pyramid inside the library, symbolizes the desire for illumination from above, the enlightenment of justice achieved.

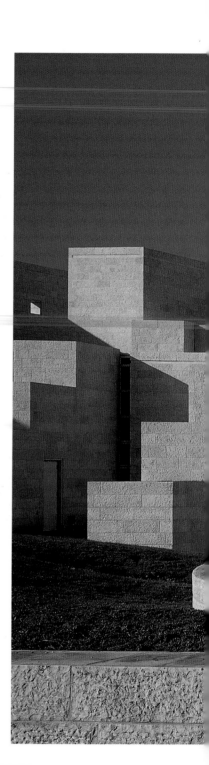

Frederick R. Weisman Art and Teaching Museum

MINNEAPOLIS, MINNESOTA, UNITED STATES

1990–93

Frank Gehry
born Toronto 1929

The work of the Canadian-born American architect Frank Gehry dominated the 1990s. Working from his studio in Santa Monica, Gehry's increasingly idiosyncratic and unusual designs – facilitated by the growing sophistication of computer technology – spread out from California during the 1980s, and by the 1990s were scattered from Prague to Paris, Japan to Germany and, most notably, Bilbao, Spain.

By 1978, Gehry had already received attention for his own house in Santa Monica (1978–79), an exploded small bungalow encased in corrugated metal, chain-link fencing and exposed studs. But the bristling pile of forms for the Manufacturing Facility and Design Museum for Vitra, the furniture makers, in Weil am Rhein, Germany (1987–89), along with the metal veneers of an equally erratic pile of forms for the Center for the Visual Arts, University of Toledo, Ohio (1987–89), drew international attention and initiated a sequence of major commissions in the 1990s. Although all have received enormous press coverage, it was with the Frederick R. Weisman Museum that Gehry first fully explored the linking of sleek curved metal forms that became his signature of the decade.

The Weisman serves as the museum and gallery of the University of Minnesota and houses a permanent collection, temporary exhibitions, offices, storage rooms, a bookshop, auditorium and workshop. Spread out on four levels, the structure overlooks the Mississippi River at a projecting point between a bridge, Memorial Plaza and a major university building, Comstock Hall. From the eastern approach, it presents a utilitarian, buttered-brick facing on the gallery volume, but around the corner, overlooking the river, peek irregular masses that extrude from the simple box – features that immediately identify the

building as a work by Frank Gehry. With their milled stainless-steel panelling of curved, carved and apparently randomly conjoined fragments, these forms capture and refract thousands of constantly shifting slivers of the surrounding riverscape. The masses jutting proudly into the sky are punctuated by windows that are the only indicators of the horizontal divisions of the interior spaces. As early as the California AeroSpace Museum, Los Angeles (1982–84), Gehry had experimented with metal panels, but until now he had always painted or somehow muted the surfaces. After considerable concern about whether an untreated surface would create too much glare, at the Weisman he made the bold decision to leave the stainless steel with a nearly mirror-like finish.

The Weisman is the first example of the concatenation of brilliant stainless-steel panels in Gehry's work and it created a sensation. For the Guggenheim Museum in Bilbao (1991–97), he used titanium panels attached with metal clips, but the swirling sculptural masses simply opened up the aesthetics explored with the Weisman. Along with the sculptural experiments of his earlier works, Gehry's designs have been responsible for a school of design that favours high-tech materials and powerful, modelled masses which, because they are conceived with only the vaguest nod to context, can be transplanted to any site.

ABOVE: Preliminary sketch by Frank Gehry

newMetropolis
National Science and
Technology Centre
AMSTERDAM, THE NETHERLANDS
1992–97

Renzo Piano
born Genoa 1937

It is difficult to imagine a more difficult location than that of the newMetropolis National Science and Technology Centre: Amsterdam harbour, amid a jumble of piers, warehouses and boats, on what is not really a site at all but the elevated space astride a highway that descends into a tunnel beneath the harbour. With his lean engineer's aesthetic, Renzo Piano was the perfect architect to tackle what appeared to be an insoluble problem, and, indeed, he pulled it off with an unusually strong form.

Among his earlier commissions, Piano worked with the English architect Richard Rogers to design the Centre Pompidou in Paris (*see pages 290–91*), best known for its display of structural and technological elements on the exterior. With the Menil Collection in Houston, Texas (1981–86), Piano revealed a far more subtle touch, inserting a modestly scaled, elegantly engineered building into a residential area with surprising understatement.

The brief and the difficulty of the site in Amsterdam encouraged greater expressive latitude, to which Piano responded by inflecting his characteristic restraint with a richer palette of colours and far bolder massing. Its raking diagonal, which recalls the prow of a ship, makes the structure appear to be eternally suspended between two possibilities, rising majestically from the water or slowly sinking into an underground tomb (hence its local nickname, the *Titanic*). The pre-oxidized copper sheets of the upper four floors help sustain the ambiguity, setting up a contrast between the polished surfaces and the deep green-blue tones of corrosion. The building grows from the fan-shaped terminus of a rounded spit of land and soars skywards just as the highway it straddles descends beneath the water. In this otherwise undistinguished setting, Piano's design is

an audacious and provocative innovation which should set the tone and inspire future neighbours. The century-old institution housed in the newMetropolis provides a variety of services, most prominently four floors of exhibition spaces, in addition to a lecture theatre, café and a black-box scientific theatre; on the ground floor are the workshop, temporary exhibition space, and an advisory centre for careers in technology.

Piano's obsession with flexible, open interiors, derived from the great exhibition halls of the second half of the 19th century, is everywhere apparent: offices and theatres occupy the perimeters of the upper floors, leaving the vast interiors open except for double rows of poured concrete columns flanking the staircases that cut through the core of the structure. Not only are the interiors open horizontally but the ramps and stairs were also designed to offer vistas from the ground to the top floor, all bathed in natural light from skylights and celebrating the vast windowless interiors.

Finally, Piano designed a ramp from the pier to a rooftop plaza with views over the harbour and city, giving the flat, low-rise city a rarity: a high spot which provides a dramatic panoramic perspective. The architect's singular achievement was to seize an impossible site and transform it into an asset.

NEWMETROPOLIS NATIONAL SCIENCE AND TECHNOLOGY CENTRE • AMSTERDAM

Phoenix Central Library

PHOENIX, ARIZONA,
UNITED STATES
1989–95

Will Bruder

born Milwaukee, Wis. 1946

When it was opened, the Phoenix Central Library was an overnight sensation in American architectural circles, but it also achieved instant popularity with residents. This rare combination of popular and widespread critical success is richly deserved, for the library is a strikingly unusual building. Like Predock's Science Center *(see pages 324–25)*, it is a key element in a programme begun in 1988 to construct buildings for the city's cultural institutions in downtown Phoenix.

Flanked on the west by a freeway, the library rises above it like an enormous copper and glass warehouse. And a warehouse was precisely the building concept the chief librarian sought – an enormous repository where books and new technologies could be stored yet would be readily available. But this warehouse is unlike any other.

A sculptor by training, Will Bruder moved to architecture in the 1970s, pursuing the discipline through practical experience on small and then larger projects. The lack of a formal architectural education freed him from the conventions and typical solutions. With Wendell Burnette (born in Tennessee in 1962), a local architect, Bruder both developed the design and undertook extensive research on materials and building systems for the library. When they could not find the products they needed, the architects persuaded manufacturers to modify standardized materials, at no extra cost, to meet their requirements and very tight budget.

Among the areas researched were ways of creating a buffer against the intense desert heat, an issue of both sustainability and energy costs. The interior is protected by delicately calibrated scallops of fabric on the glazed northern exposure, while computerized adjustable louvres shield the south elevation. Concrete walls 30 cm (12 in)

thick thermally isolate the lateral, corrugated copper elevations, nicknamed saddlebags, from the body of the building, delaying heat gain and reducing cooling costs while minimizing highway noise. The two most public areas are the ground floor, with an auditorium, children's corner and the video collection, and the top floor, with the city's vast non-fiction collection. From the top, the building offers extraordinary panoramas over the city and towards the northern mountains.

Numerous thoughtful details contribute to the richness of this building, but two features deserve special mention. First are the corrugated and perforated copper elevations, which respond to light with dramatic changes in their opacity and glow and almost dematerialize in the brilliant sun, and, at night, reveal fragments of the lighted interior like sheer fabric. The second is the diagonal 'crystal canyon' which slices through the building from east to west, tapering from the ground floor to the roof. This hollow core of frosted glass and stainless steel acts as a sound and fire barrier, a light well and a divider between public and private spaces on some floors, reading and community spaces on others. And Bruder's fascination with the infinite qualities of light led him to explore the many ways of giving it texture.

Arizona Science Center

PHOENIX, ARIZONA,
UNITED STATES
1990–97

Antoine Predock
born Lebanon, Mo. 1936

Phoenix was created in defiance of nature, with endless sun-baked, water-guzzling suburbs sprawling across the desert floor. Antoine Predock's Arizona Science Center is designed to accommodate rather than defy this hostile environment, much as he has done with projects in the southwestern United States for the past 30 years. From early schemes for adobe housing in Albuquerque, New Mexico, Predock has been inspired by the tough, arid desert and its unique light, textures, colours and flora.

His response to undistinguished settings in the sunbelt's often nondescript cities has not been to import a trumped-up architectural style but to summarize the surrounding landscape, shaping its most elemental features and fusing its best qualities into building complexes at once unique and evocative. Predock's considerable challenge in Phoenix was to create an urban presence as well as a successful science and exhibition centre. Neighbours include historic, low-scale housing in Heritage Square, the civic centre and symphony hall, a park and a pedestrianized shopping district. Phoenix's desert landscape slowly rises towards distant northern mountains, with Camelback Mountain and the downtown skyscrapers providing the only interruptions of the otherwise flat plain. The masses and peaks of the Science Center fashion a topography, one of canyons, valleys and mountains, that does not resort to cheap tricks for its power. Its concrete and glass forms rise beyond broad highways full of speeding cars with an austere, timeless silhouette, like a crusader's stronghold looming out of the shimmering heat. Of these masses, the most volatile is the huge, aluminium-clad wedge that slices through the site on the east–west axis. At times it dominates, at other times it dissolves in the harsh midday sun.

Predock always has a narrative passage in his architecture, one centred on the body and the experience of movement through different spaces and environments. Constrictions, openings, changes in ceiling heights and especially descents into cool underground areas, accented by different qualities of light, are characteristic of his public projects in the southwest. Visitors pass through the Science Center via steps and terraces that girdle massive curved walls or cut through crevices leading to a sunken entrance lobby. From here passageways lead off to a cinema, planetarium, exhibition halls and restaurant. Above the raised platform adjacent to the aluminium wedge, a trellis creates endlessly varied lattice patterns, while the subterranean entrance hall is marked by bands of light that follow the sun's trajectory.

I feel that the visual and experiential contrasts of light/dark and hot/cool created by such patterns are Predock's subtle physical signals to visitors about the transitions between searing heat and earth-cooled interiors, awakening the body to liminal spaces and sensations too often overlooked in a goal-driven culture. Striking as his buildings are, these spaces, revealing architecture's wonderful, mysterious properties, are among Predock's most inspired feats.

Naoshima Contemporary Art Museum
NAOSHIMA, JAPAN
1989–92, 1997

Tadao Ando
born Osaka 1941

Although the Japanese architect Tadao Ando first achieved recognition for city buildings, his most powerful projects are those for rural sites, often adjacent to water, such as his Children's Museum, Himeji, Hyogo, Japan (1988–89). In such an environment his designs achieve a serenity and a harmony with natural forces quite different from the aggressive armature of his urban work. The commission for a hotel and museum on an island in Japan's Inland Sea provided another open location – one which also presented constraints as severe as the tightest city plot.

The hundreds of small islands in the Inland Sea have been an inspiration to generations of artists and poets, and Naoshima had a pristine beauty. The publisher Soichiro Fukutake wanted a private gallery on Naoshima for his family's large collection of 20th-century American art, but Japanese law for the development of land designated as parkland required that accommodation be provided as well, so this was incorporated into the design.

There were two separate phases of building but, because both the owner and the architect wanted to interfere with the landscape as little as possible, Ando buried a good deal of the structure in the cliffs; less than half the museum is visible above ground. Arrival is by water, so the buildings face the sea. From the pier, visitors ascend to a small, wildflower-filled plateau and terrace, with discrete elements of the museum – cone, rough stone wall, cylindrical volume – just visible at the end of the terrace. Once in the main building, however, the central, double-height cylindrical space opens up under a brilliant light from the conical skylight above. Galleries are disposed around the cylinder from the basement up, the top two floors consisting of some of the guest rooms. These face the sky, the water and the smooth concrete walls of the museum, elements that merge with seamless elegance. In 1997 a second gallery and additional guest rooms were added at an angle to and on a hill slightly above the museum. Cleft deep into the hillside, this oval structure, which encircles a still pool, includes a gallery, cafeteria and ten guest rooms.

Ando is known for his obsessive attention to detail and for his extraordinarily deft handling of concrete; so often harsh and uncompromising, in his hands the material acquires the smoothness and depth of satin. Unlike most architects practising today, he learned his craft by travelling, observing and building, not by attending architecture school. This freed him from the tyranny of fashion, and from the need to develop a signature style. It also ensured that he would pursue his own rigorous research and that his work could not be easily imitated. His efforts have been concentrated on the creation of buildings based on a manifest logic – rendering clear what is complex – and on the sense of touch, in sensuous harmony with nature. And that is the dominant quality at Naoshima, where the island terrain is largely left as Ando found it, the buildings nestled into and merging with the setting.

NAOSHIMA CONTEMPORARY ART MUSEUM • NAOSHIMA AERIAL AND INTERIOR VIEWS

ABOVE: original plan by Tadao Ando

Thyssen-Bornemisza Museum

MADRID, SPAIN
1991–93

Rafael Moneo
born Madrid 1937

The challenge with which the Thyssen-Bornemisza Museum confronted the Spanish architect Rafael Moneo was considerable: a new interior had to be inserted into an existing building. The 200-year-old Villahermosa Palace was to be furnished with galleries to display Baron Thyssen-Bornemisza's magnificent collection of more than 800 paintings and sculptures from the medieval to the modern.

Moneo's design for the National Museum of Roman Art in Mérida, Spain (1980–85) made him an ideal choice for the commission, for he had there managed to suspend the new brick warehouse above the Roman excavations, maintaining in perfect equipoise the antique and the modern. Villahermosa Palace had undergone several dramatic and destructive transformations during its history, particularly the interiors which were gutted when it was occupied by a bank during the 1970s. Nevertheless, the austere three-storey façade, with its red bricks, simple windows, granite surrounds and pedimented central bay, was an attractive feature of Paseo del Prado and Moneo simply cleaned and tidied it up. He concentrated on the interior spaces and a new roof.

On entering, the visitor passes into a lobby which leads to a double-height, lush pink space known as a *zaguán* or place of stillness. With almost no art on the walls, the *zaguán* functions much as the landing of the grand entrance stairs of the Altes Museum in Berlin by Schinkel (*see pages 168–69*): an interim space to pause and reflect before entering the precinct of art. With the collection organized chronologically, visitors are directed to the top floor where the oldest works are displayed, followed by the others on a downward spiral. And like Schinkel's promenade in the portico of the Altes Museum, Moneo provides a wide promenade along almost the entire length of the top floor, overlooking Paseo del Prado and giving access to the galleries, so that attention is drawn on one side to the art, and on the other to the city – a delicate relationship to which Moneo is constantly attentive. Another early-19th-century structure, the Dulwich Picture Gallery (1811–14) by John Soane, inspired the pyramidal, top-lit ceilings in the main galleries, while the polished marble floors recall those of the original palace.

The delicate balance of history and the present has been a constant in Moneo's work, one which he did not abandon even during the heady days of Post-Modernism. Historical architecture inspires him, but not as a source of elements to extract from an earlier work to paste into his own; rather, he explores the dynamic relationship between a specific site, programme and structure, constants throughout architectural history, and then chooses the most appropriate concepts and design elements – such as the *zaguán* and the Dulwich Picture Gallery ceilings – but treats them to a critical reinterpretation in a modern key. For this, and for his extraordinary eye for details, finishes and sensuous materiality, he has justifiably been recognized as the most accomplished and significant Spanish architect working today.

THYSSEN-BORNEMISZA MUSEUM • MADRID *INTERIOR*

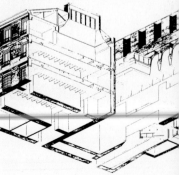

ABOVE: original elevation by Rafael Moneo.

Reichstag
BERLIN, GERMANY
1993–99

Norman Foster
born Reddish 1935

No building better illustrates Berlin's chequered political history in the 20th century than the Reichstag (1884–94; Paul Wallot, 1841–1912), the historic home of the German parliament. When the building was gutted by fire in 1933, Hitler whipped up a popular frenzy that contributed to his appointment as Chancellor. Further damaged by wartime bombs, the Reichstag was partially rehabilitated in 1960.

With the fall of the Berlin Wall, Berlin was restored as the capital of a united Germany, and the Reichstag became home to the Bundestag (the legislative assembly). Despite the multi-layered associations – democracy, infamy, Cold War stagnation, public protest, revived democracy – the government decreed that the Reichstag should retain its 19th-century shell. The English architect Sir Norman Foster won the renewal competition.

Foster's distinguished career has included major commissions throughout the world, including the Hongkong and Shanghai Bank, Hong Kong (1979–86) and the Century Tower Nunkyo-ku in Tokyo (1991). With Richard Rogers (*see pages 290–91*), he has been a leading exponent of High-Tech, in which architects celebrate the expression of production processes, high-technology materials and structural systems. For the Reichstag, Foster proposed placing a light structure surmounted by an enormous canopy held aloft by massive columns within the stone shell. He wanted people to be able to look down from above and see their representatives in parliament, so that legislative activities would be truly and symbolically transparent. Years of public debate resulted in the canopy being replaced by a dome, but the light cage of glass and aluminium, with a mirrored funnel descending from the original heavy dome,

makes the new structure alive with movement and light, the mirrors reflecting light and images back to the shell and onto the twin ramps that curve up the building to the viewing floor.

The building is designed to be sustainable, with thermal windows and a vegetable-oil-powered heating and cooling system. The mirrored funnel, as well as having an aesthetic and symbolic role, is a non-mechanical device for pulling warm air from the parliament chamber, and atmospheric levels of carbon dioxide have been reduced by a factor of 15.

Debates about virtually every feature of the Reichstag reconstruction, from its fabric to its function, were conducted among legislators, in the media and on the street. It is a wonder that it was finished at all, and given the agonizing process, the building's quality is even more remarkable. The Reichstag registers optimism in a renewed, more deeply rooted democracy, one that is soberly founded on an acknowledgement of the country's terrible recent history. Many of the scars have been left exposed on the old façade, a reminder of the country's past on the Reichstag's very skin. Despite the heightened sensitivity attached to this public building, Foster achieved a nuanced symphony of old and new with a grace and complexity that surpass the qualities of his previous, less emotionally charged commissions.

REICHSTAG · BERLIN *DETAIL SHOWING DOME*

ABOVE: original elevation by Norman Foster

Bryant House
MASON'S BEND, ALABAMA, UNITED STATES
1993–94

Auburn University
Rural Studio

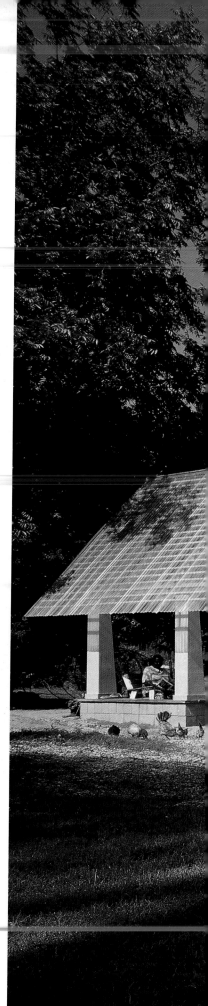

Architects in the United States rarely seek – or secure – projects for low-income clients, and even if they do, their education has not prepared them for this type of work. Occasionally tutors at isolated institutions give their students the opportunity to build small structures, and a very few assign design and construction for the poorest members of their communities. Of the last, the Bryant House is a glowing example.

Hale County, Alabama, is historically one of the most disadvantaged counties in the United States; here during the Great Depression the writer James Agee and the photographer Walker Evans recorded their timeless account of poor southern sharecropper families in the 1930s, *Let Us Now Praise Famous Men* (1941). The poverty is so acute that even federal and non-profit-making bodies refuse to provide housing for the poor, who would be unable to afford the rents. To this unpromising and challenging terrain Professor Samuel Mockbee of the nearby Auburn University brings architecture undergraduates each year, to live, study, design and work. The first group of students designed a house for an elderly couple, the Bryants, who were raising their grandchildren. They needed a house that was structurally sound, heated and with a roof that did not leak, and separate bedrooms for the children. And they had no money.

Spread over three terms, each with a different group of 12 students working on the project, the assignment was to find funding, develop a low-cost design, and build it. The county welfare agency provided $6,000; it was up to the students to find a way of building a house within that budget. The building method they chose, hay-bale construction, is not only cheap but it is ecologically sound, as hay is a renewable resource (the bales are used as insulation within a wooden

framework). The first group developed the design, presenting different proposals to the Bryant family and asking for their preferences. Each subsequent group of students worked on construction and on providing services such as electricity and heating, and each made its own contributions to the project. Details were added or modified and eventually a smokehouse (for curing meat and fish) was included, constructed from found materials: surplus concrete and bullet-riddled signs from the State highway department. No one student could claim design authorship of the project; along with the Bryants, they were all the authors, all the architects. The Bryants ended up with a home that gave each of the children a private bedroom-cum-study-nook, a smokehouse for the catfish that Mr Bryant sells to supplement their welfare benefit, and a sturdy home striking enough to be published in the most prestigious architectural magazines.

And the students gained. The design and the relationship with the clients was left in their hands, so they not only acquired unique work experience but also learned first-hand about poverty and ways in which they, as future architects, might be able to help. This project, spectacular from process to final product, gives the lie to the excuse often cited to justify architects' reluctance to engage with such issues in their work or in design courses – that socially responsible architecture is boring.

ABOVE: original section by Auburn University Rural Studio

Conclusion

Reflecting upon 2,500 years of architecture begs one big question: what form will the architecture of the future take? The 10 chapters in this book tell the story of vast changes in building technology and materials, the emergence of new architectural styles, of new building types and, indeed, the emergence and gradual consolidation of the architectural profession itself. The only really certain thing about the future is that it is unpredictable and the unexpected will happen. But, having said that, some fascinating trends are emerging which will surely give the architecture of the 21st century a distinct character.

The most obvious and dramatic developments have to do with building technologies. New materials are being created which will influence design and construction in the 21st century as powerfully as did iron and steel in the 19th and 20th centuries. Structural glass and lightweight tensile fabrics promise a minimalist architecture of light, space and air that was the dream of pioneering Modernists in the early 20th century, while new materials for cladding – such as reflective metals – will offer radical possibilities for the treatment of the exteriors of buildings. The physical flexibility of new construction and surface materials suggest that buildings in the future could break fully with the tradition of orthogonal or regular planning and construction grids and be entirely organic in form, changing to meet the needs and demands of 21st-century life.

But perhaps more important – if less visually arresting – than issues of materials and form are the concerns of ecology, energy conservation and sustainability. The quest to make buildings more environmentally friendly – utilizing renewable resources and creating less toxic waste or pollution – is beginning to have an exciting architectural consequence. It is increasingly likely that buildings of the near future will not only be organized to make maximum use of natural light and ventilation and to utilize solar energy, but will also be conceived as giant organisms that will, among many things, recycle their own waste and transform sewage into a source of energy. Buildings look set to become increasingly intelligent, working their own systems of control and management, and could maintain – or even repair – themselves. In the not too distant future it might even be possible to 'grow' buildings in the same way as marine creatures grow rock-like coral to form structures for their habitation, protection and support.

But the issue of architectural style – the great and somewhat academic debate that stretches back over the centuries – will surely not be finally abandoned in the 21st century. Even if concerns of utility, ecology and function become more dominant, questions of architectural symbolism, meaning and cultural continuity will remain. Those who feel that new buildings have to be fitted carefully and unobtrusively into historic and environmentally sensitive contexts will, no doubt, continue to promote architecture of traditional design and

RIGHT: Daniel Libeskind (architect) and Cecil Balmond (engineer), a computer-generated rendition of the proposed design for the Spiral extension to Victoria and Albert Museum, London: a sculptural presence in an urban landscape.

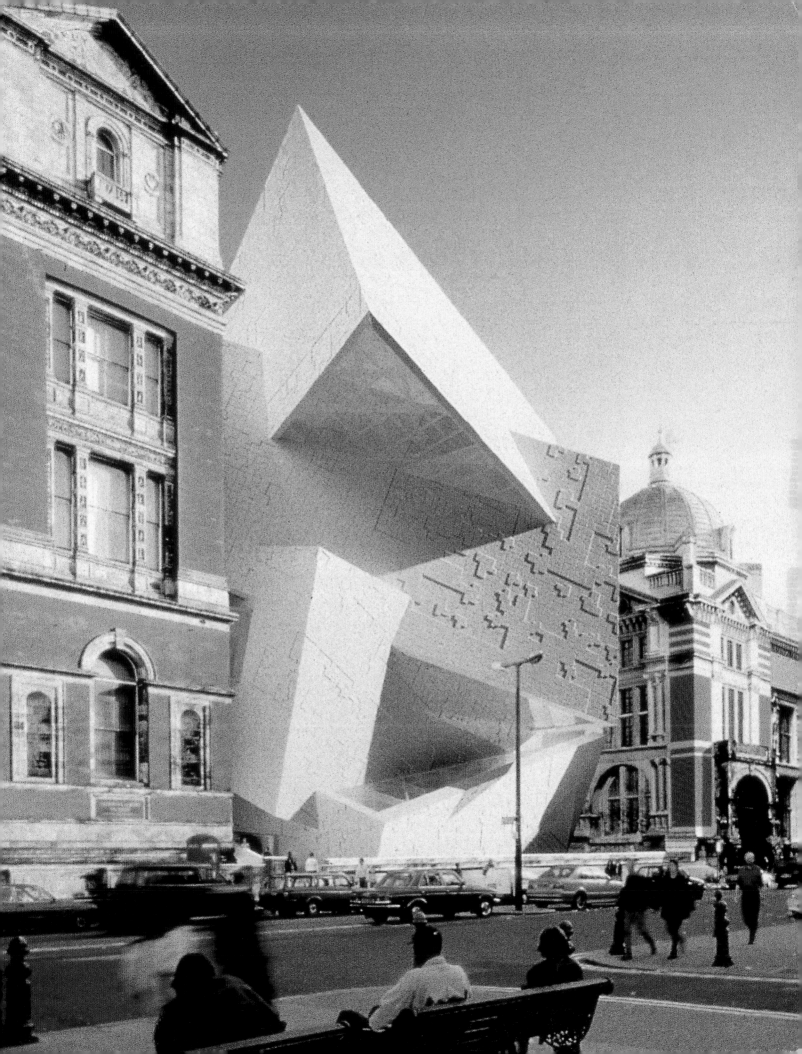

construction. The classical tradition survived through the 20th century, despite the advent of anti-historicist and anti-ornament Modernism, and there is no reason to believe that classicism will not yet again be regenerated, reinvigorated and even reinvented to meet certain needs in the 21st century.

More vulnerable than traditional construction and architecture is the established role of the architect. During the latter part of the 20th century the architectural profession – really only an invention of the early 19th century – came under pressure from other professions in the building industry. This trend is bound to continue. As architecture becomes more complex and all-embracing – including issues of engineering, cost control, planning, communications technology, sustainability and the design of specialized interiors and exteriors – it is likely that the architect's role will reduce dramatically. The architect will become just one member of a large team, probably responsible only for the external appearance of the building, with structural engineers, planners, quantity surveyors, energy consultants, interior designers and other specialists being responsible for their areas of expertise.

The demise of the architect as the lead member of the building team will be sad for those who like to think in simple terms and prefer to associate the creation of so complex an artefact as a building with the name of one person, relishing buildings created under the control of one intellect, where all issues of design represent an integrated whole. But a recognition of the architect's diminishing responsibility is not only an accurate reflection of the true state of affairs – for

some years it has been generally acknowledged that structural engineers have played an increasing role in the creation of particularly demanding structures such a Piano and Rogers' Centre Pompidou in Paris (*see pages 290–91*) – but also represents a return to an older position. Traditionally, designers of buildings were members of buildings trades, were generally capable craftsmen themselves, and were certainly greatly dependent on the contributions of other craftsmen and tradesmen for the design and execution of a building.

The notion of the all-powerful architect – a gentleman, a businessman or an artist – designing and overseeing the construction of all but executing none of the elements of the building is really a relatively modern development. Gothic cathedrals are the product of a creative and mutually respectful co-operation between many crafts and trades, building works spanning many decades and sometimes centuries; Andrea Palladio – perhaps the most influential designer of all time – was trained as a stonemason, while Sir Christopher Wren – termed the surveyor not the architect for the new St Paul's Cathedral – made it a point of principle to seek out and encourage outstanding craftsmen to construct his buildings and, whenever possible, to design those elements they were to execute.

A great building is a great corporate work of art. If the Gothic spirit of creative and democratic collaboration between all members of the building team is now to be combined with the potential offered by new building technologies, then the 21st century could see the production of some very great – and novel – architecture indeed.

LEFT: Machado and Silvetti Architects, construction mock-up of the Getty Villa, Malibu, due to be completed in 2003

Glossary

Classical Greek architecture and the orders

Mud-brick and timber were the main building materials for Greek religious structures until the 7th century BC, when TERRA-COTTA tiles were invented and cut stone was increasingly employed to support the heavy new roofs. At first stone replaced the wood of half-timbered construction for purely practical, structural reasons, but soon visual effect became a significant concern. Ancient tradition was very important to early Greek religion and influenced not only the character of the rituals but also the siting and form of the temple. Thus, stone elements of the entablature were carved to imitate the structural systems they were replacing, and the temple began to resemble a stone sculpture of traditional timber and mud-brick construction.

In the early 6th century the structural and ornamental elements of monumental temples and their position and proportions became standardized, and the classical **orders** were established. The orders are based on the decoration of the COLUMN and its ENTABLATURE. The sober **Doric** order developed on the mainland, the more elaborately decorative **Ionic** on the islands of the Aegean Sea, especially in Ionia, on the west coast of Asia Minor. The Doric column has no base and consists of a stocky, fluted SHAFT and simple bowl-shaped CAPITAL, surmounted by a plain ARCHITRAVE, a FRIEZE carrying alternating TRIGLYPHS and METOPES, and an overhanging CORNICE. The Ionic column is also fluted but is proportionately taller and narrower than the Doric, rests on a moulded base, and carries an intricate scrolled capital; above is a three-stepped architrave, a plain or DENTILLATED frieze (or a combination of the two), and an overhanging cornice. The **Corinthian** capital, with carved ACANTHUS leaves, was invented in

the 5th century BC and was used as an alternative capital in the Ionic order. In Roman times, Doric, Ionic and Corinthian capitals continued to be used, and the latter two were combined in the distinctively Roman **Composite** capital. The original architectural order of the Romans was the **Tuscan** order, inherited from the Etruscans, and its columns are similar to those of Doric but with a moulded base and no fluting on the column shaft.

From the 4th century BC, the classical orders were increasingly used for purely decorative, non-structural purposes. This use saw the development of superimposed orders, so influential in the RENAISSANCE, whose hierarchy (from bottom to top) was consistently Doric, Ionic, Corinthian.

abutment Masonry used to counteract the lateral pressure of an arch or vault.

acanthus Stylized, scalloped leaves used on CORINTHIAN and COMPOSITE capitals.

acropolis The citadel of an ancient Greek city, built on the highest ground and containing the main temples and public buildings.

acroteria The plinths carrying statues and ornaments on a PEDIMENT; also applied to the decorations themselves.

adobe Mud-brick dried in the sun, often reinforced with straw or earth. Used as a building material since ancient times.

aedicule A canopied niche, usually containing a statue; also the framing of an opening with COLUMNS, PIERS or PILASTERS carrying a pedimented ENTABLATURE.

affronted Term applied to two symmetrical figures facing each other.

agora In classical Greek architecture, a public open space in a town, usually surrounded by a COLONNADE, used as a market or meeting place; similar to a FORUM.

aisle The space at the sides of a BASILICA or longitudinally planned church, usually separated from the main area by a COLONNADE or ARCADE.

ambulatory The curved AISLE behind the high altar.

antefixae Ornaments on the edge of a roof.

anthemion A stylized honeysuckle or palmette ornament.

apse A semicircular or polygonal extension to a space, often to a CHANCEL or CHAPEL in a church.

apsidal The APSE-like termination of a CHAPEL, CHANCEL, TRANSEPT or AISLE.

arcade A series of arches carried on COLUMNS or PIERS, either freestanding or attached to a wall (a blind arcade).

arch A structure of shaped elements (such as blocks and bricks) spanning an opening, supported only from the sides. Arches take many forms, including **four-centred**: four arcs that form two shallow curves rising to a point; **pointed**: two curves meeting at a sharp angle; **segmental**: formed from a segment of a circle; **trefoil**: a round arch, broken by two steeper curves, creating three lobes. An ornamental **blind arch** in a wall frames a recessed surface, not an opening.

architrave The lowest part of an ENTABLATURE, extending between COLUMNS or PIERS; also the frame around a door or window.

archivolt Moulding on the face of an ARCH, following its contours.

arcuated A building structurally dependent on the ARCH (in contrast to TRABEATED).

Art Nouveau A decorative style that flourished in Europe at the end of the 19th century, characterized by organic and whiplash ornamentation.

Arts and Crafts English movement of the late 19th century that advocated the use of traditional building and decorative crafts and materials.

ashlar Regular masonry with flat surfaces and squared edges, forming even courses.

astylar Describes a façade without COLUMNS or PILASTERS.

atlante Also telamone. A carved male figure serving as a COLUMN.

atrium In CLASSICAL and Early Christian architecture, an open court; from the RENAISSANCE, a covered entrance hall.

attic A storey above the main CORNICE of a building; also the space within a roof.

axial plan A building planned longitudinally (in contrast to a CENTRAL PLAN).

axis An imaginary line running through the centre of a building or composition.

baldacchino Also baldachin. A canopy over an altar, throne, doorway, tomb, etc.

balustrade A series of posts, or balusters, supporting a handrail running diagonally up the side of a staircase or horizontally across, for example, a landing.

baptistery A building or room for Christian baptismal rites.

bargeboard Projecting boards, often with carved decoration, placed against a GABLE.

Baroque A style of the 17th–mid-18th centuries, characterized in architecture by exuberant decoration, a sense of drama and spatially complex compositions.

basilica A Roman longitudinal hall, developed for law courts, adopted as a building type for Early Christian churches.

bas-relief Carving in shallow relief.

Bauhaus A German school of art and architecture, 1919–33, that advocated co-operation between artists, architects and craftsmen and subscribed to an architecture of modern, stark, industrial forms and materials. A central powerhouse of MODERNISM.

bay A subdivision of a building, marked by the occurrence of COLUMNS, windows, BUTTRESSES, units of VAULTING, etc.

bay window An angular or curved projecting window; called an **oriel window** on an upper floor.

Beaux-Arts style A rich CLASSICAL style promoted by the Ecole des Beaux-Arts in Paris in the late 19th century.

belvedere A structure affording an extensive view, usually on the rooftop of a building but also a separate structure on raised ground in a landscaped garden.

béton brut ('raw concrete'); concrete left in its natural state after the removal of the FORMWORK.

boss An ornamental projection, often carved with foliage, covering the intersection of RIBS on a ceiling or VAULT.

Brutalism Also New Brutalism. A style of the mid-1950s–60s characterized by the use of concrete and weighty members, used in powerful compositions.

buttress A masonry or brickwork projection that strengthens a building.

capital The crowning element of a COLUMN, PIER or PILASTER.

caryatid A carved female figure serving as a COLUMN.

casement window A window where the opening lights are hinged at the side.

cast iron Iron shaped in moulds.

cella In classical Greek architecture, the rectangular main body of a temple.

central plan A building designed around and radiating from a central point: examples are circular and octagonal structures and those with a GREEK-CROSS plan.

chancel The part of the east end of a church where the main altar is housed; usually reserved for the clergy and choir.

chantry The part of a church for the celebration of Masses for the donor's nominees.

chapel Usually a small chamber within a church containing an altar and dedicated to a particular saint, but sometimes a separate structure, such as a **Lady chapel** which is dedicated to the Virgin.

chapterhouse In a monastery, the place of assembly for the discussion of business or for reading the chapters of the monastic rule.

chinoiserie European imitations or evocations of Chinese art, architecture and decorative forms, particularly popular in the 18th century.

choir The part of a church where the service is sung, usually part of the CHANCEL, with stalls for the singers, and separated from the NAVE and TRANSEPTS by a carved wooden or stone screen.

cladding An outer covering applied to a structure.

classical The art and architecture of ancient Greece and Rome; also used to refer to later revivals of their principles and forms.

clerestory window A window in the upper part of a wall.

cloister In a monastery, an enclosed quadrangle, open to the sky, surrounded by an ARCADE or COLONNADE and a covered passageway. It connects the church with the other monastic buildings.

cloister screen Decorative work inserted into the arcading around a CLOISTER.

coffered Describes a ceiling, VAULT or DOME that features sunken square or polygonal panels.

colonnade A row of columns carrying an ENTABLATURE or ARCADE.

column A vertical member, round, square or rectangular in section and typically slightly tapered, usually intended for support. In CLASSICAL architecture it consists of a SHAFT, CAPITAL and (other than in Greek DORIC) a base. An **engaged column** (or attached or applied column) is attached to a wall.

composite order See *Classical Greek Architecture and the Orders*, above.

console An ornamental bracket.

Constructivism A Modernist ideology from 1920s Soviet Russia advocating utilitarian simplicity, functional clarity and respect for the qualities of building materials.

coping The capping or covering of a wall.

corbel A projecting block of stone that supports a horizontal beam.

Corinthian order See *Classical Greek Architecture and the Orders*, above.

cornice The top section of an ENTABLATURE; also any crowning ornamental projection.

corps de logis The main building of a grand residence.

cour d'honneur The finest, usually front court of a grand residence where visitors were received.

crossing In a church, the intersection of the NAVE, TRANSEPTS and CHANCEL.

crypt In a church, the space beneath the main floor, generally under the CHANCEL, used for burials or for housing relics.

cupola A DOME, especially a small one crowning a turret, on a DRUM.

curtain wall A non-load-bearing external wall placed on a framed structure; also the outer wall of a medieval castle.

Deconstructivism A movement of the 1980s which proposed that there was no clear relationship between objects and meaning.

dentillation A series of small square or rectangular blocks used to decorate masonry.

dome A roughly hemispherical roof on a circular base. The section can be semicircular, segmental, pointed or bulbous.

Doric order See *Classical Greek Architecture and the Orders*, above.

dormer window A window in a sloping roof with a roof of its own.

double cube (also known as **double pile**) In a house, a rectangular block that is two equal-sized rooms deep.

drafted In stonemasonry, describes a block that has a smooth margin chiselled along one or more edges of its face as a guide for aligning the block and/or as a decorative device.

drum A vertical wall forming a circular, square or polygonal base for a DOME or CLOISTER VAULT; also a cylindrical block forming a COLUMN.

eaves The underpart of a sloping roof projecting over a wall.

elevation (see FAÇADE) An external face of a building.

en enfilade Describes the alignment of internal doors to form a vista through different rooms.

entablature The upper part of an ORDER, consisting of ARCHITRAVE, FRIEZE and CORNICE.

façade A face or elevation of a building, often used to indicate the main ELEVATION.

fenestration The arrangement of windows as seen from the outside of a building.

finial An ornament on the top of a PINNACLE, PORCH, GABLE, etc.

flashing Metal used to protect and reinforce the angles and joints of a roof.

fluting Concave vertical grooves covering the SHAFT of a COLUMN or PILASTER.

flying buttress An arched projection from the upper part of a wall or roof to an outer support, reinforcing the building.

foil A decorative lobe found in TRACERY and used in groups, for example, of three, four or five (**trefoil**, **quatrefoil**, **cinquefoil**).

formwork Also shuttering. The mould used for shaping concrete.

forum The Roman equivalent of an AGORA.

framed building A structure whose weight is carried by a framework rather than by load-bearing walls.

French window A CASEMENT WINDOW that extends down to the floor, usually used in pairs.

fretwork Geometrical ornamentation using straight lines to form a band.

frieze The central part of an ENTABLATURE; also a decorative band on an internal wall, immediately below the CORNICE.

Functionalism The theory that the form of a building should be derived from and reflect its function.

gable The triangular section of a wall at the end of a pitched roof.

gallery In a church, a storey above an AISLE, opening onto the NAVE; in secular architecture, a platform overlooking a main interior space, or a long room or corridor decorated with works of art.

giant order Also colossal order. Columns, pilasters or piers that rise through two or more storeys on a façade.

gargoyle A projecting waterspout carved into the form of a grotesque figure.

Gothic The style prevalent from the 12th to the early 16th century, typified, in church architecture, by pointed ARCHES, ribbed VAULTS, BUTTRESSES, stained glass and tall, airy spaces.

Gothic Revival A late 18th- and 19th-century movement to revive the style and structural principles of GOTHIC architecture.

Greek cross A plan of a church with four equal arms.

Greek Revival A mid-18th–19th century movement evoking the simplicity and gravity of classical Greek architecture and decoration.

groin A sharp edge or angle formed by the intersection of VAULTING surfaces.

half-timbered A building with a timber skeleton that is sometimes plastered, the spaces filled with brick or other materials.

High-Tech An approach to architecture developed in the 1970s based on engineering and state-of-the-art technologies, favouring lightweight materials and internal flexibilty, and the exposure and expression of construction and services.

I-beam A metal beam in the shape of the capital letter I, with recessed sides to receive other members.

inglenook A recess beside a fireplace containing a built-in seat.

insula A Roman multistorey apartment house.

intelligent building A building equipped with integrated computer systems to regulate functions such as heating, lighting and security and to protect the building.

Ionic order See *Classical Greek Architecture and the Orders*, above.

keep Also donjon. The main inner tower of a castle with permanent living quarters or emergency accommodation for times of siege.

keystone The central wedge-shaped stone in an ARCH or rib VAULT.

lantern A circular or polygonal turret with windows that crowns a roof.

Latin cross A plan of a church with three short arms (CHANCEL and TRANSEPTS) and one long arm (NAVE).

lintel A horizontal beam or stone that spans an opening.

loggia A roofed space or building open on one or more sides with ARCADES or COLONNADES.

lunette A semicircular window, opening, surface or panel.

Mannerism The post-High RENAISSANCE art and architecture of the 16th century characterized by stylized forms and ironic use of motifs in deliberate opposition to their original meaning or context.

mansard roof A roof with a double slope, the lower steeper than the upper.

martyrium A building or monument erected on the site where a Christian martyr is buried.

masonry Work in brick or stone.

metope The plain or carved space between TRIGLYPHS in a DORIC FRIEZE. See *Classical Greek Architecture and the Orders*, above

minaret A decorative tower attached to or near a mosque, also used to call believers to prayer.

moat A wide, deep ditch, usually filled with water, surrounding a building or town as a means of defence.

Modernism Also the New Building or International Style. Style developed in the early 20th century aiming at unadorned functional design, embracing new technologies and divorced from historical precedent.

modular construction The use of uniform components, often PREFABRICATED, in a building.

module A unit of measurement by which the proportions of a building are regulated.

mortice and tenon joint A joint formed by a projecting piece (tenon) fitting into a complementary socket (mortice).

mullioned and transomed window A window divided by vertical (mullion) and horizontal (transom) posts or bars into a number of lights.

naos In classical Greek architecture, the main chamber of a temple in which the cult image was housed.

narthex A vestibule of a church.

nave The main central part of a longitudinal church to the west of the CROSSING, usually flanked by AISLES.

Neoclassicism The 18th- and early 19th-century style of academic, geometric CLASSICISM.

oculus A circular opening.

ogee An S- or inverted S-shaped decorative line or form.

opisthodomos In classical Greek architecture, the back porch of a temple.

orders see *Classical Greek Architecture and the Orders*, above.

orientation The direction of the plan of a building. Most Western European churches have the altar at the east end, towards the rising sun. Mosques are orientated towards the holy city of Mecca in Saudi Arabia.

Palladianism A style of the 17th and 18th centuries derived from the buildings and publications of the architect Palladio and also the work of Vicenzo Scamozzi.

pantheon In CLASSICAL times, a temple to all the gods; also a monument or building honouring dead heroes.

parapet A low wall.

patera A small circular or oval ornament, often decorated with leaves or petals.

patio In Spanish architecture, an inner, open courtyard; also a paved area adjacent to a house.

pavilion A prominent structure on the main FAÇADE or terminating the wings of a grand building; also an ornamental summerhouse.

pedestal The base supporting a COLUMN or statue.

pediment In CLASSICAL architecture, a triangular GABLE at the end of a pitched roof or a similar independent, monumental feature. A **broken pediment** has a scooped space at the apex and a **segmental pediment** is curved.

pendentive The curved triangular surface formed where the angle of two flat walls meets the circular base of a DOME.

pentice A low, lean-to porch.

peristyle A continuous COLONNADE surrounding a building, open space or garden.

piano nobile The main floor of a grand building containing the principal reception rooms, usually on the storey above the entrance level.

piazza An open space surrounded by buildings or a LOGGIA.

pier A thick, freestanding masonry support; also the solid mass between doors and windows. A **compound pier** (or cluster pier) is made up of several slender SHAFTS.

pilaster A decorative rectangular COLUMN projecting only slightly from the wall, conforming with one of the ORDERS.

pile A timber, metal or concrete shaft driven into the ground to provide additional support for foundations.

pillar A freestanding member which does not conform with any of the ORDERS.

plinth The base of a PILLAR, PEDESTAL, statue or entire building.

pilotis Concrete posts or stilts, used to raise and support a building.

pointing The mortar visible between, and bonding, masonry blocks or bricks.

polychromy The combination of different coloured stones and/or marbles.

porch The covered entrance to a building.

porte-cochère A porch large enough for a coach and horses to drive through.

portico A covered entrance to a building, with a COLONNADE and PEDIMENT. It can project from or be absorbed into the building; if the latter, the COLUMNS and pediment merge into the FAÇADE.

post and lintel construction. The simplest form of construction, comprising vertical members supporting horizontal.

Post-Modernism A movement stemming from the 1970s that challenged MODERNISM through eclectic historical references, irony and bold use of colour.

prefabrication The manufacture of building components, sections or whole structures that are then brought to the building site for assembly.

presbytery In a church, the area to the east of the CHOIR containing the high altar.

prodigy houses A group of English country houses built around 1600, often extravagant in their design and decoration.

projection A geometrical drawing showing a building in three dimensions. An **axonometric projection** does not distort the plan but gives an impression from a higher vantage point than an **isometric projection**, which has lines set at an equal angle to the horizontal and so looks more perspectival, with a distorted plan.

pronaos In classical Greek architecture, the front porch of a temple.

propylaeum In classical Greek architecture, the monumental entrance to a sacred enclosure.

pylon In ancient Egyptian architecture, a truncated masonry tower that, with its pair, flanked the entrance to a temple.

quattrocento Refers to the 15th century (the 1400s) in Italian art and architecture. **Dugento** (or duecento) refers to the 13th century, **trecento** to the 14th, **cinquecento** to the 16th, **seicento** to the 17th, **settecento** to the 18th, **ottocento** to the 19th, **novecento** to the 20th century.

reinforced concrete Concrete strengthened with steel mesh or rods.

Renaissance The intellectual and artistic movement of the 15th and 16th centuries that looked to CLASSICAL models, notably, in architecture, to symmetrical forms and the ORDERS.

rendering Plaster or STUCCO applied to an exterior wall; also the first coat of plaster internally.

retrochoir In a large church, the space behind the high altar.

revetment A retaining wall; also CLADDING applied to a wall.

rib A projecting band on a ceiling or VAULT, usually structural but sometimes just decorative.

Rococo The final phase of the BAROQUE, characterized by lavish, asymmetrical, naturalistic decorative schemes and exotic motifs, often covering and merging separate architectural members. Usually refers to interior decoration.

Romanesque The style prevalent in Western architecture from the 6th to the 12th century, characterized by clear planning, massive masonry, round ARCHES and VAULTING.

rosette A rose-shaped PATERA.

rotunda A round building.

rustication The use of large, textured masonry blocks and recessed joints to give the impression of strength.

saloon Also salon or *salone*. A large hall or reception room.

sash window A window with two glazed frames, one or both of which slide up and down.

shaft The trunk of a COLUMN between the base and the CAPITAL; also, in medieval architecture, one of a cluster of slender columns in a compound PIER.

shingles Tiles, usually of wood, used to clad exterior walls; other materials such as cement are also used.

solar A private room on an upper floor of a medieval house.

spandrel The triangular space between two ARCHES or between an arch and a wall.

squinch A small ARCH or bracket built diagonally across each corner of a square or polygonal structure to form a base for a DOME or a spire.

stoa In CLASSICAL Greek architecture, a covered COLONNADE.

stucco A fine, durable, malleable plaster, used both internally and externally.

sustainable architecture Also ecological, environmental or green architecture. Developed from the 1970s, architecture that is environmentally compatible, using natural, renewable materials such as earth, wood, hay and turf that do not cause pollution in their preparation, and energy-efficient techniques such as solar power and ample insulation, with minimal impact on the site.

terra-cotta Clay moulded and baked to a hard finish, used to make roof tiles, bricks, CLADDING and ornamentation.

thermae Roman public baths, which included gardens, gymnasia, lecture halls and libraries as well as pools and rooms of different temperatures.

thermal window Also Diocletian window: a semicircular window with three lights. In 20th- and 21st-century architecture also refers to a window using insulation technology to keep out heat or cold.

trabeated Constructed on the POST AND LINTEL principle (in contrast to ARCUATED).

tracery Ornamental interweaving stonework or woodwork, typically found in the upper part of GOTHIC windows, but also in screens, panels, blank ARCHES and VAULTS.

transept The transverse arms of a cruciform church.

triglyph The grooved blocks between METOPES in a DORIC FRIEZE.

triumphal arch A freestanding monumental Roman gateway.

Tuscan order See *Classical Greek Architecture and the Orders*, above.

vault An arched ceiling of stone, brick or concrete. Vaults take many forms, including **barrel** (or tunnel or wagon): a continuous arch, semicircular or pointed in section; **cross** (or groin): the intersection at right-angles of two barrel vaults; **rib**: a framework of diagonal arched RIBS with compartments between them; **fan**: an elaborate rib vault in which all the ribs have the same curve and fan out; **segmental**: a shallower curved barrel vault.

Venetian window Also Serliana or Palladian window. A window with three openings, the central one wider and arched. The form can also be applied to a door or an arch.

vernacular architecture Buildings in indigenous styles using traditional practice and forms, usually constructed from local materials.

Vitruvius, Pollio Roman architect and theorist of 1st century BC whose treatise on architecture in ten books, *De architectura* (the only surviving architectural text from antiquity) had an enormous influence on the development and expression of CLASSICAL architecture from the RENAISSANCE onwards.

Vitruvian door A doorway in which the sides slope inwards slightly, giving it a heavy, Egyptian appearance. Windows can take a similar form.

voussoir A wedge-shaped block forming one of the units of an ARCH.

wrought iron Iron hammered or rolled into shape.

Bibliography

Penguin Dictionary of Architecture and Landscape Architecture (first published as the *Penguin Dictionary of Architecture*, 1966), 5th ed., Penguin, London and New York, 1998.

Banister Fletcher, *A History of Architecture* (18th ed., revised by J.C. Palmes), Athlone Press, London and Charles Scribner and Sons, New York, 1975.

Trewin Copplestone (ed.) *World Architecture*, Hamlyn, London, New York, Sydney and Toronto, 1963.

Bibliography

CLASSICAL ARCHITECTURE

Berve, H, Gruben, G, and Hirmer, M, *Greek Temples, Theatres and Shrines,* Thames and Hudson, London, 1985

Boethius, A, *Etruscan and Early Roman Architecture,* Penguin, London and New York, 1978

Brown, FE, *Roman Architecture,* George Braziller, New York, 1961

Coulton, JJ, *Greek Architects at Work,* Cornell University Press, Ithaca, N.Y., 1977

Dinsmoor, WB, *The Architecture of Ancient Greece,* 3rd ed., WW Norton, New York, 1975

Lawrence, AW, *Greek Architecture,* 4th ed., Penguin, London, 1983

MacDonald, WL, *The Architecture of the Roman Empire, vol. 1,* An Introductory Study, revised ed., Yale University Press, New Haven and London, 1982

MacDonald, WL, *The Architecture of the Roman Empire, vol. 2, An Urban Appraisal,* Yale University Press, New Haven and London, 1986

Pollitt, JJ, *Art and Experience in Classical Greece,* Cambridge University Press, Cambridge, 1972

Rhodes, RF, *Architecture and Meaning on the Athenian Acropolis,* Cambridge University Press, Cambridge, 1995

Rhodes, RF, *A Story of Monumental Architecture in Greece,* Cambridge University Press, Cambridge, forthcoming

Robertson, DS, *Handbook of Greek and Roman Architecture,* 2nd ed., Cambridge University Press, Cambridge, 1969

Scranton, RL, *Greek Architecture,* George Braziller, New York, 1962

Scully, V, *The Earth, the Temple and the Gods,* Yale University Press, New Haven and London, 1962

Sear, F, *Roman Architecture, revised ed.,* Batsford Academic and Educational Ltd, London, 1989

Ward-Perkins, JB, *Roman Imperial Architecture,* Penguin, London and New York, 1981

EARLY CHRISTIAN, ROMANESQUE AND GOTHIC

Bideault, Maryse and Lautier, Claudine, *Ile-de-France Gothique 1,* Picard, Paris, 1987(first of a series of regional guides to French Gothic; also *Ile-de-France Gothique 2,* 1988; *Lorraine Gothique,* 1989; *Aquitaine Gothique,* 1992)

Bony, Jean, *French Gothic Architecture of the 12th and 13th Centuries,* University of California Press, Berkeley, 1983

Focillon, Henri, *The Art of the West, vol. 1: Romanesque, vol. 2: Gothic,* Phaidon, London, 1963

Frankl, Paul, *The Gothic: Literary Sources and Interpretations through Eight Centuries,* Princeton University Press, Princeton, N.J., 1960

Harvey, John, *English Medieval Architecture: A Biographical Dictionary down to 1550,* Alan Sutton, Gloucester, 1984

MacDonald, William, *Early Christian and Byzantine Architecture,* George Braziller, New York, 1964

Mark, Robert, *Experiments in Gothic Structure,* MIT Press, Cambridge, Mass., 1982

Radding, Charles M and Clark, William W, *Medieval Architecture, Medieval Learning: Builders and Masters in the Age of Romanesque and Gothic,* Yale University Press, New Haven and London, 1992

Rodley, Lyn, *Byzantine Art and Architecture, an Introduction,* Cambridge University Press, Cambridge, 1994

Ruskin, John, *'The Nature of Gothic' from The Stones of Venice (1851–53),* Library Edition, ed. Cook and Wedderburn, George Unwin, London, 1903–12 (also printed separately by William Morris's Kelmscott Press)

Simson, Otto von, *The Gothic Cathedral,* Princeton University Press, Princeton, N.J., 1988

Wilson, Christopher, *The Gothic Cathedral: The Architecture of the Great Church, 1130– 1530,* Thames and Hudson, London, 1992

Zodiaque series of regional guides to Romanesque architecture in France, Italy and Spain, La nuit des temps, Pierre-qui-Vire

THE RENAISSANCE

Boucher, Bruce, *Andrea Palladio,* Abbeville, New York, 1999

Heydenreich, IH, *Art and Architecture in Italy 1400–1500,* Yale University Press, New Haven and London, 1994

Howard, Deborah, *Jacopo Sansovino: Architecture and Patronage in Renaissance Venice,* Yale University Press, New Haven and London, 1975

Lotz, Wolfgang, *Art and Architecture in Italy 1500–1600,* Yale University Press, New Haven and London, 1995

Palladio, Andrea, ed. Isaac Ware, *The Four Books of Architecture,* Dover, New York, 1983

Saralman, H, *Filippo Brunelleschi: The Buildings,* Thames and Hudson, London, 1993

Summerson, John, *The Classical Language of Architecture,* Thames and Hudson, London, 1980

Summerson, John, *Architecture in Britain 1530–1830,* Yale University Press, New Haven and London, 1994

Summerson, John, *Inigo Jones,* Yale University Press, New Haven and London, 2000

Tavernor, Robert, *Palladio and Palladianism,* Thames and Hudson, London, 1990

Tavernor, Robert, *On Alberti and the Art of Building,* Yale University Press, New Haven and London, 1999

Wittkower, Rudolf, *Architectural Principles in the Age of Humanism,* Academy Editions, London, 1988

THE BAROQUE

Blunt, A, *Art and Architecture in France 1500–1700,* Penguin Books, Harmondsworth, 1957

Downes, K, *English Baroque Architecture,* London, 1966

Fox, HM, *André Le Nôtre,* London, 1968

Fürst, V, *The Architecture of Sir Christopher Wren,* London, 1956

Hempel, E, *Baroque Art and Architecture in Central Europe,* Penguin Books, Harmondsworth, 1965

Hibberd, H, *Bernini,* Penguin Books, Harmondsworth, 1965

Kubler, G and Savia, M, *Art and Architecture in Spain and Portugal,* Penguin Books, Harmondsworth, 1966

Lavedan, P, *French Architecture,* Penguin Books, Harmondsworth, 1956

Millon, H, *Baroque and Rococo Architecture,* New York, 1961

Norberg-Schulz, C, *Late Baroque and Rococo Architecture,* New York, 1985

Norberg-Schulz, C, *Baroque Architecture,* New York, 1986

Portoghesi, P, *The Rome of Borromini,* New York, 1968

Summerson, J, *Architecture in Britain 1530–1830,* Penguin Books, Harmondsworth, 1953

Tapié, V, *The Age of Grandeur,* New York, 1966

Wittkower, R, *Art and Architecture in Italy 1600–1750,* Penguin Books, Harmondsworth, 1958

CLASSICAL VISIONS

Bergdoll, Barry, Karl Friedrich *Schinkel: An Architecture for Prussia,* Rizzoli, New York, 1994

Colvin, Howard, *A Biographical Dictionary of British Architects 1600–1840,* Yale University Press, New Haven and London, 1995

Darley, Gillian, John Soane, *An Accidental Romantic,* Yale University Press, New Haven and London, 1999

Downes, Kerry, *Hawksmoor,* Thames and Hudson, London, 1970

Downes, Kerry, *Vanbrugh,* Zwemmer/Philip Wilson Publishers, London, 1977

Harris, Eileen, 'Home House: Adam Versus Wyatt', Burlington Magazine, vol. 139, May 1997 pp308–21

Harris, John and Snodin, Michael (eds), *Sir William Chambers, Architect to George III,* exhibition catalogue, Yale University Press, New Haven and London/Courtauld Gallery, London, 1996

Hitchcock, Henry-Russell, *Architecture: Nineteenth and Twentieth Centuries,* Pelican History of Art, London, 1958

Middleton, Robin and Watkin, David, *Neo-classical and Nineteenth-Century Architecture, 2 vols,* Faber and Faber, London, 1980

Mordaunt Crook, J, *The Greek Revival,* John Murray, London, 1972

Pierson, William H, Jr, *American Buildings and their Architects; the Colonial and Neo-classical Styles,* Doubleday, New York, 1970

Saumarez Smith, Charles, *The Building of Castle Howard,* Faber and Faber, London, 1990

Stroud, Dorothy, *George Dance, Architect,* Faber and Faber, London, 1971

Turner, Paul Venable, *Campus: An American Planning Tradition,* MIT Press, Cambridge, Mass. and London, 1984

Watkin, David, *Sir John Soane, Enlightenment Thought and the Royal Academy Lectures,* Cambridge University Press, Cambridge, 1996

THE MACHINE AGE

Atterbury, Paul and Wainwright, Clive (eds), *Pugin, A Gothic Passion,* Yale University Press, New Haven and London, 1994

Bergdoll, Barry, *Architecture: Neo-Classicism to Art Nouveau,* Oxford University Press, Oxford, 2000

Brooks, Chris and Saint, Andrew (eds), *The Victorian Church,* Manchester University Press, Manchester and New York, 1995

Cunningham, Colin and Waterhouse, Prudence, *Alfred Waterhouse 1830–1905: The Biography of a Practice,* Clarendon Press, Oxford, 1992

Dixon, Roger and Muthesius, Stefan, *Victorian Architecture,* Thames and Hudson, London, 1978

Ferriday, Peter (ed.), *Victorian Architecture,* Jonathan Cape, London, 1963

Goodhart-Rendel, HS, *English Architecture since the Regency,* Constable, London, 1953, reprinted by Century, London, Sydney, Auckland and Johannesburg, 1989

Hitchcock, Henry-Russell, *Early Victorian Architecture in Britain, 2 vols,* Architectural Press, London and Yale University Press, New Haven, 1954

Middleton, Robin and Watkin, David, *Neo-Classical and 19th-Century Architecture,* Harry N Abrams, New York, 1976

Middleton, Robin (ed.), *The Beaux-Arts and Nineteenth-Century French Architecture,* Thames and Hudson, London, 1982

Mordaunt Crook, J, *The Dilemma of Style,* John Murray, London, 1987

345

Muthesius, Stefan, *The High Victorian Movement in Architecture 1850–1870,* Routledge and Kegan Paul, London and Boston, 1972

O'Gorman, James F, *Three American Architects, Richardson, Sullivan and Wright, 1865–1915,* University of Chicago Press, Chicago and London, 1991

Stamp, Gavin, *Alexander 'Greek' Thomson,* Laurence King, London, 1999

Thompson, Paul, *William Butterfield,* Routledge and Kegan Paul, London, 1971

ART NOUVEAU

Curtis, William JR, *Modern Architecture since 1900, 3rd. ed.,* Prentice-Hall, Upper Saddle River, N.J., 1996

Etlin, Richard A, *Frank Lloyd Wright and Le Corbusier: The Romantic Legacy,* Manchester University Press, Manchester, 1994

Ford, Edward R, *The Details of Modern Architecture,* MIT Press, Cambridge, Mass., 1990

Gravagnuolo, Benedetto, *Adolf Loos: Theory and Works,* Rizzoli, New York, 1982

Hitchcock, Henry-Russell, *In the Nature of Materials: The Buildings of Frank Lloyd Wright, 1887–1941,* Da Capo Press, New York, 1975

Latham, Ian, *Joseph Maria Olbrich,* Rizzoli, New York, 1980

McCoy, Esther, *Five California Architects,* Reinhold Publishing Co., New York, 1960 (Richard Etlin is indebted to Esther McCoy for her account of Bernard Maybeck's First Church of Christ Scientist for his description of the building)

Münz, Ludwig, and Künstler, Gustav, *Adolf Loos: Pioneer of Modern Architecture,* Frederick A. Praeger, New York, 1966

Rheims, Maurice, Hector Guimard, Harry N Abrams, New York, 1988

Russell, Frank (ed.), *Art Nouveau Architecture, Academy Editions,* London, 1979; Arch Cape Press, New York, 1986

Sullivan, Louis, *The Public Papers,* ed. Robert Twombly, University of Chicago Press, Chicago, 1988

Tafel, Edgar, *Years with Frank Lloyd Wright: Apprentice to Genius,* Dover Publications, New York, 1979

Van Rensselaer, Mariana Griswold, *Henry Hobson Richardson and his Work,* Dover Publications, New York, 1969

Wit, Wim de (ed.), *Louis Sullivan: The Function of Ornament,* WW Norton, New York, 1986

Wright, Frank Lloyd, An Autobiography, Horizon Press, New York, 1977

MODERNISM I

Banham, Reyner, *Theory and Design in the First Machine Age,* Architectural Press, London, 1960

Blake, Peter, *The Master Builders,* Gollancz, London, 1960

Conrads, Ulrich, *Programmes and Manifestos on Twentieth-Century Architecture,* Lund Humphries, London, 1970

Curtis, William J, *Le Corbusier, Ideas and Form,* Phaidon, London, 1986

Curtis, William J, *Modern Architecture Since 1900, 3rd ed.,* Phaidon, London, 1996

Frampton, Kenneth, *Modern Architecture, A Critical History,* Thames and Hudson, London, 1980

Gössel, Peter and Leuthäuser, Gabriele, *Architecture in the Twentieth Century,* Benedict Taschen, Cologne, 1991

Levine, Neil, *The Architecture of Frank Lloyd Wright,* Princeton University Press, Princeton, 1996

Midant, Jean-Paul (ed.), *Dictionnaire de l'architecture du XXe siècle,* Hazan, Paris, 1996

Sharp, Dennis, *A Visual History of Twentieth-Century Architecture,* Heinemann/Secker and Warburg, London, 1972

Weston, Richard, *Modernism,* Phaidon, London, 1996

MODERNISM II

Ahlin, Janne, *Sigurd Lewerentz,* MIT Press, Cambridge, Mass. and London, 1987

Banham, Reyner, *The New Brutalism,* Architectural Press, London, 1964

Buchanan, Peter, *Renzo Piano Building Workshop: Complete Works,* Phaidon, London, vol. 1, 1993, vol. 2, 1995, vol. 3, 1997

Frampton, Kenneth, *Modern Architecture: A Critical History,* Thames and Hudson, London, 1985

Jones, Peter Blundell, *Hans Scharoun,* Phaidon, London, 1995

Kroll, Lucien, *The Architecture of Complexity,* Batsford, London, 1986

Neumeyer, Fritz, *The Artless Word: Mies van der Rohe on the Building Art,* MIT Press, Cambridge, Mass., 1991

Pehnt, Wolfgang, *German Architecture 1960–1970,* Hatje, Stuttgart and Architectural Press, London, 1970

Powell, Kenneth, *Richard Rogers: Complete Works,* Phaidon, London, vol. 1, 1999, vol. 2, forthcoming

Ronner, Heinz and Jhaveri, Sharad (eds), *Louis I. Kahn: Complete Work 1935–74,,* ETH, Zurich, 1977

Schulze, Frank, *Mies van der Rohe: a Critical Biography*, University of Chicago Press, Chicago, 1985

Weston, Richard, *Alvar Aalto,* Phaidon, London, 1995

Wilford, Michael, *James Stirling: Buildings and Projects,* Architectural Press, London, 1984

Zevi, Bruno, *Towards an Organic Architecture,* Faber and Faber, London, 1950

Zucchi, Benedict, *Giancarlo De Carlo,* Butterworth-Heinemann, Oxford, 1992

CONTEMPORARY ARCHITECTURE

Adjmi, Morris, *Aldo Rossi: Architecture 1981–1991,* Princeton Architectural Press, New York, 1992

Davis, Sam, *The Architecture of Affordable Housing,* University of California Press, Berkeley and Los Angeles, 1995

Dutton, Thomas A, and Mann, Lian Hurst (eds), *Reconstructing Architecture: Critical Discourses and Social Practice,* University of Minnesota Press, Minneapolis and London, 1996

Farmer, John, *Green Shift: Towards a Green Sensibility in Architecture,* Butterworth Architecture, Oxford, 1996

Frampton, Kenneth, *Modern Architecture: A Critical History, 3rd ed.,* Thames and Hudson, London, 1992

Ghirardo, Diane, *Architecture After Modernism,* Thames and Hudson, London, 1996

Ghirardo, Diane, *Out of Site: A Social Criticism of Architecture,* Bay Press, Seattle, 1991

Hawkes, Dean, *The Environmental Tradition: Studies in the Architecture of Environment,* E and FN Spon, London, 1996

Hays, Michael, *Architecture/Theory since 1968,* MIT Press, Cambridge, Mass., 1998

Rice, Peter, *An Engineer Imagines,* Artemis, London, 1994

Slessor, Catherine, *Eco-Tech: Sustainable Architecture and High Technology,* Thames and Hudson, London, 1997

Toy, Maggie (ed.), *Visions for the Future,* Academy Group, London, 1995

Tzonis, Alexander and Lefaivre, Liane, Architecture in Europe since 1968, Thames and Hudson, London, 1996

Index

Picture acknowledgements